DR. J.M. JUSSAWALLA'S DRUGLESS HEALING

Nature Cure

Rajendar Menen

Published by

F-2/16, Ansari Road, Daryaganj, New Delhi-110002
☎ 011-23240026, 011-23240027 • *Fax* 011-23240028
Email info@vspublishers.com • *Website* www.vspublishers.com

Regional Office Hyderabad
5-1-707/1, Brij Bhawan (Beside Central Bank of India Lane)
Bank Street, Koti, Hyderabad - 500 095
☎ 040-24737290
E-mail vspublishershyd@gmail.com

Branch Office : Mumbai
Jaywant Industrial Estate 1st Floor–108, Tardeo Road
Opposite Sobo Central Mall, Mumbai – 400 034
☎ 022-23510736
E-mail: vspublishersmum@gmail.com

Follow us on   

All books available at **www.vspublishers.com**

ISBN 978-93-505706-0-9

Edition: 2020

Printed at Param Offseters Okhla New Delhi-110020

Dedication

The book is dedicated to Dr. J.M. Jussawalla and the Nature Cure movement. "*Be careful about reading health books. You may die of a misprint*," said Mark Twain. Since the purpose of this book is to benefit humanity, I thank the publishers for making it error free.

Dr. J.M.Jussawalla's sons Adil and Firdausi wish to honour him, the staff of Natural Therapy Clinic, Bombay, and their beloved mother Mehera through the pages of this book.

Acknowledgements

I thank my parents and immediate family for letting me be. I must also thank Bob Snyder for his critical eye and painstaking efforts at perfection.

Preface

The awareness that health is dependent upon habits that we control makes us the first generation in history that to a large extent determines its own destiny.

– ***Jimmy Carter***

Yogis have long understood that the mind and body are thoroughly interwoven, each affecting the other. The mind and body are not in fact separate and distinct but are interdependent components of the whole person. Throughout the ages, the Yogis have taught methods for creating balance. They have long understood that what we think affects the way we feel, and that what we eat, drink and do to our bodies affects the way we think. There can be no separation of function, except for the enlightened adept who has transcended the limitations of the body/mind by assiduous practice of meditation.

– ***Chris Kilham, Take Charge of Your Health: The Mind/Body Relationship***

I began reading about health and nutrition very early in life. As a schoolboy, I kept wondering why people fell ill. And whenever I fell ill, I took the prescribed medication to get well. I was too young, ignorant and scared to question the need for medication. But the big question – why does the human body go off the rails so often? --- remained, hovering over me like a heavy load. And, of course, I didn't want to fall ill ever again!

As I grew up, became a journalist and travelled the world, I kept with my search for an answer. I read possibly every book on the subject, met with medical professionals, *sadhus*, saints, *sants*, *sanyasis*, yogis, mendicants, gurus, *babas*, *godmen*, alternate therapists, medicine men, *shamans*, *tantriks*, miracle men, gypsies, nomads, Bedouins, quacks, intellectuals, and anyone with even a slight slant on the causes and cure of disease.

I also experimented with myself, sometimes with disastrous consequences. I fasted for days on end eschewing even water, adopted auto-urine therapy, checked out the virtues of distilled cow urine, ate different foods, went on all sorts of diets, tried various forms of *alternate therapy*, did *yoga*, ran and walked miles, dipped into martial arts, weight training and other exercise regimens, and pushed my body, mind and soul to the extreme.

I lived dangerously.

After decades of research and lifestyle changes, there are a few answers.

For one, you are what you eat. Most diseases are born of *auto-intoxication.* Watch what you put into your body. Everybody's *prakriti* is different. So before you decide what is good for you, a little experimentation is necessary. Eat a little less than your stomach can hold, eat on time, eat natural, seasonal, organic, unprocessed food; which means you junk everything that is packed, bottled or even re-heated. Have a wide spectrum of foods focussing on fruits, nuts and vegetables, and after you binge (you are only human), just remember to fast when you feel that you have had it till there!

Exercise is vital. The human body is made for movement. If you don't use it, you lose it.

Organise your life around a healthy schedule with moderation as the key. We all have our vices and we are all different; no one is smaller or greater than the other. *Adorn your day with awareness.*

Live in gratitude and love. Enjoy the fellowship of fellow travellers, birds, animals, flowers, trees, the sun, the moon, the wind, water and the stars. After all, we are a part of the cosmos.

Allow your body to heal when you fall ill. The body knows what to do and sends the appropriate signals. Heed them. The human body is made for health and not ill-health. Body intelligence is nature's intelligence. Respect it.

In sickness, look for options that are not particularly aggressive or intrusive. The human body is a miracle and works in mysterious ways. It can heal on its own. You need to bite the 'bullet' only in dire circumstances.

Take adequate rest and relaxation. Do not try to change the world; it is unnecessary stress. Start by changing yourself and you will see how difficult – and worthwhile -- it is.

Live with acceptance, in celebration and joy.

Bear no grudges, and trash negativity. Forget, forgive, and ask for forgiveness. Save your soul. *'Allow the highest aspiration to organise your life' (The Mother).*

Each patient carries his own doctor inside him.

— Norman Cousins, Anatomy of an Illness

Dr. Jussawalla who, in a sense, pioneered 'modern' naturopathy in India was a visionary. India has a rich legacy of natural healing, but it was *Dr. Jussawalla who married the latest knowledge with appropriate gadgetry.* Natural therapists were earlier scattered, went unrecognised, worked in oblivion, and their home grown remedies were rarely documented. There were no systems in place. They had no credible voice and were often dubbed quacks and easily dismissed. It was *Dr. Jussawalla who gave Nature Cure a respectable, educated, influential and urbane voice.* He was the Indian face, the poster boy of a movement that would soon spread all over the world and give conventional medicine a run for its money. (I say this deliberately as medicare has become one of the biggest businesses in the world grossing billions of dollars annually!)

Mahatma Gandhi, Jawaharlal Nehru, Morarji Desai and several other statesmen and people of stature came to Dr. Jussawalla to heal their tired bodies. The word spread, and as India awoke to freedom, the Nature Cure Movement spearheaded by him took a new pedigree.

Dr. Jussawalla was inclusive in his approach. He wanted all the systems of medicine to work together; this way one could easily dip into the other's pharmacopoeia for the right cure. He saw the merits in allopathy and knew that it could be a life saver. He was against the taking of life to adorn the palate, and was strident in his opposition to vaccination. He was on several government bodies and made his views known unequivocally.

In 1989, at the age of 82, he was presented the **Dhanvantri Award**, the *first naturopath to receive the prestigious award.*

This book is a tribute to Dr. Jussawalla and the Nature Cure Movement.

I begin with Dr. Jussawalla's life and times for a young audience that may not know him, look at his methods, trace the origins of the Nature Cure movement globally, dwell on the latest, cutting-edge findings, and ponder, finally, the possibility of a 'disease-free' man in the future.

The book is filled with contemporary research culled from every available source.

I hope it will benefit the reader.

How to Use the Book

At the outset, I must insist *that this is not a self-help book.* If you have an ailment, please visit a *medical professional for treatment.* If you are on medication of any kind, do not stop it without expert advice. *The views expressed here should not be interpreted as a substitute for conventional medical treatment.* Research in medicine opens new vistas all the time, and we have highlighted some of them. As you know, disease can be a complex process without easy answers.

This book explains, in some detail, the tenets of *Naturopathy.* Nature Cure has a rich legacy and posits *that you are what you eat.* The mind, body and soul work in tandem. Imbalances happen and you fall prey to disease. Allow your body to repair itself with the right food, thoughts and surroundings. The healing may not be instant, but it is profound and long lasting. Sickness is as ancient as creation. But modern lifestyle -- with its refined foods, excesses, insufficient exercise and stress – is particularly toxic. Step back, return to nature and simplify your life.

Many Naturopathic methods have been outlined here. Naturopathy has also changed with the times. There is new gadgetry to restore the body to health, and new theories for rejuvenation. Quite appropriately, in our strife-torn times, the importance of wellness has emerged from the woodwork. The circle is now complete. Modern man is tapping ancient repositories of knowledge for answers; along with contemporary scientific research, he is looking at a future with infinite possibilities, even at eternal youth and immortality!

This book will help understand the methods used by Naturopathy which was given a new definition in India by Dr. Jussawalla several decades ago.

There are tips on how to lead a healthy life. You can see why Mahatma Gandhi, Jawaharlal Nehru, Morarji Desai, J.R.D.Tata, the Birlas, the Mafatlals, Meena Kumari and several other well-known people resorted to Nature Cure. This book may help you decide if you need allopathy for immediate relief, or *if it is a better bet to change your lifestyle and remove the cause of disease altogether from the root.*

You will get to know the therapeutic uses of water, sunlight, air, massage, other Naturopathic methods, the right diet, the benefits of fasting, the virtues of vegetarianism, the importance of regular exercise, the value of sleep, the need for fellowship and a mind at peace with itself, the effects of colours, herbs, minerals, vitamins, even the zodiac, the harm from Genetically Modified (GM) foods, and so on. You can also decide if you need to be vaccinated as the dangers of vaccination are being hotly discussed all over the world now. This book will open a window to the latest research on health, nutrition and fitness sourced from the most authentic and – sometimes -- even irreverent health *gurus* who oppose mainstream beliefs with sound empirical knowledge.

Finally, this book will help you look deep within yourself and, hopefully, make for a healthier, happier you. If that were to happen, we will have succeeded in our efforts.

Contents

Chapter 1

Dhanvantari Award

At times our own light goes out and is rekindled by a spark from another person.
Each of us has cause to think with deep gratitude of those who have lighted the flame within us.

--Albert Schweitzer

Quoting from the Citation

Dhanvantari Foundation is honoured, happy and proud to make its 17th Dhanvantari Award, symbolic of recognition of the highest merit to you, Dr. J. M. Jussawalla an eminent naturopath.

Sir, you have the distinction of being the first practitioner of naturopathy in which hoary discipline of medicine you are a pioneer in modern times to be chosen for the prestigious DHANVANTARI AWARD recognised as representing the highest honour conferred on a doctor in India.

Sir, you have devoted a life-time to nature cure and are a naturopath of world fame, who at the ripe old age of 80 plus, go on propagating the principles of drugless method of curing diseases and demonstrate its efficacy through its application on a large scale. It is not for us to discuss and compare the merits of various ways of therapeutics. Suffice it to say that it occupies a high place in the community of kind interests, namely the health and physical welfare of mankind.

In popularising the long-neglected naturopathy, you, Dr. Jussawalla, have played a most notable part. You strongly believe and not without any basis that nothing cures like sunshine, fresh air, hygienic living, simple food which are the keys with which to unlock the hidden resources of strength and vitality in one's body to remain healthy. The body itself is both a recreation ground and a mobile hospital.

To give a biographical sketch born in 1907, you graduated from Davidson College of Natural Therapeutics in England and was appointed an assistant to Dr. V. Stanley Davidson of Lindhlar College, U. S. A. After returning to India, you found in 1938, the Natural Therapy Clinic in Bombay, of which are still the director. In 1947 you were elected the All India Official Delegate to the Golden Jubilee Congress of the American Naturopathic Association. You were also appointed a member of the Planning Commission on the Health Panel of the Government of India and an adviser to the Government of India on Nature Cure, and served on the Nature Cure Advisory Board of the Government of Gujarat State.

You are a Director and President in India, of the International Federation of the Scientific Research Society for the Prevention of Diseases by Drugless Methods and Fellow of the Naturopathic Forest University where you received your doctorate in physical medicine in 1957.

The honorary director and lecturer at the Physiotherapy Centre for the Blind in Bombay, you are the Vice-President of the All India Nature Cure Federation (Akhil Bharatiya Prakritik Chikitsa Parishad) and a practicing member of the Health Practitioners Association of London, after attaining by examination the required standard in naturopathy, iridiagnosis, osteopathy and chiropractic. You are also a permanent member of the American Naturopathic Association since 1947 and have been appointed a Special Representative of the International Society of USA Naturopathic physicians for India. You are the vice-chairman of the Vegetarian Society, Bombay, President of Nature Cure Practitioners Guild (Bombay), and a member of the Governing Body of the Central Council for Research in Yoga and Naturopathy. You are a member of the Scientific and Financial Advisory Committee (Naturopathy) of the Central Council for Research in Yoga and Naturopathy.

In these various capacities, besides pioneering in the field of naturopathy you have rendered yeoman services in the cause of its progress in India, which had spearheaded its development in ages gone by. Sir, we hope that your recommendation to the Union Government which has recognised nature cure should set up a separate board or panel for the system under the Central Council for Research in Yoga and Naturopathy for training and registration will be implemented. And also your desire for the establishment of a Nature Cure College with the status of a University in New Delhi with a Hospital attached will be fulfilled before long. Once such centres are opened, the new comers in the field will be enabled to be equipped with the necessary qualifications to tend patients and handle cases with confidence and authority, you further opine. Your advocacy for a uniform code of ethics for practitioners of all systems of medicine too will not be in vain, we feel.

Dr. Jussawalla, in conformity with your philosophy of life, you have remained a man of simple living and high thinking, besides being a pragmatist, your austerity, kindness to all living creatures, your humane approach to every problem, virtuosity in your calling and faithful adherence to the Hippocratic oath embodying the duties and obligations of physicians, constitute a model for others to follow.

May God grant you long life, health and happiness.

With the above citation, I, as the President of the Governing Council of Dhanvantari Foundation, am pleased to hand over this Award in the shape of a Statuette of Dhanvantari, primogenitor of all medical sciences, to be presented to you now by the Chief Guest of this ceremony His Excellency Shri K. Brahmanand Reddy to you, Sir, with prayers for a further long period of service to the medical profession and the well-being of society.

The citation, named after *Dhanvantari*, the *God of Health* and one of the *24 avatars of Vishnu*, was signed by K. Brahmanand Reddy, Governor of Maharashtra, Jawaharlal Darda, Minister for Public health, Sushilkumar S. Shinde, Minister for Finance and Industries, Suresh Chaturvedi, Secretary General of the Dhanvantari Foundation, and Dr. B. K. Goyal, its Founder President.

The *Dhanvantari Award* was presented to Dr. Jussawalla at a glittering function in Mumbai on Saturday, October 28, 1989. He became the first naturopath to receive the prestigious award and joined an elite band of previous awardees that included Dr. Rustom Jal Vakil, Dr. B.N.Purandare, Dr. C.Gopalan, Dr. B.Ramamurthi, Dr. L.H.Hiranandani, Dr. Christian Bernard, heart transplant surgeon, and Dr. Denton A.Cooley of Houston, Texas, the renowned cardiac surgeon.

Dr. Jehangir Jussawalla was 82 years old.

Chapter 2

A Pioneering Doctor

The Nature Cure man does not 'sell a cure' to the patient. He teaches him the right way of living in his home, which would not only cure him of his particular ailment but also save him from falling ill in future. The ordinary doctor or vaidya is interested mostly in the study of disease. The Nature Curist is interested more in the study of health. His real interest begins where that of the ordinary doctor ends; the eradication of the patient's ailment under Nature Cure marks only the beginning of a way of life in which there is no room for illness or disease. Nature Cure is thus a way of life, not a course of 'treatment'. It is not claimed that Nature Cure can cure all diseases. No system of medicine can do that or else we should all be immortals.

-- Mohandas Karamchand Gandhi, Harijan, 7-4-1946

Naturopathy has captured the world's imagination today. Alternate therapies are slowly replacing conventional medicine as the first line of medical treatment. But what has now snowballed into gigantic proportions globally began with tiny baby steps. Dr. Jussawalla could well be called one of the pioneers who set the ball rolling. Without a doubt, he was the first to give the naturopathy movement in India a modern touch.

Dr. Jussawalla understood the complexities of the human body well, which, in a way, would always defy comprehension. It would always stay a step ahead of all the medical marvels science threw up. Despite his successes, he made no grandiose claims about naturopathy; he never claimed that it had all the cures for all the ills of the flesh. He insisted, on the contrary, that no system can be a cure-all or even claim to have a monopoly on the truth. Throughout his career, he tried to synchronise different systems of medicine in his theory and his practice.

His major contributions to what he called 'the art of healing' were in the fields of accurate, often intuitive diagnosis, diet and a variety of treatments like massage, hydrotherapy, sitz baths, jet and needle baths, sun-lamp therapy and colonic irrigation. Long before the current boom in fitness centres, he offered systematic programmes for weight gain and weight loss through diet and exercises. For most of his six decades of practice at the Natural Therapy Clinic, he offered natural methods of treatments not found in other clinics in Bombay (Mumbai). His aim was to provide every possible form of Nature Cure treatment under one roof. The rash of clinics these days calling for a return to nature as a panacea is ample evidence that what he began -- with some amount of uncertainty and a great deal of opposition -- works!

As his stature as a doctor grew, Dr. Jussawalla was invited to Nature Cure conferences abroad and given important positions. In 1947, he was India's official delegate at the *Golden Jubilee Congress* of the *American Naturopathic Association, USA*. He was on the Planning Commission for the Third Five-Year plan, on the Health Panel of the Government of India and was on the Nature Cure Advisory Board to the Gujarat State Government. He was also an advisor on Nature Cure to the Government of India for many years. He also tirelessly worked with the students of the *Victoria Memorial School for the Blind in Bombay (Mumbai)* and made several of them successful professional masseurs.

Apart from practising naturopathy, Dr. Jussawalla also believed in spreading the message of Nature Cure and wrote several books, monograms and booklets. He also had the humility to encourage and not debunk or ridicule local systems of medicine which often came up with miraculous cures at a fraction of the cost and time conventional medicine would take to affect a cure. He wanted them to be systemised, and insisted that the cures attributed to such systems should be scientifically investigated and not be castigated as mere 'quackery'.

To systemise natural healing, Dr. Jussawalla made a strong pitch for the promotion of Nature Cure in the Third Five-Year Plan. Way back on August 18, 1960, as a member of the Health Panel, Government of India Planning Commission, he emphatically stated that, "There is a prime need for a teaching and treating institute to standardise the science of nature cure, so that this valuable system as well as its accredited practitioners may secure the legal recognition they deserve as well as the confidence of the public." In a brochure presented to the government of India he added, "It is high time that the state considered this system that has forged its way to the front on the sheer merits of its commonsense and logic, as well as its intellectual appeal, and recognised its claim. In the interests of public health it has become absolutely imperative that the State does so. Besides improving the health of mankind by pure, simple, natural and harmless remedies, it will lift practitioners from the quagmire of quackery. It will standardise therapeutics and give its seal of a qualified status to nature cure professionals. Once the standard is set, the newcomers in the field will be equipped with the necessary qualifications to handle a case with authority, confidence and safety to the patient. Nature cure is providing as much a thing of public utility as any other medical service."

Naturopathy has millions of adherents today. Its enormous success as a viable, non-invasive and non-violent healing modality is a tribute to the hard work and determination of a young Parsi doctor who braved the odds, stepped out of line, and spent his entire life living his dream with a rare passion.

Chapter 3

Early Years and Influences

Life isn't about finding yourself. Life is about creating yourself.

--George Bernard Shaw

To get to know more about his early life and influences, I am with Adil, his eldest son and well-known poet, writer and editor, at his Cuffe Parade residence in Mumbai. Sparrows chirp in the balcony as the evening sun patterns artful designs on the wall. We sip green tea and talk.

Dr. Jehangir Jussawalla was born on November 18, 1907 in Temple Road, Lahore, Pakistan, (then British India) to Aimai and Merwan in the Parsi month of Khordad. Aimai was from the well-known Dhanjibhoy Commodore family. Her father was a Khan Bahadur who was almost knighted for his loyalty to the British during the Afghan wars, the Boer War and the Boxer Rebellion. He ran a well equipped Tonga, Mail and Carrying Agency called Dhanjiboy & Son. Thanks to its efficiency, the journey from Rawalpindi to Srinagar, the capital of Kashmir, a distance of 200 miles, which earlier took about 14 days could be completed in a mere 24 hours! His tonga transport service and a pony drawn ambulance, called the Tonga Ambulance also often bailed the British out of tight situations during the wars. The British, of course, were more than grateful for all this.

The Khan Bahandur was a colourful personality and wore many hats. He was also a Governor of the Hindu Technical Institute, in Lahore; a member of the Muree Municipal Committee for 25 years, and its Vice-President for about 12 years; he was an Honorary Magistrate for the District, exercising First Class powers, for about nine years. In addition to several other positions, he was also appointed a Life Honorary Member of the Calcutta Light Horse.

He received many awards. In addition to being made a Khan Bahadur, he was bestowed the title -- Companion of the Most Eminent Order of the Indian Empire, and for his public services, he was conferred the Kaiser-i-Hind First Class Gold Medal. Additionally, he also had a distinguished Masonic career. "He was a successful, popular and wealthy man. He died in 1911," says Adil.

The Khan Bahadur had a son and three daughters. He had also expanded his business interests and bought land and property in Mumbai. Aimai, one of the daughters, married Meherwanjee. Later, in 1914, she left Lahore and her husband and came to Pune and later Bombay (now Mumbai) with her four sons --- Savak, Kakku, Jehangir and Eruch. One daughter died in infancy. "Bombay wasn't new to her as she made frequent visits to the city and had many friends. From Bombay she moved to Pune which was cooler, less populated and had more open space," continues Adil. Jehangir was seven when he came to Mumbai. "By the 1930s the family moved to Hill Crest, Salsbury Park, in Pune. For about 15 years, they lived in different places in Pune. Kakku wanted to be an agriculturist and he bought land in Pune and ran a successful poultry farm in the 1940s. Later, in Bombay, Savak, the eldest, ran an electric shop at Gowalia Tank and Erach ran an air-conditioning set-up. It could easily be said that we were migrants to Mumbai and were a second generation nuclear family."

Scout Movement

Jehangir had his early education in Lahore and Murree Hills after which he continued his education in Pune. He was a good student but there was nothing exceptional about his early life that could provide a window to the meteoric trail he would later blaze as a naturopath of consequence. But, looking back, circumstances were forging him in that direction.

Jehangir never seriously considered becoming a doctor until he was in his twenties. As a schoolboy, he cycled, swam, played the violin and spent the rest of the time in study. He was shy and kept to himself. To overcome his natural introversion, he was advised to become a Scout which he reluctantly did. The Scout movement inspired him, he liked being a Scout, and after passing a scoutmaster examination when he was 15, was made assistant scoutmaster of the Second Poona Parsi Troop. He also led the Scouts of the Bombay Presidency to a world jamboree in Liverpool.

"When I was at school I used to spend most of my time studying, reading, building up my body and learning," he mentions in a diary he maintained. *"One day the head teacher of the class complained to my brother, who was mainly responsible for bringing me and my three brothers up, that I was keeping aloof from my schoolmates and that I should mix with them and take more active part in school life. I reluctantly joined the Scouts. I was soon wholly involved in the Scout movement. Its principles and laws greatly impressed me. They emphasised, temperance, character building and self- help."* Much later, he would acknowledge his years as a scout along with the other influences that shaped his life, *"My years in the scout movement, physical culture and Nature Cure have all helped me to realise this -- that man's most rational approach to himself and his problem has always lain along the path of self-control, self- discipline and self-denial."*

Physical Culture

Jehangir, quite like the great *yoga guru B.K.S.Iyengar* in his younger days, had a somewhat frail constitution. His eyesight deteriorated as a schoolboy and he began wearing glasses which he didn't particularly like. He also took to physical culture, which was a fad among young Parsis in the 1920s, to build his frail physique. "Father's heroes were Rustom Pehlwan from an earlier time, to be replaced in the 1950s by the wrestlers Dara Singh and King Kong," remembers Adil. At age 20, after training at the Southern Command military centre in Poona, he became a physical training instructor at Deccan College. "*The hard work and strict discipline of the military roughened me. This made a positive change in my outlook on life and was one of the first steps towards a crucial point in it later,*" adds the diary jottings.

But remarkably, a few months before becoming a physical instructor, he found he didn't need glasses. Jehangir had been in contact with Dr. Bernard MacFadden, the American "father of physical culture" and was prescribed a course of eye exercises. His eyesight was restored to normalcy. If this wasn't a miracle it was, at the very least, proof that natural methods of healing worked. He could see this clearly. This could well have sowed the seeds of natural healing and given his career aspirations a clear plank to build on. He mentions in his diary: "*I used to correspond with Bernard Macfadden and received many encouraging letters concerning the maintaining of health and physical fitness without the use of drugs. His response made me study his eight volumes on physical culture and drugless healing.*"

Fateful Contact

In 1929, when Dr. Dinshah K.Mehta, arguably the pioneer of naturopathy in India, who, reportedly, discovered at the age of seven, that "the purpose of life is perfection", started his Nature Cure Clinic, "with a tap of cold water and a galvanised tub," as his biographer Sundri P. Vaswani put it, Jehangir was paradoxically one of his first patients. A physical culturist in his younger days, Mehta had a great body which helped enhance his magnetic personality. He posed easily to show off his musculature and also performed feats such as having a car run over him. Later, as he evolved spiritually, he metamorphosed from a conservatively dressed doctor to *Dadaji*, resplendent in saffron robes, his full white beard reaching halfway down his chest. Mehta also conceived of the *Bhagwan Bhojan*, *Ram Roti* and *Sita Soup* meals which were nutritious and within the means of the masses. These "spiritual meals" were served for eight years in both Houses of Parliament. Mehta also established the Society of Servants of God.

Jehangir had earlier trained under Mehta at his physical culture centre and knew him well. But this time the circumstances were different. He had fallen in love with Nergish, his first cousin, and when his feelings weren't reciprocated he was distraught. Two bad attacks of influenza had weakened his heart. He needed to get well and reposed faith in Dinshah Mehta to get him back on his feet. His diary dated "October 31, 1929," reads, "*Treatment of fasting, milk diet, exercises under Dinshah (sic) Mehta in Poona.*" He adds, on an earlier occasion, "*When I heard about Dr. Dinshah K. Metha's Nature Cure Clinic in Poona I joined it, chiefly interested in exercise there. Later he himself introduced me to the principles of Nature Cure. That was the main turning point in my life. I took a firm decision at a crossroads. But at what cost? Nature Cure at that time (1931) was totally misunderstood and misinterpreted. I went against the wishes of everyone, save my mother. My superiors, relatives and the medical gurus under whom I was going through my pre-medical studies were horrified. So prejudiced were they against this science that my chief doctor-professor warned me not to take such a foolish step, as he called it, towards 'sheer Quakery'. He considered all practitioners of Nature Cure, nothing less than charlatans.*"

Again, Jehangir recovered, and along with the success of the eye exercises was more than convinced that naturopathy worked. He was now well set for a career in naturopathy despite all the initial opposition and scepticism; the opposition, if anything, seemed to have made him more determined. (It must be mentioned here that the Nature Cure Clinic and Sanatorium run by Dr. Dinshah K. Mehta was later converted to the National Institute of Naturopathy (NIN) in 1986 located at Bapu Bhavan on Tadiwala Road. Bapu Bhavan is named after Mahatma Gandhi who had made this Institution his home whenever he was in Pune. The All-India Nature Cure Foundation Trust was established here and Mahatma Gandhi became its life-long Chairman.)

Another Twist

As destiny would have it, this decision to reach out to Dinshah Mehta had far reaching consequences. Jehangir was deeply impressed by Mehta's personality and principles, and began to take Nature Cure seriously. In February 1931, he joined the clinic as a helper. Jehangir learnt fast and impressed Dinshah with his diligence and hard work. The next year he was put in charge of the Bombay branch of the clinic, at Wassiamal Building, Grant Road. He was asked to manage the Poona clinic in 1934, then the Bombay clinic in 1935. Dinshah was a shikari and would often go on *shikars* hunting panthers which invaded nearby villages, leaving Jehangir in charge. (Apparently, he discussed the issue of killing panthers with Gandhiji who reportedly told him that the taking of life was necessary in this case.) Jehangir got to know Dinshah's sister Mehera well during a tiger shoot in Sinhagad, the romance blossomed, and the two got married.

Despite the relationship now taking a new turn, their professional association didn't last much longer. Jehangir resigned in 1935 itself much to Mehta's dismay. But he had other plans. He wanted to branch out on his own. By this time, Gandhiji used to regularly come for nature therapy and stayed at Dinshah's Bapu cottage. Other political leaders also found solace in Dinshah Mehta's nature cure which grew rapidly in popularity.

To mark his own imprint, Jehangir decided to update his naturopathy skills. He enrolled in the Davidson College of Natural Therapeutics in Newcastle Upon Tyne for a triple-barrelled ND, DO, DC (Doctor of Naturopathy, Doctory of Osteopathy, Doctor of Chiropractic). It was a one-year course and he left in October 1936, exactly a year after his marriage, and returned in October 1937. He went on a Wadia scholarship accompanied by Mehera. The Tatas funded her. Both of them did well and Mehera qualified as a masseuse and assisted Dr. Davidson for a while.

Elite Clientele & Encounters

As time passed, Dr. Jussawalla's naturopathy was being wooed by the elite of the country. With success and growing accolades, naturopathy became his greatest passion, the very meaning of his existence. His practice thrived, and there was no looking back.

His *Natural Therapy Clinic,* started at *Petit House, Gowalia Tank*, on *February 15, 1938* and later at *Sunama House, Cumballa Hill,* drew a wide range of patients. The list included Mahatma Gandhi, Jawaharlal Nehru, Morarji Desai, Vallabhai Patel, Vijaylakshmi Pandit, J.R.D. Tata, Rukmini Devi, the Birlas, the Bajajs, the Mafatlals, Leela Naidu, Prithviraj Kapoor, Madhubala, Nargis, Pradeep Kumar, Shashi Kapoor, Meena Kumari, Raj Kapoor, Yusuf Meherally, Governors, MPs, MLAs, business magnates, lawyers, students, film stars, medical professionals, dancers, writers, yogis, wrestlers, high ranking police officers and a large chunk of middle-class professionals and housewives. There were all types: some wanted to put on or lose weight, others just came for the enemas and bowel washes. Many patients needed special kinds of massage for muscular and joint pains, and there were those who came for moral and emotional guidance. Dr. Jussawalla believed in treating the whole patient with diet and nutrition. He believed, as he said in his acceptance speech when he was given the Dhanvantari Award, not just in normal health, but ABSOLUTE POSITIVE HEALTH.

Yusuf Meherally came to him "a dead man," in Dr. Jussawalla's words, a terminal case too late to save. He spent six months at the clinic and died there. Morarji Desai, whose fasts he sometimes supervised, was a good patient but difficult to like. He admired Jawaharlal Nehru despite being roundly scolded by him once on account of Morarji. "You're playing fast and loose with the CM's life! You're starving him!" Nehru shouted on the grounds of a house in Juhu where Morarji was temporarily staying. Dr. Jussawalla tried to explain that fasting wasn't starving, and before he could offer an explanation Morarji arrived on the scene, his face glowing. He had gone for a brisk walk. Nehru relented. Adil recounts the event. "Nehru landed in a helicopter and asked about Morarji. Father explained that the fast was to eliminate poisons and before he could complete the explanation, Morarji Desai came in from his early morning walk pink faced and glowing. Nehru, a trifle flustered, said, 'Okay, okay, carry on'. Morarji Desai was kept on a fast of distilled water, juices and raw vegetables for ten days."

After the Indo-china war in 1962, Nehru was not keeping well and whenever he was in Bombay, Dr. Jussawalla was at hand to treat him. "One day I received a call from Vijaylakshmi Pandit asking me to intervene and not to allow Panditji to go out," he reminisced in an interview. When Dr. Jussawalla approached him, Nehru told him: *Jusswalla, maine vada jo kar diya* (I have given my promise). That evening, despite his frail health, thanks to Dr. Jussawalla's 'first aid', Nehru managed to attend the dance performance of Vyjantimala Bali.

Dr. Jussawalla's clients also included the cream of Hindi cinema. "Meena Kumai used to visit the clinic along with her sister and one day after the session she didn't return home. She married a man old enough to be her father. Newspapers made a hue and cry that she was last seen at my clinic," he recollected light-heartedly to a reporter. So popular was he with Bollywood that Dilip Chitre, the well known writer, painter and filmmaker, once quipped to Adil, "The starlets owe their complexion to Jehangir uncle. He was the natural cosmetologist."

Mahatma Gandhi & Naturopathy

Dr. Jussawalla had the highest praise for the Father of the Nation who was a great believer in naturopathy. I quote from his diary: *"The greatest Naturopathy in our country was no less a person than Mahatma Gandhi. I had an opportunity of coming into contact with Gandhiji in connection with a Nature Cure treatment he was going through and was greatly impressed by his faith, self-control, moral courage, selflessness, and simplicity -- the qualities of greatness. Gandhiji's attitude to Nature Cure was positive and forthright. After the various long fasts he undertook, he benefited a great deal from Nature Cure. This set him thinking about how to bring its benefits within reach of the poorest villages. He was greatly worried by the high quality of medical treatment. Nature Cure became for him one of his experiments with truth. He opened a Nature Cure centre in a modern size village about 150 miles from Bombay. His aim was to make treatment as inexpensive as possible by getting from Nature her many gifts of healing which those living in big cities had lost."*

In a magazine interview many years later, Dr. Jussawalla adds about Gandhiji, "He did his 21-day fast from a spiritual point of view. I was there with him. Even when his urine started showing acetone, he flatly refused any food. So I put lime juice in his enema, so that he would retain something at least. But that man had such strength -- he had something higher than just physical strength."

He recounts that he was once scolded by Gandhiji who sent for him occasionally when he was fasting. "Jussawalla, I don't like this," he said more than once. "Your clinic is for the rich. It should serve the poor." And when he was preparing to leave for New York, to attend the Golden Jubilee Conference of the American Naturopathic Association to which he had been invited, Gandhiji wrote in his typical Gujarati on a post card: "By going, you are not helping India. Stay here and serve."

Whenever Gandhiji was in Bombay (Mumbai), a messenger would arrive at the Jussawalla Clinic to summon him either to the Congress House or the Jamnalal Bajaj's cottage at Juhu. "Whenever I visited him, I would be in my suit which was objected to by his followers. One day I asked him about it and Gandhiji laughed it off. He used to tell me that my clinic was for the rich, but I used to retort that it is open for all," he remarked in another newspaper interview.

Life and Times

What was Dr. Jussawalla like as a father and husband? With his passion for work and the long hours he put in, did he have time for the family? "Despite all the distractions, his domestic life wasn't as bad as one would have imagined," notes Adil. "But in all honesty I suspect mother felt left out and unloved as he was always more fond of his mother, he was devoted to her, (*for motherhood there is no substitute*, his dairy would read. *It is the golden cord that unites the creatures of this earth to God.*) Mother did love father but his responses to her were more often cold and hurtful. There was also a period of separation. Most school vacations were spent without him. His work took up all his time. He'd be in his consulting room by six, some times five-thirty in the morning, ready to meet his first patients. He'd be there till eight in the evening, sometimes later, long after his nursing staff had gone home. His patients called him at all times of the day or night to visit them in their homes. Sometimes family outings, planned for a Sunday, would have to be cancelled because one of his patients called. Slowly, inexorably, his patients took him away from us. It took us some time to accept this and I don't think my mother ever did. But he organised and joined us once on a two-week trip to the north which he thoroughly enjoyed."

Mehera understood Jehangir's mission (she was a trained masseuse) and tried her best to beautify the clinic with hand-painted copies of Amrita Sher Gils. Despite the occasional marital discord, she supported and encouraged Jehangir in his work. She had trained at Shantiniketan too and had an artist's eye. "She transformed the clinic's waiting room from a dowdy box hung with photographs to an art gallery," says Adil. "Mother was always very giving and I suspect often misunderstood. Father was unable to show kindness and affection to close family members but he was very good to everyone else he met. But despite being admired and extremely popular he could never nurture a close friendship. Maybe, he just didn't have the time! But his neo-Gandhian, Brahminical-Calvinist work ethic, that's the one label I can think of, didn't infect the clinic. The place frequently rang with laughter from all quarters. He laughed and joked easily."

An Indulgent Father

As a father he was almost faultless. "He wanted happiness, peace, prosperity for the family. But, most important, he wanted health for all of us," continues Adil. "He had a disgust for dirt and didn't encourage street food, but he never imposed his will on our eating habits even if he was disappointed with them. He was calm unlike mother and was generous with money. We always got more than what was needed. He loved knowledge and would get the best encyclopaedias for us. He wanted us to have the very best in education and would invest in it. He made it a point to find time for us on weekends when we went to the movies. He loved *The Hunchback of Notre Dame*, *Jungle Book*, *The Life of Emile Zola*, *The Count of Monte Cristo*, *King Kong*, Chaplin and Garbo films, and such classics. He was an indulgent father."

Dr. Jussawalla was on several committees and was also saddled with several man management issues at the clinic. "But he was never really an ideal committee man," notes Adil. "For one thing he didn't like leaving his clinic for a minute unless it was for house calls. Meetings in New Delhi and Calcutta sometimes left him agitated for days." Adil recalls, "Father was outspoken and would speak his mind even at important meetings with eminent people. But he had the rare ability to engage in discussions with people he would disagree with. At the height of the clinic's success, between the late 1950s and early 1970s, he had 25 assistants, women and men. In the months before his crippling fall in 1993, he had none. Every patient of his that I've met has told me that, as a masseur, he had wonderful hands. But, like every ambitious doctor, he knew he needed more than his hands to succeed; he needed assistants."

He was loved by his patients, had excellent bedside manners and was regarded as a kind and patient doctor. As I sift through the countless letters of appreciation, I can clearly see all this. An introvert even after being courted by success, Dr. Jussawalla would look for time to reflect, to disengage from the many demands of his professional life. "He disliked society and luckily mother too shared this distaste. They wouldn't throw or even attend parties," continues Adil. "But despite not being a sociable person, he made sure he dressed well. He had fine shoes and classy suits. He was clean shaved and well turned out. His favourite colour was silver grey. During the day, he wore his doctor's white clothes with mother-of-pearl buttons. He dressed well for official functions."

In 1952, he became honorary director of the *Victoria Memorial School for the Blind in Tardeo.* He taught them *physiotherapy.* Oozing energy, propelled by his passion to heal, Dr. Jussawalla always kept active. His life radiated the words from the Vedanta – *Intense work is rest*. "He would walk up and down the clinic, going to all the cubicles, and meeting all the patients and those who wanted his time for whatever reason. He practised what he preached," adds Adil. "Father was always working but was never fatigued. Now the blind school ate up whatever spare time he had. It was an activity very close to his heart. He was proud of those students who went on to become professional masseurs and was greatly distressed when the physiotherapy department closed. Sometimes, he even missed the *qawalis* he liked listening to on Sundays after lunch. If he had any spare time on a weekend it went in writing and taking sun-baths. One of my most vivid memories of father is of him sitting on the west facing balcony outside his bedroom, bare-chested, his skin glowing in the sun. He seemed content, his eyes closed, moving his body almost imperceptively, basking in the sun, resigned to its healing."

How did he find the time for everything, particularly his books? "He used to write at the clinic, he used to write at home," says Adil. "He would always be making notes and taking down quotes for the many books he penned. He wrote for many of the journals of his time, including *The Illustrated Weekly of India*, *Eve's Weekly* and *Kaiser-e-Hind*. Between 1949, when he brought out his first pamphlet *The Message of Nature Cure to Suffering Humanity* to 1994, when he brought out his last book *Nature's Materia Medica,* he published more than 30 books and booklets, many for Jasu Shah's Vegetarian Society to which he was committed." Dr. Jussawalla wanted the message of natural healing to spread. "*It is essential that the knowledge we gain through books and experience be imparted by teaching, training, writing and research to help suffering humanity and people at large*," he would say in his diary.

Milk & Vegetarianism

A man of strict habits, Dr. Jussawalla didn't smoke, drink or even have tea and coffee. His favourite meal was chana daal and dhudi with ginger-garlic in it. He avoided fried food and potatoes with rice. "He fell ill just once in late middle age when he overdid eating grapefruit and paid the price with uncontrolled diarrhoea," recalls Adil. "Cooking for him, with his strict dietary compartments was a thankless task, especially since he showed no appreciation for the meals mother made for him, in the beginning with the help of a cook, later on her own. A home-cooked *dabba* (tiffin) was impossible since he usually left by six in the morning, sometimes by 5.30. His lunch at the clinic was sparse: nuts, dates, *dahi* or *lassi*, sometimes cornflakes and milk and always, during the mango season, mangoes and milk. Milk was an essential part of his diet. He never stopped talking about the wholesomeness of milk or the benefits of a milk diet."

Dr. Jussawalla was a firm believer in the goodness of milk. The ingestion of milk has had its share of controversy in recent times but it worked well for him. The milk diets fattened his underweight patients and when surgeons cut open his flesh after he fell at his clinic at the age of 85, to pin together a femur which had shattered, they were amazed his bones were so strong. In one of his books he extols the virtues of milk, "Milk contains proteins, carbohydrates, fat, salts and vitamins and has been termed a complete food. The great nutritional value of milk is due to the high quality of its proteins, its richness in mineral element and vitamins, and the easy digestibility of its fats. It protects against nutritional failure and therefore is classed among the protective foods." There are all types of milk available these days, and the quality of locally available non-packaged milk is debatable. But, without a doubt, high quality, unadulterated raw milk is considered a healthful, living food. It is filled with over 60 digestive enzymes, growth factors, and immunoglobulins. It is also rich in beneficial raw fats, amino acids, vitamins, protein, and conjugated linoleic acid (CLA). Dr. Jussawalla was obviously referring to uncompromised high quality milk which is sadly in short supply today.

As time passed, he was convinced that being vegetarian was necessary for spiritual growth. "I remember him having chicken when we lived at the clinic. That went, sometime in the 1950s, I think. A little later went eggs," notes Adil. Vegetarianism, for him, was a conscious decision made on rational principles. "Vegetarianism has so many facets; there are aesthetic concerns, concerns for sanctity of life, moral concerns, and scientific ones. I was initiated into vegetarianism at the Doctor Davidson college of Natural Therapeutics when we studied matters like autotoxemia," he would explain in one of his books.

Allopathy *vs* Nature Cure

What about all the criticism to Nature Cure, and how did he take it? There was opposition all along, even when he embarked on a career in naturopathy. **"Fad, humbug, quackery: nature cure was called worse things. But drugless systems of healing worked for him and for many of his patients.** They worked for mother who, in 1957, was suspected of having a cancer; in her case the cure was Christian Science. They worked for Firdausi, my younger brother, who was narrowly saved from an operation on one of his kidneys by father's intervention. They worked for my wife Veronik whose jaundice went with the daily supply of *paan* and a powder father secretly obtained and delivered. I once had to take antibiotics to get me through broncho-pneumonia when I was eight. But that I guess is testimony to father having an open mind to all systems of medicine," points out Adil.

Dr. Jussawalla always maintained that he was not entirely opposed to allopathy. He admitted that it has been the fountainhead of much important scientific discovery. But what he opposed was the misuse of it. **"Antibiotics have cured so many diseases, have saved so many lives. But the unrestrained use of antibiotics has its disadvantages too,"** he would say. He was particularly upset by the closed-mindedness of allopaths. "They do not see the merits of systems of thought that are old and deeply empirical. They do not seem to care about prevention of disease. They do not seem to understand that the alternative forms of medicine are not inimical to allopathy, but complementary to it. There are two methods of treating disease; combative and preventive. We emphasise the preventive."

This was evident at the Universal Health Institute on Lamington Road where he was the honorary director. There were ayurveds, homeopaths and allopaths working together. **After the patient went through a thorough examination, they would sit together and discuss the case and choose the modality of treatment. Despite being a successful naturopath, he didn't boycott allopathic medicines. He was open to the other healing arts and would resort to antibiotics if they were absolutely necessary.** He read the papers and medical journals thoroughly and made it a point to be abreast of the latest in medical trends in conventional medicine. If allopathy could save life or alleviate pain and there was no other option in non-invasive therapies, he would use it. I quote from his diary. "*A physician has rightly said, 'There is so much good in all systems of healing that it would be a crime to belittle or ignore any of them, but there is so much bad in the best of a single method to fight all others methods'. I believe that co-operation between practitioners of different systems of healing is needed. The object, after all, is to relieve suffering. A closed mind and healing don't go together.*"

Gizmos & Indulgences

In modern lingo, Dr. Jussawalla may have been called a gizmo freak. In an era, when even a phone connection was sheer luxury in India, his clinic had many space-age contraptions that sent out infrared and ultraviolet rays with a faint buzz; steam-bath and radiant-heat cabinets, on which patients' heads rested; sun lamps; a sitz bath; a needle bath; a python-like hose that ejected water with great force, a jet bath; and glassy, tubed contraptions for bowel washes. His Natural Therapy Clinic was a one-stop shop where you bought the treatment you wanted depending on the doctor's diagnosis. He had all sorts of health apparatus imported from England, USA and Germany and was specially known for his water treatments.

He also had his indulgences. In June 1947, just before Indian independence, he went to New York for the International Nature Cure Conference to celebrate the golden jubilee of the American Nature Cure Congress and brought a left-hand-drive silver-grey Chevrolet to Bombay. "He drove it for years. Later, he got himself a second hand Dodge and finally a Maruti," remembers Adil. "He also had a fondness for new gadgets and took to the electric shaver. He had a collection of western classical and Hindustani music. He liked the violin and was fond of high-end watches and pens. For a man with a scientific bent of mind, he was also into numerology and astrology. He dabbled in medical astrology which he may have used in diagnosis." **When critics pointed out that astro-medicine could well be a pseudo-science, he retorted, "Never utter, these words: 'I do not know this therefore it is false'. One must study to know, know to understand, understand to judge."** He also made use of teletherapy which involves curing the patient using a photograph or a signature. "Cosmic rays are radiated to the photographs reaching to the patient, penetrating his aura, which is considered the place of the disease," he explained in an interview.

Despite his successes, Dr. Jussawalla always remained rooted. He had given himself to a higher power to guide him along the way and there was no room for arrogance or the false triumphs that come easily to ordinary mortals. But in a lighter vein, according to Firdausi, his youngest son, actor and airline executive, "When father heard that he had won the Dhanvantari Award, he thought he had won the *Padma Shri* and there was a spring in his walk." He also "loved to draw donkeys and rabbits on odd bits of paper and once he dreamt he was wandering as a ghost in J.B.Petit sanatorium!"

End Times

In 1994, at the age of 84, Dr. Jussawalla was the sole medical worker in his clinic and still accepting very difficult cases for treatment. He was also preparing to write more volumes, one on teaching blind students physiotherapy, when he had a fall that broke his right thigh-bone.

Adil recalls making a phone call to him around the same time. In a magazine article he says, "He (father) said of himself that he would die in harness and others have admiringly said that of him too. In January 1993 he almost did that. His patient low-pitched voice, during the course of a chance call I made to the clinic, told me that he'd fallen and couldn't move. There was nobody else around. We found him on the floor, after a break-in with the help of neighbours. He was lying just outside his consulting room, a telephone next to him. He had fallen in the room just before seven in the morning. It had taken him more than three-and-a-half hours to drag himself from his room to the place where the phone was. He had, with great difficulty, managed to pull it down with a stick. He was trying to call someone but couldn't.

"He had fractured his upper thigh. It was repaired. He went back to work, had another fall two years later, and fractured his other thigh. Later he had a stroke. He used to say of himself that he was a fighter and he still is. He fights with the nurses who care for him, he fights with us. That's when he resists being fed, otherwise he sleeps. He fights like a trussed bull, in bed, his stunned brain unable to have him sit upright on his own, unable to stand upright for long unable to recover. He struggles with himself, with unconsciousness, with an unseen foe, and falls back exhausted. He said of himself that he'd live past 90. His body, still strong, says yes but the unseen foe commands No."

Despite occasionally asserting that he'd never die, did he feel his age? The answer is Yes. In a note in his diary, he says: *"Looking back from the high watchtower of old age on the past years of my life and all the complications of my paths, they seem to wind themselves sometimes on the brink of an abyss; but they lead against all expectation to the glorious heights of vocation and finally attain them, and I have every reason to praise the tender and wise ruling of providence, the more so as the paths which according to human ideas seemed to be sad and leading to death, showed to me and numberless others the opening to new life."*

Dr. Jussawalla died on the morning of December 5, 1997. He was 90 years old. Mehera died a few years later in 2006 at the age of 94.

Looking Back, Looking Forward

Was it all worth it -- A lifetime spent in caring for the sick!? A diary jotting is eloquent. "*It was an uphill task to begin with facing strong criticism, trying to gain the confidence of patients against all odds, and especially while treating those who had been rejected by other systems of medicine. But as my practice grew, I was brought into contact with a variety of people -- the rich, the poor, political leaders and businessmen. They came to me with their illnesses and their personal problems -- the father with his anxieties the mother with her hidden grief, the daughter with her trials and the son with his follies.*"

The hand of destiny had also most certainly rocked Dr. Jussawalla's cradle. Like with most of us, new paths open without much prodding. In his case, he seemed to be born entrusted with the role of curing the diseased. I quote from his diary: "*Just as on a tree no leaf resembles perfectly to another, so also do men's destinies differ one from the other. If every man were to write a sketch of his own life, we should have as many different tales as there are men. Intricate are the ways twisting themselves in our life in every direction, sometimes like an inextricable ball of confused silk, the threads of which seem to be laid without plan or purpose. So it frequently seems; but it never is so in reality. Faith darts its enlightening beam; into the darkness, and shows how all these paths serve wise purposes and how all of them lead to one end, designed and fixed by the all-wise creator from the beginning. The ways of providence are wonderful.*"

Drugless & Bloodless

After decades as a naturopath and witnessing the miracles it brought to ailing humanity, he was even more convinced of the efficacy of Nature Cure as a valuable system of healing. He notes, "*Naturopathy, as Nature Cure is often called, is not the invention of any one human mind. Its origin can't be traced to any specific date, but is the accumulation of knowledge of natural methods of living and healing throughout the centuries. In our own country we can say that Naturopathy is one of the ancient Indian civilization's gifts to the world. Centuries before Plato, Aristotle and Hippocrates were born, Indian yogis and sages expounded certain principles of natural healing. It can be said that Nature Cure was practiced by holy men and their disciples as a means of purifying body, mind and soul. It called for great will power and self-control. Fasting, Sattvic diet, hydrotherapy, massage, the various asanas were all, in a way, a means to make the body invincible to disease.*

Noting how great the benefits were and how low the cost of treatment was, certain yogis devised a means of making the system available to the humblest. To the lessons of Naturopathy, they lent the great authority of Religion, so that its principles could be followed with reverence and zeal."

He underscored the fact in every interview he gave that Nature Cure was an independent system of medicine, that it was a distinct system of healing, based upon its own philosophy of life, health and disease. "It is by no means a collection of fads and notions, as is popularly supposed, nor is it a scheme for returning to a wild life in the woods. It is restoration and maintenance of health, and correction of body disorders without the use of poisonous drugs. Naturopathy is not a rigid system. Though fundamentally 'drugless' and 'bloodless' it does admit the use of both natural medicines and surgery, when it conforms to the basic principles of nature cure." He also never stopped repeating that the "participation and co-operation of the patient is the most important factor in healing."

Dr. Jussawalla always insisted that **"Nature Curists were not against medicine. We are not against surgery. We are not against drugs. But there are so many antibiotics needlessly being given, so many poisonous drugs. This is what we object to. Where surgery is absolutely necessary, by all means go to a surgeon. You can't expect a miracle cure. Suppose you have a hemorrhage, a blood transfusion has to be given. We won't say go on a fast!"** He elaborated, "Nature cure deals with auto-intoxication or self-poisoning. Our bloodstream must remain two-thirds alkaline and one-third acidic. Our diet should therefore be more alkaline. The balance within the bloodstream, two-thirds alkaline and one-third acidic, has to be maintained." He consistently harped on the Unity of Disease and Unity of Cause because, **"Practically all diseases are due to not looking after yourself. That can bring about so many things -- that is Unity of Disease. In the same way the Unity of Cure is that if you find that not looking after yourself causes disease, then treat it from that point of view -- don't treat the disease."**

Dr. Jussawalla maintained that allopathy or conventional medicine treated only the symptoms of the disease and not the cause of the problem. "Suppose you have a strong pain and you just take a tablet and you find that your pain has gone. This is only symptomatic treatment. Whereas, we go to the cause of the disease. Why do you get this sort of pain? Why indigestion? Why stomach ache? Even in a case of appendicitis, if we can help the patient without surgical interference we try and help him. Otherwise we send him to a surgeon. Please remember that we do a lot of investigations in Nature Cure before deciding on the course of treatment."

Healing from Within

Dr. Jussawalla's concept of health was not just about being free from disease but also about having the vitality to live life to the full. "When I talk of health, I mean sound health, not this artificial health created by vaccinations and innoculation. That is not health. Positive health is the body's natural immunity against disease. Healing is from within. Let the body try to heal itself. Even with diseases like smallpox, or typhoid, the body will fight it out. You see there are laws governing health, just as there are laws governing everything else in the world. Nowadays there are so many hazards – pollution, food adulteration and so on. Until you get rid of hazards like these how are you going in enjoy your health?"

He firmly believed that the future belonged to Nature Cure. **"People are getting sick of antibiotics but they are not prepared to change their habits. They come to us only when everything else has failed, when they have completely damaged their bodies.** I get cases of arthritis full of cortisone. We can't cut down the cortisone completely or he will be bed-ridden! The same thing happens with those who come to me with high insulin. We have to be very careful in putting the patient on a fast because he might go into a coma. The main cause of most problems is tension. It is a killer. Tension can lead to hyperacidity. Hyperacidity can lead to ulcers, and ulcers, if not properly treated, can lead to cancer. That's why we say you have to treat the *cause.* Today if a patient has a nervous breakdown, he is given depressive drugs. People become so habituated to them. I have people coming to me who have been on these drugs for years when all that needed to be done was to remove the source of tension. There are no incurable diseases, there are only incurable cases. It all depends on the vitality of the patient, how much vitality he has to fight the disease out."

He recounted a case of a VIP that worked out well thanks to the inherent vitality of the patient. "Once, I was treating a Chief Minister here. I had put him on a water fast for ten days because he had high fever, low-blood pressure, colitis, and a urinary infection. He flatly refused any medical help and insisted on Nature Cure. I told him that I didn't want any interference. For ten days I put him on bowel washes, distilled water, fomentations -- the fever came down, but the infection was still there. Then his urine started showing acetone -- a sign of starvation -- so I had to end the fast and put him on fruit juices. After four to five days on fruit juices, the acetone disappeared."

But he was also quick to point out that if the patient has been brought in too late and if a lot of damage has already been done he would have to take recourse in the conventional course of treatment. **"Suppose you have a case when due to too much surgical interference, or over-drugging, or the kidneys fail completely. What are you going to do? That's why I have written in favour of transplantations and surgery, though many Nature Curists are against it. What can you do when the organs are absolutely finished?"**

Dr. Jussawalla insisted that no modality of treatment was complete in itself. **"No science is perfect and there are limitations not only of the science but also of the practitioner. That's why there are so many different doctors. Otherwise, there would only be one doctor curing everybody."**

He recalled Meena Kumari's case. "She used to come to me at the beginning. At that time she was a young girl. She went through a little stress and started drinking. I told her. 'Look here, this is where you must stop'. But there was one doctor who said, 'No. let her have a little alcohol'. And then it started. Alcohol, alcohol, alcohol. There was no limit. She even went to England for treatment, and then it was too late." **Nature Cure also involves psychological counselling. The patient needs to relax, to be at peace, to enable the healing process. "I have certain patients who come here to relax. I give them a soothing massage, put them completely to sleep. The psychological aspect is very important."**

The world has changed, science has taken gigantic strides, and there are new discoveries both of new microbes and powerful medication. The stranglehold of conventional medicine has spread wider and man is arguably living longer if not healthier. I quote his diary, "We are living in a world of rapid change and much of that unfortunately lies in overlooking certain basic principles of life. We find the world moving in two directions. In many fields, chiefly science, we are really moving forward. But, in spite of the advances in the world of healing, disease and sickness are on the increase. How can we explain this except by saying that our chief approach to disease is wrong, that it is based on combative methods and mass medication not only for those who are ill, but for those who are healthy too (a reference to the mass vaccinations which we will go into later in the book). Natural health, which has the ability to resist disease, is entirely different from artificial health. Natural health is something which can only be achieved by strict adherence to hygiene, sanitation, health foods, fresh air, sunshine and exercise. In other words- -- by sticking to the laws of health which govern body and mind. The principles and physiology of Nature Cure have helped me treat the body and mind as a whole."

Chapter 4

Origins of Naturopathy

Nature Cure treatment brings us nearer to God. I will have no objection whatever if we could do even without it. But why be afraid of fast or avoid pure air? The meaning of Nature Cure is to go nearer Nature -- God.

-- From a letter written by M.K. Gandhi, Sevagram, 9-1-1945

A lot has been written on naturopathy, and yet a lot remains to be written. Let us look at this science in some detail, at the origins of naturopathy, hear relevant voices and contemporary trends, and then focus on the methods used by Dr. Jussawalla.

Naturopathy, or Naturopathic Medicine, is a type of alternative medicine based on a belief in *vitalism*. According to the medical dictionary, *vitalism* is a doctrine that the processes of life are not explicable by the laws of physics and chemistry alone and that life is in some part self-determining. It is believed that living organisms are fundamentally different from non-living entities because they contain some non-physical element often referred to as "vital spark", or "*élan vital*".

Vitalism has a long history in medical philosophies. Traditional healing practices posited that disease results from some imbalance in the vital energies. In the Western tradition founded by Hippocrates, these vital forces were associated with the four temperaments and humours. Eastern traditions mention similar forces called *qi* in China, *prana* in India, *ki* in Japan, *mana* in Polynesia and *Lüng* in Tibetan Buddhism. It is what the great poet Kabir referred to when asked, "Where is God?" His answer was simple. "He is the breath within the breath." To fully grasp the import of his words, we have to look beyond the physical composition of breath and beyond mere inhalation and exhalation. Kabir was talking about *prana*, the universal vital energy. *All that exists in the three heavens rests in the control of prana. As a mother her children, oh prana, protect us and give us splendour and wisdom,* says the ***Prashna Upanishad II.13*** *Prana* has many levels of meaning from the breath to the energy of consciousness itself. The entire universe is considered a manifestation of *prana*, which is the original creative power. In Hinduism, even *Kundalini Shakti*, the serpent power or inner power that transforms consciousness, is said to develop from the awakened *prana*.

These vital forces are present all over the universe both in macrocosm (space) and microcosm (bodies of living beings). Its proper flow in our bodies is essential for good health. Alternative medicine works on healing the body by stimulating this life force. The term "naturopathy" is derived from Greek and Latin, and literally translates as "nature disease."

Naturopathic practitioners are divided into two groups -- traditional naturopaths and naturopathic physicians. Naturopathic physicians employ the principles of naturopathy within the context of conventional medical practices, while naturopathy (practised by naturopaths) comprises many different treatment modalities which may or may not be fully accepted by the conventional medical community. Naturopathy has many arms: from standard evidence-based treatments, to homeopathy, ayurveda, siddha, unani and other seemingly esoteric practices.

Wisdom of Nature

Naturopathy is as old as man and is practised in every culture in every country. When cosmic time prevailed and when science was a distant dream, ancient man had no other option but to seek out the wisdom of nature for answers. Long before Hippocrates, who lived in 450 B.C., was Aesutaptes, son of the Sun God, described by Homer as a 'blameless physician'.

Excavations have revealed that even as early as the 5th century bathing houses had steam baths and massages. Hippocrates' idea on the use of water was picked up by Gallenus. Paracelsus, another great healer, born in 1493 in Switzerland, was also renowned for his natural healing methods.

To quote Paracelsus, "It was the book of nature which I studied, not those of scribblers, for each scribbler writes down the rubbish that may be found in his head." Each one handed the baton to his followers; each one of them had his own methods, and over time it all coalesced into the science of natural healing.

Since no particular date can be set to the origin of nature cure, it could well have originated thousands of years ago in a primal form. Ancient man knew how to call on nature for cures. There were herbalists, ayurveds, babas, medicine men, shamans and witch doctors. There were also epidemics and deadly accidents which took a toll, but ancient man tapped the plant world for efficacious cures for everyday ailments, accidents, poisonous bites and stings, and several more serious diseases.

But as civilization progressed, new diseases were born. Food habits changed, processed food and synthetic medicines entered the bloodstream, there was more pressure on the land and it started losing its nutrition thanks to chemical fertilizers and multiple cropping. The entire genetic structure of man, animal and plant began slowly changing. (Now, there is Genetically Modified Food which we will briefly touch later in the book). Along with modernism, came technology and radiation. *Science and its marvels became a double-edged sword.*

Modern Naturopathy

Modern Naturopathy grew out of the Natural Cure Movement of Europe. The term was coined in 1895 by John Scheel and popularised by Benedict Lust, the "father of U.S. naturopathy." The concepts of Sebastian Kneipp (1821-1897), Louis Kuhne who expounded the 'unity of disease and unity of cure' theory (1844-1907), Adolf Just (1838-1936), and Henry Lindlahr (1853-1925) played a prominent role in shaping it.

It is believed that Father Kneipp, a German priest, opened a 'water cure' centre after becoming convinced that he and a fellow student had cured themselves of TB by bathing in the Danube. Lust was treated by Kneipp.

In 1895, Lust went to the USA to promote the system there. Lindlahr further systematised naturopathy and opened a sanatorium and school in a Chicago suburb. John Harvey Kellogg (1852-1944), whose name is synonymous with Kellogg's cornflakes, was an American naturopath who wrote books on hydrotherapy and massage. Adolf Just also wrote many books to popularise the system, one of them being *Return to Nature*, which propelled Mahatma Gandhi to take a closer look at nature cure.

Since there is no exact date to the origin of nature cure, it can be reasonably assumed that it was a long process that evolved over time. The ancient Romans, the Egyptians, the Greeks and the Indians among others practised nature cure. But it was in Germany that nature cure was first recognised as a science. Vincient Priessnitz founded a sanatorium in

Grafenburg, a small village in the Silesian mountains in Germany, well over a century ago with great success. He drew patients from all over the world and his success with water cure laid the foundation for drugless therapy. Practitioners from everywhere became his students and the baton of knowledge passed on. The lamp was now lit and the flame would spread far and wide over time.

Louis Kuhne cured the sick with sunshine, steam and sitz baths. His slogan was simple: "Only cleansing can heal." In diagnoses, he relied on "facial expression", and his doctrine of the Unity of Disease is a pillar of Modern Nature Cure. Father Kneipp, another follower of Priessnitz, was a great advocate of water treatment, medicinal herbs and plants.

The Americans, who can never be left behind, caught on. Dr. Trall, Dr. Kellogg, Dr. Benedict Lust, Dr. Henry Lindlahr and others became students of Priessnitz. Dr. Lindlahr propounded the theory which every naturopath observes: "Every acute disease is a healing effort of nature." He was the first nature cure physician to co-ordinate all the different forms of natural treatment into one exact and complete science.

Several others improved on existing knowledge. Dr. Stall invented osteopathy, the scientific manipulation of the body structure, muscles, nerves and nerve centres. Dr. Tilden pioneered the right diet and firmly believed that wrong eating was one of the main causes of disease.

Dr. Palmer introduced chiropractic, a system of spinal manipulation to relax contracted tissue, replace dislocate bones, liberate and stimulate the flow of blood and nerve impulses and thereby work on removing the mechanical cause of disease. Dr. Kellogg introduced hydrotherapy in a scientific manner.

It may also be appropriate to mention The Feldenkrais Method here named after its originator, Dr. Moshe Feldenkrais, D.Sc. (1904-1984), a Russian-born physicist, judo expert, mechanical engineer and educator.

He had a serious knee injury and was faced with a 50 per cent chance for recovery and possible long-term confinement to a wheelchair. To recover, he developed a programme of therapeutic movement called the Feldenkrais Method based on the principles of physics and biomechanics, an empirical understanding of human physiology and the connection between mind and body. The method uses gentle movement and directed attention to increase ease and range of motion, improve flexibility and coordination.

The Feldenkrais Method helps ease stress and tension and is useful in the rehabilitation of stroke victims and in neurological injuries like brain tumours, head trauma, multiple sclerosis and ataxia. It can also be used in correcting poor posture or painful movement, eating disorders and even psychiatric conditions like depression and anxiety. It is gentle and non-invasive. Several methods of bodywork that focus on the musculoskeletal system -- including massage, manual manipulation, and acupuncture – along with yoga, tai chi or qigong can be used in conjunction with the Feldenkrais method to augment flexibility of movement.

Chinese Medicine

China has a rich legacy of indigenous healing. Traditional Chinese Medicine (TCM) is a healing system developed in China more than 2,000 years ago to "dispel evil and support the good." In addition to treating illness, TCM focusses on strengthening the body's defences and enhance its capacity for healing.

TCM encompasses how the human body interacts with all aspects of life and the environment, including the seasons, weather, time of day, diet and emotional states.

It believes that the key to health is the harmonious and balanced functioning of body, mind and spirit. According to TCM, the balance of health depends on the unobstructed flow of *qi* or "life energy" through the body, along pathways known as meridians.

TCM practitioners see disease as the result of disruptions in the circulation of *qi*. TCM can be particularly effective for complex diseases with multiple causes, including metabolic diseases, chronic and degenerative conditions and age-related diseases. According to Dr. Weil, many Chinese remedies appear to have significant therapeutic value and that some work on conditions for which Western doctors have no pharmaceutical drugs. Some TCM formulas combine eight to 12 herbs and may be prescribed in pill or extract form or as dried herbs to make a tea.

Moxibustion: Here, a burning cigar-shaped moxastick, usually made of the herbs mugwort or wormwood, is held near acupuncture points to stimulate them with heat and improve the flow of *qi*. It is used along with acupuncture and TCM practitioners may recommend it for improvement of general health as well as for the treatment of cancer, arthritis and digestive disorders.

Qigong: This is a 5,000 year-old mind-body practice as well as an energetic form of movement done to enhance the flow of *qi* in the body. By integrating posture, body movements, breathing and focused intention, Qigong is designed to improve mental and physical health.

Tuina (pronounced tway-na): A form of manipulative therapy, tuina aims to open the body's blockages and stimulating movement in the meridians and muscles.

Practitioners may brush, knead, roll, press and rub the areas between the arm and leg joints (known in TCM as the eight gates) and then use range of motion, traction, massage, with the stimulation of acupressure points. Tuina is used in TCM for treatment of both musculoskeletal and non-musculoskeletal conditions.

Acupressure: Here, TCM uses pressure (not needles) to stimulate the acupuncture points and meridians in order to release tension, promote blood circulation and *qi*. A popular manifestation of acupressure is the use of wristbands that press on a meridian point to prevent or reduce seasickness, as well as nausea from any cause.

Cupping: This 2,500-year-old practice involves placing special cups filled with heated air on painful areas of the body. As the cups cool, the volume of air within them shrinks, creating suction on the skin that increases blood flow to the area. It is commonly used to ease aches and pains, relieve respiratory problems, mitigate coughs and wheezing, improve circulation and reduce menstrual symptoms.

There are other natural therapies too. With time, new methods and apparatus have been added to the rich repertoire of Naturopathy.

Relevant Voices

Fed up and, at times, defeated by conventional modes of treatment, humanity is now looking at alternate cures with some urgency. Modern man in the Aquarian Age is looking at a lifestyle more in tune with a higher consciousness.

All life is yoga, said Sri Aurobindo. *Food cooked more than three hours before being eaten, which is tasteless, stale, putrid, decomposed and unclean, is food liked by people in the mode of ignorance*, says the

Bhagavad Gita (Chapter 17, verse 10). Evidently, food for the supramental man or the man of the higher consciousness is food that stimulates *Prana*!

Sadguru, the contemporary mystic and founder of *Isha Yoga*, believes that health has to happen within yourself. "Health is not something that you invented. Health is not your idea. When life processes are happening well, that is health. If at all we have created anything, it is ill-health," he says. "Use your body, use your head and use your energies. If these three things are well exercised and balanced, you will be healthy.

If your body is working well, your mind is working well and your energy is supporting the two, making sure nothing goes wrong, that is health. In yoga, when we say "health," we don't look at the body; we don't look at the mind; we only look at the energy -- the way it is. If your energy body is in proper balance and full flow, your physical body and mental body will be in perfect health."

H.K. Bakhru, Mumbai-based author of several naturopathy books, who retired as chief PRO with the Central Railways, India, adds, "Nature cure is a constructive method of treatment which aims at removing the basic cause of disease through the rational use of natural diet and elements freely available in nature."

Bakhru kept falling sick and underwent several surgical procedures until he decided to get to the root cause of his illnesses and not just hand over his body to physicians to experiment with. He researched naturopathy, adopted its ways, and was free of the intrusion of medicine until his demise after a long and well lived life.

"It is the oldest mode of treatment. When an animal injures itself, it will hasten to dip the injured part in water," says S. Swaminathan, a Delhi-based minimalist naturopath. "Nature cure is synonymous with nature care and is essentially concerned with the care of the mind, body and spirit.

Nature cure is a harmonised amalgamation of the basic sciences like physiology, applied psychology, nutrition, sanitation and immunity. There is an ingrained power of healing within the body that has to be activated by following certain simple doctrines. Not only does it improve the condition of a diseased person but it also enhances the immunity of a healthy person.

Nature cure is nature's prerogative and cannot be imposed. Those who live in tune with the laws of life keep their body and mind clean and maintain health. Human health, as everything else in the world, is governed by the laws of nature. One of them is cause and effect."

Healing in India

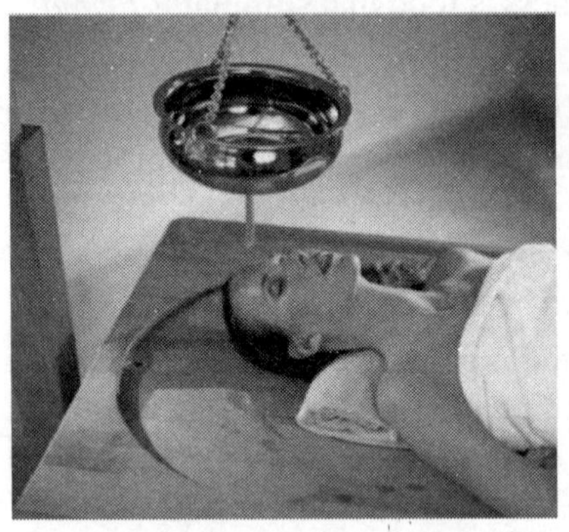

India, ancient and rich in culture and knowledge, was a forerunner in Nature Cure thanks to its rishis, yogis, saints, mendicants and visionaries. Yogis could fast endlessly, contort their bodies effortlessly, were immune to heat and cold, and were considered to live with vigour for well over a hundred years. They worked on their mind and body to withstand pain and deprivation. Modern medicine hadn't made inroads and so naturopathy and ayurveda or healing with herbs according to the *prakriti* of the body was widely practised. Cow products which include urine and *gobar* were also well used in cures. India had a powerful and reliable healing system in place. There were countless healing practices spread over this large, populous and diverse land. But it wasn't well documented and didn't fall under a single reliable, authentic and credible umbrella with easy access to a vast populace.

During the Vedic period there were clear ideas about the medicinal uses of water. The Ganga, among other holy rivers, was considered pure and it was believed that its waters could cure many diseases, a belief that holds good even today despite the high pollution levels. Scientists in the UK have isolated an enzyme in its waters that kept it pure. In the *Rig Veda*, fasting was advocated as the supreme medicine to eliminate accumulated toxins. The *Manu Smriti* had clear ideas about personal hygiene and the maintenance of good health. The *Bhagawad Gita* detailed the types of foods and its effects on the human body and mind. India was and is still filled with curative hot and cold springs. There were world famous baths in the forts and palaces of yore. Rajgir in Bihar was well known for its hot springs packed with sulphur ions.

But, of course, the greatest naturopath of India was none other than Mahatma Gandhi, the Father of the Nation. He would undertake several fasts (not only for political reasons) and also spend time in ashrams and naturopathy centres to heal his tired body. When modern medicine slowly made its inroads into India, the Mahatma opened a nature cure centre in Urli Kanchan, a small town about 250 kms from Mumbai. The centre has grown and draws patients from all over the world.

Today's India, despite the widespread use of conventional allopathic medicine, is dotted with naturopathy centres and is a haven for cures of all kinds. Home grown and well documented alternate healing methods dot the land from Kashmir to Kanyakumari. India has given birth to the world's largest homoepathy chain in Dr. Batra's, and has unani, siddha and ayurvedic practitioners who perform miracles. Yoga and therapeutic massage are also widespread. India is also a hub for medical tourism as peoples from all over the world come here to tap the life saving skills of its medical practitioners. The world has shrunk and conventional medicine has a massive presence. But, along with it, is the natural healer who is resorted to when everything else fails; and now, increasingly, also as the first choice of treatment.

Conventional Medicine *vs* Alternative Therapies

Thanks to the rapid advances in medical science, the stranglehold of allopathy or conventional medicine -- which relies solely on evidence-based medicine (EBM)—is all-pervasive today. Without a doubt, conventional medicine has been able to wipe away epidemics from the face of the earth and ensure better health and greater longevity for both mankind and domesticated birds and animals. Cutting edge discoveries in research laboratories around the world have made miracles happen: from cloning animals and humans and even playing God by making new body parts, creating life, and even cheating death. The future only beckons infinite possibilities.

But, possibly because of all this, conventional medicine, which is also a multi-billion dollar business and growing by the nano second, tends to go overboard in its quest for profits. The miracle cures are heady, and the infinite possibilities that beckon the future so charmingly can dispatch ethics to the bin. The media brims with such occurrences. Mankind is desperately seeking the youth and immortality pill. There is money to be made from miracle cures. Life is a one-time jab, fast and fleeting. 'Live fast and young forever' is the new credo. A little greed may be pardoned if the end, even if it is a bit unethical, is met. Finally, the buck never stops!

Alternate healers, on the other hand, seemingly more humane and sensitive, goaded by concerns not just pecuniary, claim that that the human being is a complex maze of emotions and EBM alone may not be the answer to most diseases. They want the human being to be seen more holistically.

They want prevention of disease and softer, more complete and lasting, less 'violent' cures without side-or after-effects. Many naturopaths have even opposed vaccination saying it goes against the body chemistry resulting in severe damage to the body. The views against vaccination, expressed unequivocally by Dr. Jussawalla decades ago, have grown more strident in recent times and we will highlight that later in the book.

But despite the growing global approval of naturopathy, the world of conventional allopathic medicine has not been really encouraging of naturopathy. The reasons are quite obvious as the pharmaceutical industry makes a killing (the pun is your call) raking in the big bucks! Plus, as the monetary incentive is so huge, conventional medicine is also prone to unethical practices. In his book *Bad Pharma*, Ben Goldacre highlights how drugs enter the market and are promoted as effective by pharmaceutical companies and doctors, even when trials have shown then to be ineffective and, often, unsafe. It is estimated that medical errors kill the equivalent of four jumbo jets' worth of passengers every week, but the death toll is being largely ignored. Also, that up to 30 per cent of all medical procedures, tests and medications may be unnecessary – at a cost of at least $210 billion a year. This, of course, does not include the unquantifiable cost of emotional suffering and related complications. Possibly to safeguard its interests, The American Cancer Society has even remarked, "Available scientific evidence does not support claims that naturopathic medicine can cure cancer or any other disease, since virtually no studies on naturopathy as a whole have been published."

Growing Popularity

But even in the face of such pronouncements, alternate therapies are growing in popularity with homeopathy being officially accorded the status of the most popular method of treatment globally after allopathy! A U.S. survey by the National Center for Complementary and Alternative Medicine (NCCAM) and the National Center for Health Statistics found that over 36 per cent of American adults use complementary and alternative medicine. That number jumps to more than double when prayer used specifically for health reasons is included in the definition. The reasons for alternative medicine's popularity, according to an article titled *Why Patients Use Alternative Medicine* by John A. Astin, Ph.D, in the *Journal of the American Medical Association* explains that people seeking alternative medicine aren't necessarily dissatisfied with conventional medicine, but they find "these health care alternatives to be more congruent with their own values, beliefs, and philosophical orientations toward health and life."

In recent times, there has been a significant evolution towards a more proactive, holistic view of well-being. "Conventional medicine has a lopsided view of the physical, mental, and spiritual body," surmises Andrew Weil, M.D., who has locked horns with the medical mainstream with what he calls integrative medicine. His definition of the term is very straightforward: healing-oriented medicine that takes into account the whole person (body, mind, and spirit), including all aspects of lifestyle. In 1994, Weil was instrumental in creating The University of Arizona Medical School's Program in Integrative Medicine, the first comprehensive, continuing-education fellowship to give physicians the chance to learn about alternative therapies such as botanicals, acupuncture, Reiki, massage, diet, and meditation -- and how they can be used to enhance medical care, prevent illness, and improve quality of life. "We are looking at the whole body, at lifestyle, at the relationship between the practitioner and the patient," Weil explains. "Not only is this the kind of medicine patients want, but it has the potential to restore the core values of medicine in an age of managed care."

Medical schools in the United States now also offer some kind of elective integrative medicine curriculum. They have accepted the fact that naturopathic philosophy is based on the concept of the healing power of nature and that the earliest doctors and healers worked with herbs, foods, water, fasting and bodywork. In the U.S. today, certification follows study at a four-year, graduate-level, naturopathic medical school which includes the basic sciences studied by M.D.s. Additionally, students are taught holistic and non-toxic approaches to therapy with a strong emphasis on optimising wellness and disease prevention. Apart from following a standard medical curriculum, the naturopathic physician is required to complete four years of training in clinical nutrition, acupuncture, homeopathic medicine, botanical medicine, psychology and counselling. Naturopathic physicians then take professional board examinations before being licensed by a state or jurisdiction as primary care general practice physicians (identified as an ND or NMD).

Leading hospitals have also recognised alternative therapy. Sloan-Kettering's integrative medicine centre has included bedside therapists and massage, meditation, hypnotherapy, and yoga sessions. At the

Bendheim Integrative Medicine Center, Sloan-Kettering's outpatient integrative medicine facility, crystals and *mandala* art grace the walls. There is herbal tea, fruit, or juice breaks. Additionally, yoga classes, hypnotherapy, meditation, massage, acupuncture, *qi gong* and other therapies are on offer.

Evidently, *alternate therapies* have come to stay.

Chapter 5

Dr. Jussawalla's Methods

Alter Your Ride
Alter Your Vehicle
Alter Your Journey
For Your Sacred Vehicle... whatever, whoever, wherever that may be
--- Vedi Vaahans by Vyana Yoga

Nature Cure, according to Dr. Jussawalla, is the term applied to any method of treating disease which cooperates with nature and augments the defence mechanism of the body or its natural ability to fight disease. Nature cure, he says simply, is a way of life in tune with the vital life-giving forces; it is about living in harmony with the supreme force which acts on every atom, molecule and cell of the human body. It is about the right food, water and thought processes that ensure optimal health.

Naturopathy, on the other hand, is the system of medicine that uses air, light, water, heat and other natural modalities to diagnose and treat diseases. The essential difference between the two is that nature cure is a broader term that incorporates a way of life to augment the body's life energy or *prana* or inherent intelligence. It can be used as a preventive process. *Naturopathy, on the other hand, is the method that uses nature to heal a diseased body.*

All healing is from within, emphasises Dr. Jussawalla. It is nature that heals and cures. The naturopath only interprets nature's law to aid in the healing process. The human body is a wonderful mechanism and can repair itself. Naturopathy helps trigger the healing processes, the vital force within us, and helps restore balance.

Naturopathy helps remove wastes, toxins and foreign substances from the body. It stimulates the organs of purification and elimination. It frees nerves, blood vessels and the lymphatic system from obstruction. It balances glandular activities, relieves nervous and muscular tensions, and restores to the diseased organs and tissues their normal blood supply. Naturopathy also helps to supply the body the cell salts it lacks, corrects abnormalities of the tissues, organs, muscles, joints, bones and skin. It helps make necessary and vital life changes and provides solutions to live with the natural laws of health. This way the inherent healing processes of the body are stimulated, and the return to good health made permanent.

Causes of Diseases

Dr. Jussawalla underscores the fact that there is only one cause of disease, though it may manifest in several forms and in different degrees of severity. The primary cause of all disease, he says, is the violation of nature's law. Whatever the malady, disease is a unit, and is simply the result of conscious or unconscious transgression. He also explains that every disease is a self-purifying effort on the part of nature. And by suppressing disease with drugs, the foundation is being laid for deep-seated and chronic disease. All diseases represent nature's efforts to remove morbid matter from the system.

"Give me fever and I will cure every disease," said Hippocrates, the father of medicine, who formulated the 'fundamental law of cure' over two thousand years ago. His views were echoed much later by Dr. Henry Lindlahr, the pillar of the nature cure movement. "Every acute disease is the result of a cleansing and healing effort of nature," he stated in concurrence.

The natural state of the human body is one of perfect health. All living beings have a life force which tries its best to realise perfect health. Inherent in the body are curative forces. As soon as remedial measures for optimum health are provided, the body naturally heals itself. That is the bedrock of naturopathy.

Fundamental Principles

According to Dr. Jussawalla, there are three fundamental principles of nature cure:

- ❑ **The first principle is that all forms of disease are due to the same cause.** If the organs of elimination are not functioning properly and there is a build-up of waste material in the body, the body becomes highly toxic. It is like a drain which is clogged with garbage and refuse. The system gets clogged and this results in auto-intoxication or toxaemia. This is the fundamental cause of ill-health.
- ❑ **The second principle is that acute diseases are an attempt on the part of the body to discard the accumulated waste materials.**

If this is further suppressed or treated symptomatically, it leads to chronic diseases.

- **The third principle of nature cure is that the body contains within itself the power to right itself.** Given the right conditions, it will move in the direction of perfect health.

Health and disease – from the nature cure perspective – is based on the two fundamental principles:

- *Vis Medicatrix Naturae* (the healing power of nature), and
- *Non Nocere* (the measures employed in the treatment of disease must cause no harm).

Therefore, it must be remembered that all healing takes place from within. The cause of the disease is more important than the symptom. Treat the body and mind together. *Since toxaemia is one of the major causes of diseases,* there can be no cure without cleansing the system. Return to the fundamentals of nature and prevent disease. Know yourself, know your body, and heal yourself. Allow the body's healing instinct to kickstart the healing process.

Advanced Naturopathy

The advanced naturopathic system has been broadly classified in a three-fold manner to cover three fields of treatment. They are:

- Psychological (man's emotional, mental and psychic state)
- Physiological (the body, its anatomy and functions), and
- Chemical (substances which compose the body cells, tissues). The scientific means employed for healing in these three fields are:
- **PSYCHOTHERAPEUTIC** – In the form of constructive suggestions to correct wrong habits, psychosomatic treatment for guiding the reciprocal influences of mind and body.
- **PHYSIOTHERAPEUTIC** – Articular, spinal and muscular manipulations, massage and vibration, exercises and rest, orthopedics, gymnastics, hydrotherapy, neurotherapy, zonetherapy,

sunlight, air, water, earth, heat and cold, light and colour rays, electrotherapy, etc.

- **CHEMICALS AND MATERIALS**—Nutritional control, dietetics, external applications, minerals, cell salts, vitamins and herbs.

The progressive system of natural therapeutics combines the best features of methods like fasting, the proper combination of natural foods, mono-curative diets and other dietetic measures, massage, curative gymnastics, physical exercises, osteopathy, chiropratic, spondylotherapy, hydrotherapy (water treatment), electrotherapy, sun and air baths, scientific relaxation, mental and magnetic therapeutics, and so on. Naturopathy has also made tremendous advances in recent times. Oxidative therapies such as ozone therapy, ultraviolet blood irradiation therapy, and intravenous hydrogen peroxide therapy are also being resorted to. They are beneficial for treating a wide range of conditions ranging from viral and fungal infections to joint pain and arthritis. Oxidative therapies work by stimulating the immune system, enhancing mitochondrial processes and facilitating healing with virtually no side effects. Oxidative medicine can be used as a treatment as well as for a preventive, anti-aging health strategy.

There is also Animal Assisted Therapy (AAT) which uses trained animals to enhance an individual's physical, emotional and social well-being. The use of AAT reportedly dates back to the 1940s, when an army corporal brought his Yorkshire Terrier to a hospital to cheer wounded soldiers. There was such a positive response that the dog continued to comfort others for 12 more years. Animal-assisted activities include providing seeing-eye dogs to the visually impaired and therapy in which the emphasis is on psychological support and physical healing. Research has demonstrated that animals have a calming effect, reducing blood pressure and anxiety. There are many different animals used in AAT, from dogs and cats to horses and even dolphins.

Evidently, there are many methods, and they are growing in number by the day, but a strong line is drawn to exclude 'dangerous' or 'harmful' medication, uncalled for surgical operations, administration of diseased products and destructive suggestions. There is, therefore, a combination and selection from everything that is good, practical and efficient -- all that conforms to the fundamental laws of cure without harmful or destructive after effects.

As no single remedial adjunct of naturopathy or its forms of treatment is broad enough to be efficacious as a cure for every disease and condition, the progressive naturopathic physician selects from his large therapeutic armamentarium the particular form of treatment best suited to the needs of the case in hand. Modern naturopathy has therefore kept pace with the progress made in other fields of science. There are several add-ons to what the pioneers of the movement initiated. The individual modalities and techniques employed vary with the degree of intelligence, training and clinical experience of the practitioner. But the essence remains the same -- live in accordance with nature's laws and allow the body to unlock its *prana*. This unchanging fundamental truth will ever remain the bedrock of naturopathic practice. This is the essence of nature cure.

As explained earlier, nature cure has basically two groups of practitioners. One group takes into consideration only the five elements of nature: sunlight, air, fire, water and earth. The other group also includes in its practice therapeutic methods like electrotherapy, osteopathy, chiropratic and so on.

Naturopathy is primarily 'drugless' and 'bloodless' – emphasises Dr. Jussawalla -- but, yet, sometimes natural medicines and surgery are needed when their use is in conformity with the basic principles of Nature Cure.

Chapter 6

Various Drugless Therapies

Water is the driving force in nature.

--Leonardo da Vinci

HYDROTHERAPY: USING WATER TO HEAL

Nature cure includes several systems of *drugless therapy*. One of them is hydrotherapy or water treatment. In this therapy, water is used in every form – internally as a beverage and externally as a bath, through breathing vapours, steam, as a cleansing agent in douches and enemas, as an ingredient in mud baths and clay packs, and as an exercise and therapeutic medium in swimming pools.

Simply put, hydrotherapy is the use of water to revitalise, maintain and restore health. Hydrotherapy treatments include saunas, steam baths, foot baths, sitz baths, and the application of cold and hot water compresses.

Father Sebastian Kneipp, a 19th century Bavarian monk, is said to be the father of hydrotherapy (Cathy Wong in *Alternate medicine Guide*). Kneipp believed that disease could be cured by using water to eliminate waste from the body.

Hydrotherapy is popular in Europe and Asia, where people "take the waters" at hot springs and mineral springs. In North America, it is often recommended as self-care by naturopathic doctors.

There is a physiological basis to hydrotherapy. The cold is stimulating, and it causes superficial blood vessels to constrict, shunting the blood to internal organs. Hot water is relaxing, causes blood vessels to dilate, and removes wastes from body tissues. Alternating hot and cold water also improves elimination, decreases inflammation, and stimulates circulation.

Different Types of Hydrotherapy

- **Sitz bath -** There are two adjacent tubs of water, one hot and one cold. You sit in one tub with your feet in the other tub, and then alternate. Sitz baths are recommended for hemorrhoids, PMS and menstrual problems, cystitis, polyps.
- Warm water baths - Soak in warm water for up to 30 minutes, depending on the condition. Epsom salts, mineral mud, aromatherapy oils, ginger, moor mud, and sea salts may be added.
- **Sauna -** Dry heat
- Steam bath or Turkish bath
- Compresses - Towels are soaked in hot and/or cold water.
- Wraps - Cold wet flannel sheets are used to cover the person who is lying down. The person is then covered with dry towels and later blankets. The body warms up in response and dries to wet sheets. This is used for colds, bronchitis, skin disorders, infection, and muscle pain.
- Wet sock treatment - Used for sore throat, ear infections, headaches, migraines, nasal congestion, upper respiratory infections, coughs, bronchitis, and sinus infections.
- Hot fomentation - For treatment of acute conditions such as chest colds and coughs. It seems to relieve symptoms but also decrease the length of the illness.

Hydrotherapy or hydropathy is also a part of occupational therapy and physiotherapy that involves the use of water for pain relief and treatment. The term encompasses a broad range of approaches and therapeutic methods that take advantage of the physical properties of water, such as temperature and pressure, for therapeutic purposes, to stimulate blood circulation and treat the symptoms of certain diseases. Various therapies today employ water jets, underwater massage and mineral baths (e.g. balneotherapy, Iodine-Grine therapy, Kneipp treatments, Scotch hose, Swiss shower, thalassotherapy) and/or whirlpool bath, hot Roman bath, hot tub, Jacuzzi, cold plunge and mineral bath.

Long History

From ancient records, it is believed that various forms of hydrotherapy have been employed in ancient Egypt, Persia, Greece and Rome. Egyptian royalty bathed with essential oils and flowers, while Romans had communal public baths for their citizens. Iranians classified spa waters according to its effects. Hippocrates prescribed bathing in spring water for sickness. Other cultures noted for a long history of hydrotherapy include China and Japan. After an apparent oblivion during the Middle Ages, hydrotherapy was rediscovered during the 18th and 19th centuries by people such as J.S.Hahn, MD, (1696-1773), Philippe Pinel, Vincent Priessnitz (1799-1851), Professor E.F.C. Oertel (1764-1850), and J.H. Rausse (1805-1848).

In the 19th century, a popular revival followed the application of hydrotherapy around 1829, by Vincenz Priessnitz, a peasant farmer in Gräfenberg, then part of the Austrian Empire. This revival was continued by a Bavarian priest, Sebastian Kneipp (1821–1897). In Wörishofen (south Germany), Kneipp developed the systematic and controlled application of hydrotherapy for the support of medical treatment that was delivered only by doctors at that time. Kneipp's book *My Water Cure* was published in 1886 with many subsequent editions, and translated into many languages.

From the 1840s, hydropathics were established across Britain. Initially, many of these were small institutions but by the later nineteenth century the typical hydropathic establishment grew in size and facilities. Baths and recreation rooms under the supervision of fully trained and qualified medical practitioners and staff were added. In Germany, France and America, and in Malvern in England where Dr. James Wilson followed by James Manby Gully set up their clinics using Malvern water, hydropathic establishments multiplied with great rapidity.

Hot & Cold

Hydrotherapy, especially as promoted during the height of its Victorian revival, has often been associated with the use of cold water. However, not all therapists limited their practice of hydrotherapy to cold water. The specific use of heat was often associated with the Turkish bath. This was introduced by David Urquhart into England on his return from the East. The Turkish bath became a public institution and became one of the most noteworthy contributions by hydropathy to public health. Until around 1840, hydropathy was not common in the United States although it was popular in Europe in the 19th century. But in *Nature's Cures*, Michael

Castleman wrote that hundreds of 'water cures' were located in the countryside during the American Civil War.

Cold water immersion or ice bath is another form of hydrotherapy used by physical therapists, sports medicine facilities and rehabilitation clinics. Proponents claim improved return of blood flow and by-products of cellular breakdown to the lymphatic system and more efficient recycling.

Alternating the temperatures, either in a shower or complementary tanks, combines the use of hot and cold in the same session. This results in improvement in the circulatory system and lymphatic drainage. Experimental evidence suggests that contrast hydrotherapy helps to reduce injury in the acute stages by stimulating blood flow.

Hydrotherapy & Tourism

The growth of hydrotherapy, and various forms of hydropathic establishments, resulted in a form of tourism right across Europe. At least one book listed English, Scottish, Irish and European establishments suitable for each specific malady. In Europe, the application of water in the treatment of fevers and other maladies had, since the 17th century, been consistently promoted by a number of medical writers, and spa tourism was popular for a long time.

In the 18th century, 'taking to the waters' became a fashionable pastime for the wealthy classes who decamped to resorts around Britain and Europe to cure the ills of over-consumption. With improved knowledge of physiological mechanisms, practitioners wrote specifically of the use of hot and cold applications to produce "profound reflex effects", including vasodilation and vasoconstriction.

There are interesting examples of hydrotherapy applications. Before World War II, various forms of hydrotherapy were used to treat alcoholism, and it is used today in alternative medicine. Apparently, Bill Wilson, the co-founder of AA, was treated by hydrotherapy for his alcoholism in the early 1930s. The use of water to treat rheumatic diseases has a long history. It continues to be used as an adjunct to therapy, including in nursing. Hydrotherapy is also widely used for burn treatment.

Therapeutic Springs

Water has been used as a therapeutic agent from ancient times. The *hamams* or the royal baths spread all over India are famous. The thermal springs of Europe have for centuries helped combat disease either by effective cures or by prevention. Of varied mineral and chemical compositions, these springs provide a wide range of therapeutic treatments thanks to the presence of one or more of the following -- sulphur, carbon, phosphorous, magnesium, arsenic, iodine, calcium, copper, silica, selenium and so on. Rare gases like helium, argon and krypton are also present in these waters.

During their passage through the soil and the sub-soil, the waters of the thermal springs become charged with certain radioactive substances like radium, thorium, actinium, plutonium and uranium. The hydro-mineral spas are classified according to their predominating chemical properties and therapeutic qualities.

The father of water cure, though, is believed to be Vincient Priessnitz. In the United States, Dr. John H. Kellogg of Michigan systemised water treatment with some success. Times have changed but water treatment has not lost its followers. But it must be remembered, Dr. Jussawalla cautioned, that water is a double-edged sword. It should be used with care and wisdom.

It is a simple and natural remedy and a very powerful therapeutic agent. Water has great power in absorbing heat. It is a universal solvent, and is available in three forms – liquid, solid and gas (steam). It also adapts to the form of the container.

In therapy, water is the most flexible medium for producing thermic and mechanical effects and can be applied to limited areas and also to the whole body. Water can not only absorb heat but it can also give off heat.

So it can be used to take away body heat and also to give the body heat. Being a universal solvent it can be used internally in enemas and colonic irrigation to get rid of clogged waste. Steam applications and saunas are also invaluable. In many part of the world water baths with cleansing algae are very popular.

The principle is simple. Cold water helps improve the tone of muscles and blood vessels. Warm water relaxes and dilates. Both cold and warm water produce hyperaemia or an increase of blood to the body part. Cold water is a tonic and warm water is essentially a relaxant. Cold water application to a body part contracts the small blood vessels.

But as soon as the application is withdrawn the contracted blood vessels expand and suffuse the parts with an increased amount of blood. So, if the person has high vitality the secondary effect of the cold application increases vigour thanks to the force with which the blood rushes to all parts of the body. But if the vitality of the person is low, cold water applications may prolong depression.

Hot Water Application

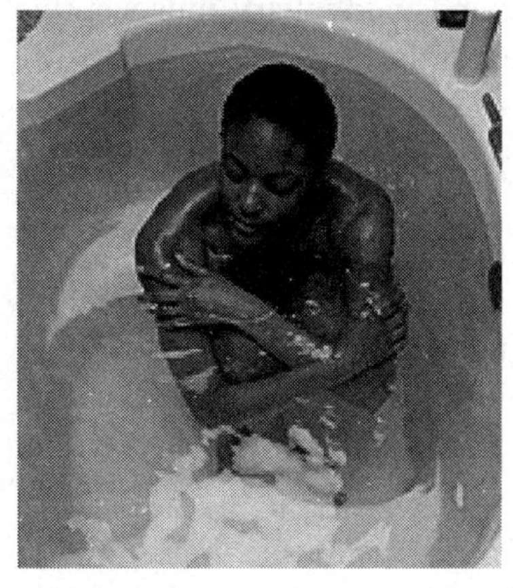

The great value of hot water application is that it prepares the body for the application of cold water.

This is very beneficial for those suffering from fatigue, rheumatism and anaemia. Hot baths relax the tissues, soothes the body and relieves pain. Hot water can be used to excite or depress the nervous system. But very hot baths may result in dizziness, nervousness, headache, nausea etc, and so the water temperature should be carefully monitored.

Continued exposure to hot water can also result in exhaustion. But water slightly below body temperature, if used for over and hour or so, helps insulate the nerve centres and takes the form of a sedative. The alternate hot and cold bath is most stimulating. This helps in reducing congestion without disturbing the heat balance of the body. It must also be mentioned that whether one uses hot or cold water, the pressure of the water is also important. The right pressure enhances the application.

Nature cure therapists know that the mucus membranes can endure water ten to fifteen degrees hotter than the skin can. The warm water in rectal irrigation can be comfortably borne in the rectum but it may be painful for the skin. In a steam or vapour bath, water temperature up to 120 degrees F is generally employed. In Turkish hot air baths the usual temperature is 140-180 degrees F and is sometimes raised to 220-250 degrees F without being injurious.

The sweat boxes, which induce perspiration, are invaluable in the treatment of rheumatism, gout, urticaria, toxaemia, diabetes and obesity. Recent advances in hydrotherapy include whirlpool baths and underwater exercises.

This helps in the treatment of paralysis and poliomyelitis thanks to the buoyancy of water. Whirlpool baths were first employed during the World Wars in the treatment of painful stumps after amputation. Sprains, dislocations, peripheral vascular diseases, arthritis and infected wounds of the extremities have been greatly benefited by whirlpool baths. The baths are especially significant for improving circulation, relieving pain and stiffness and preparing the body for massage. The nerve centres, the heart and blood vessels, the voluntary and involuntary muscles, the digestive system, every organ, tissue and cell of the body is affected by the application of water.

Dangers of Saunas

"Sweat bathing" is often recommended to cleanse the skin, soothe sore muscles, or simply relax. Sweating in dry or wet heat has been found to be beneficial to patients with arthritis, asthma, or respiratory infections. Sweating rids the body of excess sodium and other unwanted substances, including drugs and toxins, thus reducing the workload of the liver and kidneys.

While the benefits are many from "sweat bathing", a few precautions are necessary. To avoid overheating, limit one's time to 20 minutes at a stretch. Ensure that one drinks plenty of water before, during and after saunas to restore fluids. Those with high blood pressure or heart disease may do well to check with their doctor before a "sweat bath" plunge.

The main risk of sweat bathing is staying in too long and fainting from overheating, but there are other accidents too. According to an analysis of data on hot tub injuries collected by The National Electronic Injury Surveillance System in the U.S., in the 18 years between 1990 and 2007, more than 80,000 people were injured in hot tubs or whirlpool baths seriously enough to wind up in an emergency room; nearly half the injuries stemmed from slipping or falling.

However, in 10 per cent of all cases, the problem was heat overexposure. In addition, the Consumer Products Safety Commission reported in 2009 that more than 800 deaths associated with hot tubs occurred from 1990 to 2009, nearly 90 per cent of them in children under age three. The researchers who analysed the injury data for a study published in the December 2009 issue of the *American Journal of Preventive Medicine* recommended that hot tubs be used for just about 10 to 15 minutes, at a temperature no higher than 104 degrees.

Balneotherapy, a form of therapeutic bathing, has been practiced since the days of the ancient Greeks and Romans to preserve health and treat a range of ailments from injuries to eczema. As one soaks in the tub, the blood vessels dilate, the circulation increases, the muscles relax, and the nervous system chills out. According to Jonathan P. DeVierville, vice-president of the International Society of Medical Hydrology and Climatology and director of the Alamo Plaza Spa in San Antonio, Texas, "Submersion in warm water calms the physiological part of the fight-or-flight response."

It should be clearly understood that the human body is made up of 70 per cent water. So, quite naturally, when your water stores dry up or become depleted, your body can't function at optimum efficiency. Water is the primary transportation system for all the nutrients and vital elements in the body.

For the metabolism to function at its highest level, the blood needs to be thin and strong so it can flow more freely and rapidly throughout the body. The lymphatic system also has to be clean and free of all toxins absorbed from the environment through breathing, etc. The systems in the brain, the metabolic system, and the nervous systems also need to function at optimal capacity. Water helps all this happen.

Many naturopaths and practitioners of conventional medicine advise drinking one cup of water for every 14 to 20 pounds of body weight. For metabolic enhancement and looking and feeling younger, healthier and firmer, it is advised to consume about eight ounces of plain, fresh water for every 14 to 20 pounds. Those who habitually drink vegetable juices on a regular basis manage to get their supply of water. It must be emphasised that water is the body's number one ally to promote longevity, fat loss, and metabolic health. Indeed, water is one of the most powerful agents known to mankind.

MAHATMA GANDHI ON HYDROTHERAPY

To fall ill should be a matter of shame for anyone. Illness implies some error or other. He whose body and mind are perfectly sound, should never suffer from illness.

- M.K.Gandhi, Sevagram, 26-12-'44

Hydrotherapy is a well-known and ancient form of therapy. Many books have been written on the subject but, in my opinion, the form of hydrotherapy suggested by Kuhne is simple and effective. Kuhne's book on nature cure is very popular in India. He has written a good deal about diet as well, but here I wish to confine myself to his experiments in hydrotherapy.

Hip bath and sitz bath are the most important of Kuhne's contributions to hydrotherapy. He has devised a special tub for use, though one can do without it. Any tub thirty to thirty-six inches long according to the patient's height generally serves the purpose. Experience will indicate the proper size. The tub should be filled with fresh cold water so that it does not overflow when the patient sits in it. In summer the water may be iced, if it is not cold enough, to give a gentle shock to the patient. Generally, water kept in earthen jars overnight answers the purpose. Water can also be cooled by putting a piece of cloth on the surface of the water and then fanning it vigorously. The tub should be kept against the bathroom wall and a plank put in the tub to serve as backrest. The patient should sit in the tub, keeping his feet outside. Portions of the body outside water should be kept well covered so that the patient does not feel cold. After the patient is comfortably seated in the tub, gentle friction should be applied to his abdomen, with a soft towel. This bath can be taken for five to thirty minutes. When it is over, the body should be rubbed dry and the patient put to bed.

Hip bath brings down the temperature in high fever, and given in the manner described above it never does any harm, and may do much good. It relieves constipation and improves digestion. The patient feels fresh and active after it. In cases of constipation, Kuhne advises a brisk walk for half an hour immediately after the bath. It should never be given on a full stomach.

I have tried hip baths on a fairly large scale. They have proved efficacious in more than 75 cases out of 100. In cases of hyperpyrexia, if the patient's condition permits of his being seated in the tub, the temperature immediately invariably falls at least two to three degrees and the onset of delirium is averted.

Accumulation of Waste

The rationale of hip bath, according to Kuhne, is this: Whatever the apparent cause of fever, the real cause in every case is one and the same, i.e., accumulation of waste matter in the intestines. The heat generated by the putrefaction of this waste matter is manifested in the form of fever and several other ailments. Hip bath brings down this internal fever so that fever and other ailments which are the external manifestations thereof subside automatically.

How far this reasoning is correct I cannot say. **The speciality of Nature Cure methods lies in the fact that being natural, they can be safely practised by laymen. If a man, suffering from headache, wets a piece of cloth in cold water and wraps it round his head, it can do no harm. The addition of earth to cold water enhances the utility of the cold pack.**

Now about the sitz or friction bath. The organ of reproduction is one of the most sensitive parts of the body. There is something illusive about the sensitiveness of the glans penis and the foreskin. Anyway, I know not how to describe it. Kuhne has made use of this knowledge for therapeutic purposes. He advises application of gentle friction to the outer end of the external sexual organ by means of a soft wet piece of cloth, while cold water is being poured. In the case of the male the glans penis should be covered with the foreskin before applying friction. The method advised by Kuhne is this: A stool should be placed in a tub of cold water so that the seat is just about the level of the water in the tub. The patient should sit on the stool with his feet outside the tub and apply gentle friction to the sexual organ which just touches the surface of the water in the tub. This friction should never cause pain. On the contrary the patient should find it pleasant and feel rested and peaceful at the end of the bath.

'I Have Been Lax'

Whatever the ailment, the sitz bath makes the patient feel better for the time being. Kuhne places sitz baths higher than hip baths. I have had much less experience of the former than of the latter. The blame, I think, lies mostly with myself. I have been lax. Those whom I advised sitz bath, have not been patient with the experiment, so that I cannot express an opinion on the efficacy of these baths, based on personal experience. It is worth a trial by everyone. If there is any difficulty about finding a tub, it is possible to pour water from a jug or a lota and take the friction bath. It is bound to make the patient feel rested and peaceful.

A few words about wet sheet packs will not be out of place. It is very useful in pyrexia and insomnia. The method of giving wet sheet packs is this. Spread three or four thick broad woollen blankets on a cot and on top of them a thick cotton sheet dipped in cold water with the water wrung out. The patient lies flat on the wet sheet with his head resting on a pillow outside the sheet. The wet sheet and the blankets are wrapped round the patient covering the whole body, except the head which is covered with a damp towel treated after the manner of the wet sheet. The sheet and the blankets are wrapped round the patient, so that outside air cannot get inside. Though the patient feels a gentle shock when first laid in the wet sheet pack, he finds it pleasant afterwards. In a minute or two he begins to feel warm, unless the fever has become chronic; in about five minutes it begins to come down with sweating. In resistant cases I have kept the patient wrapped in the wet sheet pack up to half an hour. This has finally resulted in sweating. Sometimes, there is no sweating, but the patient goes off to sleep. In that case, he should not be awakened. The sleep indicates that the wet sheet pack has produced a soothing effect and he is quite comfortable. The temperature invariably falls at least by one or two degrees as a result of the wet sheet pack.

Wet sheet packs are also useful in the treatment of prickly heat, urticaria, other forms of skin irritation, measles, smallpox etc. I have tried them on a fairly large scale for these ailments. For smallpox and measles cases, I added enough potassium permanganate to the water to give it a light pink colour. The sheet used for these patients should afterwards be sterilized by soaking it in boiling water, and leaving it in it till it cools down sufficiently and then washed with soap and water.

Ice Massage for Circulation

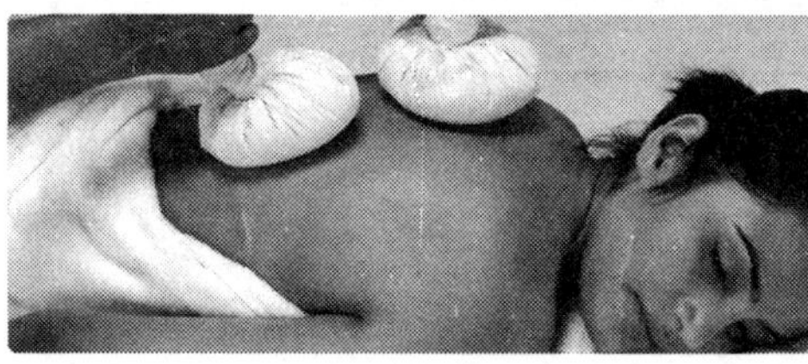

In cases where circulation has become sluggish, the leg muscles feel sore and there is a peculiar ache and feeling of discomfort in the legs, an ice massage does a lot of good. This treatment is more effective in summer months. Massaging a weak patient with ice in winter might prove a risky affair.

Now a few words about the therapeutics of hot water. An intelligent use of hot water gives relief in many cases. Application of iodine is a very popular remedy for all sorts of injuries and the like. Application of hot water will prove equally effective in most of these cases. Tincture of iodine is applied on swollen and bruised areas. Hot water fomentations are likely to give equal relief, if not more.

Again, iodine drops are used in cases of earache. Irrigation of the ear with warm water is likely to relieve the pain in most of these cases. The use of iodine is attended with certain risks. The patient may have an idiosyncracy towards the drug. Iodine mistaken for something else and taken internally might prove disastrous.

But there is no risk whatsoever in using hot water. Boiling water is as good a disinfectant as tincture of iodine. I do not mean to belittle the usefulness of iodine or suggest that hot water can replace it in all cases. Iodine is one of the few drugs which I regard most useful and necessary, but it is an expensive thing. The poor cannot afford to buy it, and moreover its use cannot be safely entrusted to everybody. But water is available everywhere. We may not despise its therapeutic value because it is obtained so easily. Knowledge of common household remedies often proves a godsend in many a crisis.

Hot Water & Steam

In cases of scorpion bite where all remedies have failed, immersion of the part in hot water has been found to relieve the pain to a certain extent. A shivering fit or a rigor can be made to subside by putting buckets of hot boiling water all round the patient who is well wrapped up or by saturating the atmosphere of the room with steam by some other device. A rubber hot water bag is a most useful thing, but it is not to be found in every household. A glass bottle with a well-fitting cork, filled with hot water and wrapped in a piece of cloth, serves the same purpose. Care should be taken to choose bottles that would not crack on hot water being poured into them.

Steam is a more valuable therapeutic agent. It can be used to make the patient sweat. Steam baths are most useful in cases of rheumatism and other joint pains. The easiest as well as the oldest method of taking steam bath is this.

Spread a blanket or two on a sparsely but tightly woven cot and put one or two covered vessels full with boiling water under it. Make the patient lie flat on the cot and cover him up in such a way that the ends of the covering blankets touch the ground and thus prevent the steam from escaping and the outside air from getting in. After arranging everything as above, the lid from the vessels containing boiling water is removed and steam soon gets on to the patient lying between the blankets. It may be necessary to change the water once or twice.

Usually in India people keep an *angithi* under the pots to keep the water boiling. This ensures continuous discharge of steam but is attended with risk of accidents. A single spark might set fire to the blankets or to the cot and endanger the patient's life. Therefore, it is advisable to use the method described by me even though it might seem slow and tedious. Some people add neem leaves or other herbs to the water used for generating steam. I do not know if such an addition increases the efficiency of steam. The object is to induce sweat and that is attained by mere steam.

In cases of cold feet or aching of the legs, the patient should be made to sit with his feet and legs immersed up to the knees in hot water as he can bear. A little mustard powder can be added to the water. The foot bath should not last for more than fifteen minutes. This treatment improves the local circulation and gives immediate relief.

In cases of common cold and sore throat a steam kettle which is very much like an ordinary tea kettle with a long nozzle can be used for applying steam to the nose or throat. A rubber tube of required length can be attached to any ordinary kettle for this purpose.

--Excerpted from Key to Health, pp. 63 to 75(written while in jail from 1942-44)

Chapter 7

Electrotherapy: Electrical Stimulation for Pain Relief

I happen to have discovered a direct relation between magnetism and light, also electricity and light, and the field it opens is so large and I think rich.

---Michael Faraday

Electrotherapy is the use of electrical energy as a medical treatment. It can apply to a variety of treatments, including the use of electrical devices such as deep brain stimulators for neurological disease. The term has also been applied specifically to the use of electric current to speed wound healing. The term "electrotherapy" or "electromagnetic therapy" encompasses a wide range of alternative medical devices and treatments.

Electrical stimulation has for long been used to decrease both acute and chronic pain. It is believed that electrical stimulation blocks the transmission of pain signals along nerves. It is also believed to provoke the release of endorphins -- the body's natural painkillers. Commonly used electrical stimulation devices apply electrical stimulation to nerves and muscles via adhesive pads placed on the skin. Some devices use alternating current, while others use direct current. Electrical stimulation should be avoided on sensitive areas as a precaution; the doctor in attendance will determine that.

Several Uses

The applications of electricity in nature cure are many. According to Dr. Jussawalla the effects may be classified as mechanical, thermic, actinic and psychic. Through different electrical currents and modalities, powerful muscular contractions of voluntary and involuntary muscular fibres are caused, the nerves are stimulated, pain relief is possible, faulty metabolism is corrected, waste products like urea, uric acid, carbon dioxide, solidified lime deposits are eliminated, artificial respiration is made to happen, and so on. In diagnosis too, electrotherapy has many uses. The naturopath can use it to differentiate different forms of paralysis (whether it is due to a brain lesion or a lesion in the spinal cord), is able to test muscular degeneration, locate foreign bodies, structural dislocations and malpositions within the body, and so on.

The nature cure physician uses electrotherapy in several forms -- galvanic, faradic, sinusoidal, high frequency currents, radiant heat baths, ultrasonic or ultra sound therapy and so on. The galvanic and faradic currents help in the diagnosis of many conditions affecting the nerves and muscles. Sinusoidal or alternating current differs from the faradic current for stimulating nerves or muscles especially when the current is rhythmically cut off and restored (known as rhythmic interruption) by an instrument.

The heating of the deeply situated organs can only be done with the help of diathermy during which heat is produced in the body at the desired depth and place to be treated. Ultra sound, or sound transmission, is a special form of sound which passes in continuous succession of pressure waves causing strong movements in the tissue particles. This technique has excellent response in nervous diseases like neuritis, neuralgia, sciatica and other health issues.

Dr. Jussawalla concludes that *electrotherapy is not a cure-all. But it can be used very effectively as an adjunct.*

Chapter 8

Heliotherapy: Sunlight for Better Health

If I had to choose a religion, the Sun as the universal giver of life would be my God.

-- Napoleon Bonaparte

Heliotherapy is medical therapy involving exposure to sunlight. Heliotherapy is commonly known as light therapy and is a recognised scientific system. Sunlight is a fundamental biological need and both natural and artificial sunshine are of great value in therapeutic work. It has been scientifically proved that without access to adequate sunlight, all life, especially man, would wither away and die.

In Greek mythology, *Helios* was the God of the Sun, the charioteer who drove the sun across the sky each day. Hippocrates was a great advocate of the sun's healing properties. Although heliotherapy traditionally refers to treatments that use natural sunlight, the term is also applied to artificial sources of ultraviolet, visible or infrared light radiation.

From the late 1800s, heliotherapy, also called *phototherapy* and *climatotherapy,* became a key part of certain treatment regimes for tuberculosis (TB), notably TB of the bones, joints and skin, as prolonged exposure to sunlight can kill the bacteria which cause the disease. Even today, exposure to sunlight, the right medication and a high protein diet is the advised regimen for TB which is making an aggressive comeback with strains resistant to drugs; multi-drug resistant TB is the greatest medical threat today as it is often a symptom of a depressed immune system, often caused by HIV/AIDS.

Recent studies show how and why the 'sunshine' vitamin D can speed recovery in TB patients, helping explain the success of heliotherapy in the pre-antibiotic era. From the late 1800s -- well before the development of antibiotics in 1930s -- TB patients were often sent to retreats where they were encouraged to soak up the sun's rays in what was known as heliotherapy. A study by British researchers has found that high doses of vitamin D -- which is made in the body when exposed to sunlight -- appears to help patients recover more quickly. According to Adrian Martineau, a senior lecturer in respiratory infection and immunity at Queen Mary University of London, high doses of the vitamin dampen the body's inflammatory response to infection and reduce damage to the lungs, in this case – pulmonary TB.

As sunlight was not available at all times in many parts of the word, artificial alternatives were developed that could mimic the sun's beneficial effects. The Finsen lamp, invented by Faeroese physician Niels Ryberg Finsen, is perhaps the best-known example. An ultraviolet lamp, it allowed flexible treatment in all seasons and its rays could be concentrated onto the most affected parts of a patient's body. Its greatest success was in the treatment of tuberculosis of the skin for which Finsen was awarded a Nobel Prize in 1903.

Natural sunlight contains many wavelengths of light besides visible light. There is also invisible ultraviolet radiation. Heliotherapy makes simple use of intentional direct exposure to natural sunlight to get the therapeutic benefits of the included ultraviolet radiation.

Heliotherapy has a long history. It was used a long time ago in India, China and Egypt to treat diseases, including psoriasis, vitiligo and other skin diseases. Ancient Greeks also used natural sunlight as therapy. As far back as 3,000 years, medical practitioners were advanced enough to use sunlight-sensitising chemicals before sun exposure -- a primitive version of today's photochemotherapy or PUVA.

Several Benefits

Heliotherapy has many uses. In rickets there is a softening of the skeleton and deformity as a result of the deficiency of Vitamin D. This vitamin facilitates the absorption and deposition in the bone of calcium and phosphorous. In anaemia, ultra-violet rays are the most effective antirachitic rays and are of definite value. Their radiation imparts an increased appetite, better sleep and greater sense of well-being.

In ultra-violet radiation, the skin goes through many changes. It must be remembered that long exposure to the sun results in sunburn, and adequate precautions have to be taken. Even exposure to the powerful rays of the sun at noon in a non-therapeutic setting is best avoided. India is blessed with sunshine and heliotherapy is the ideal treatment for the masses. Natural sunshine may not be available in sufficient intensity and duration in the prevention and treatment of disease. So heliotherapy has become useful in nature cure.

The importance of sunlight is best underscored by Seasonal Affective Disorder or SAD which is a form of depression that occurs in the fall and winter months when there is a shortfall of sunlight. Researchers affirm that between four to six per cent of people in the U.S. are believed to suffer from SAD. Another 10-20 per cent experience a milder form of winter-onset SAD. Symptoms include fatigue, lack of interest in normal activities, social withdrawal, weight gain, and a craving for carbohydrate foods. According to the American Psychiatric Association (APA), SAD has been linked to a biochemical imbalance in the brain prompted by shorter daylight hours and a lack of sunlight in winter. The sleep-related hormone melatonin may also be implicated since it is produced at night, and longer hours of darkness can lead to greater production of melatonin. A drop in levels of serotonin, a brain chemical (neurotransmitter) that affects mood, may also play a role as reduced sunlight can cause serotonin levels to fall. The treatment for SAD includes exposure to bright light daily via a special (full-spectrum) light source or light therapy.

Additionally, every day new research highlights the benefits of vitamin D. It is now believed to help with waist-to-hip ratio (a potent risk factor for heart disease), type 2 diabetes, age-related macular degeneration, Alzheimer's disease, pneumonia, and epilepsy. The European Food Safety Authority has raised the RDA for vitamin D supplementation to levels far beyond American guidelines. New guidelines call for 4,000 IU's/day for adults and children over the age of 11; 2,000 IU's/day for children aged 1-10; and 1,000 IU's for infants. But, of course, the ideal way to optimise one's vitamin D levels is through appropriate sun or safe tanning bed exposure.

Dr. Jussawalla fully understood the need for light and used heliotherapy with great success. He worked in a tropical climate but heliotherapy had its seasonal uses.

Chapter 9

Chromotherapy:Fortifying Health with Colours

The more ugly, older, more cantankerous, more ill and poorer I become, the more I try to make amends by making my colours more vibrant, more baanced and beaming.

--Vincent van Gogh

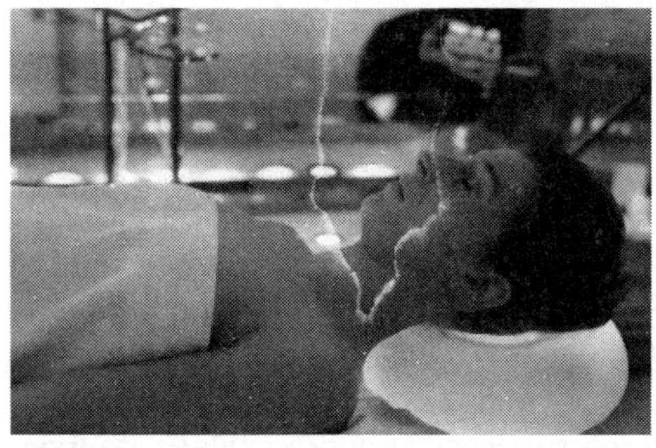

Chromotherapy, another healing modality of Dr. Jussawaalla, is the method of treating disease with sunlight and colours. The chemical rays of the sun when applied through coloured glass can not only preserve health and energy but also cure diseases in accordance with nature's law of healing. Scientific experiments have revealed that the chemical rays of the sun, when applied through coloured glass, can even treat heart disease.

Even pure water if kept in coloured glasses and subjected to the rays of the sun for a few hours will acquire healing properties and can be used medicinally. The 'composure' of water can be changed depending on where it is sourced and how it is preserved; in peaceful climes the molecules of water reflect the serenity of the environment and in war-torn areas the molecules are in flagrant disarray! Food and drink can also be charged with ultra-violet rays to fortify it with vitamins and minerals to help cure diseases.

Chromotherapy is centuries-old and has been used to cure various diseases. Apparently, every creature is engulfed in light that affects its health. The human body, according to the doctrine of chromotherapy, is basically composed of colours. The body comes into existence from colours, is stimulated by colours and colours are responsible for the correct working of the various body systems. All organs and limbs of the body have their own distinct colour. All organs, cells and atoms exist as energy, and each form has its frequency or vibrational energy. Each of our organs and energy centres vibrates and harmonises with the frequencies of these colours. When various parts of the body deviate from these expected normal vibrations, it is assumed that the body is either diseased or at least not functioning properly. The vibratory rates inherent in chromotherapy balance the diseased energy pattern found in the body. Light affects both the physical and etheric bodies. Colours generate electrical impulses and magnetic currents or fields of energy that are prime activators of the biochemical and hormonal processes in the human body.

Origin

Phototherapy or light therapy was practised in ancient Egypt, Greece, China and India. The Egyptians utilised sunlight as well as colour for healing. According to ancient Egyptian mythology, the art of chromotherapy was discovered by the god Thoth. In the hermetic traditions, the ancient Egyptians and Greeks used coloured minerals, stones, crystals, salves and dyes as remedies and painted treatment sanctuaries in various shades of colours. The ancient Ayurvedic physician Charaka, who lived in the sixth century BC, recommended sunlight to treat a variety of diseases. In ancient Greece, colour was intrinsic to healing. They adopted direct exposure to sunlight as well as indirect healing in which they used stones, dyes, ointments and plasters as the medium.

It is also believed by alternate therapists that the body has seven *chakras*, even referred to as spiritual centres located along the spine. Each of these *chakras* is associated with a single colour along with a function and organ or bodily system. The *chakras* can become imbalanced and result in physical diseases. But with the application of the appropriate colour these imbalances can be corrected. Each *chakra* energises and sustains certain organs. The balance of the seven *chakras* activates healing by transmitting energy to the electromagnetic field around the body. *Chakras* located at the sites of the major endocrine glands corresponds to particular states of consciousness, personality types and endocrine secretions.

Walker M. in *Power of Colours* sums it up: "You realise you are part of the hologram of life, surrounded by an aura or energy field that radiates distinct colour and vibrations. The aura fingertips your soul and reflects your goodness, wellness, mental stability, maturity, emotional/inner turmoil or peaceful fulfilment. More of each of these qualities, peace, wellness, stability, maturity and fulfilment may become your ever present precious possession by the application of colour's power in our daily living."

Chapter 10

Chiropractic: Employing the Right Healing Pressure

The best lightning rod for your protection is your own spine.

-- Ralph Waldo Emerson

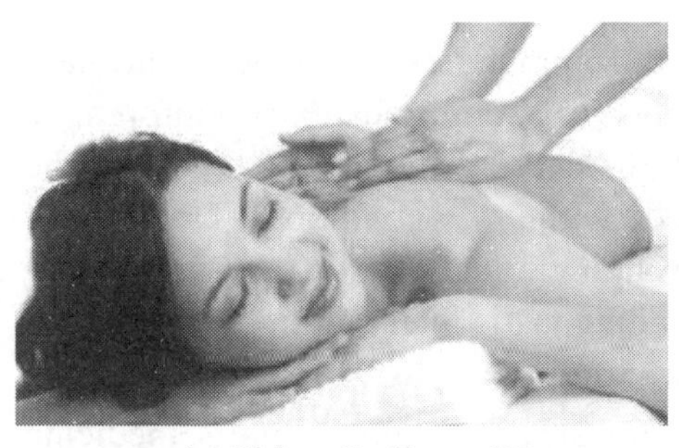

The word, 'chiropractic' is originally Greek meaning "done by hand." Although it was formally introduced in 1895, chiropractic, along with osteopathy, follows the tradition of hands-on manipulation that dates back to ancient systems of treatment in China, India and Egypt.

Chiropractic is concerned with the diagnosis, treatment and prevention of disorders of the neuromusculoskeletal system and the effects of these disorders on general health. The main chiropractic treatment technique involves *manual therapy*, including *manipulation of the spine,* other *joints,* and *soft tissues*. Treatment also includes exercises and health and lifestyle counselling.

D.D. Palmer founded chiropractic in the 1890s, and his son B.J. Palmer helped to expand it in the early 20th century. It has two main groups: 'straights', in the minority, who emphasise vitalism, innate intelligence and spinal adjustments, and consider vertebral subluxations to be the cause of all diseases, and 'mixers' who are open to mainstream views and conventional medical techniques, such as exercise, massage, and ice therapy.

Although a wide diversity of ideas currently exists among chiropractors, they share the belief that the spine and health are related in a fundamental way, and that this relationship is mediated through the nervous system. Chiropractors examine the biomechanics, structure and function of the spine, along with its effects on the musculoskeletal and nervous systems and what they believe to be its role in health and disease.

Chiropractic philosophy includes the following perspectives:

- ❑ Holism assumes that health is affected by everything in an individual's environment; some sources also include a spiritual or existential dimension.
- ❑ Conservatism considers the risks of clinical interventions when balancing them against their benefits. It emphasises non-invasive treatment to minimise risk, and avoids surgery and medication.
- ❑ Homeostasis lays store on the body's inherent self-healing abilities.

Primary Treatment

In lower back pain and such cases, chiropractic care may be the primary method of treatment. When other medical conditions exist, chiropractic care may complement or support medical treatment by relieving the musculoskeletal aspects associated with the condition. Doctors of chiropractic may assess patients through clinical examination, laboratory testing, diagnostic imaging and other diagnostic interventions to determine when and if chiropractic treatment is appropriate.

This treatment is often used by physical therapists, sports medicine doctors, orthopedists, physical medicine specialists, doctors of osteopathic medicine, naturopaths and massage therapists. Chiropractors may also use other treatments like mobilisation (a technique in which a joint is passively moved within its normal range of motion), massage therapy, heat and ice, ultrasound, electrical stimulation, rehabilitative exercise, magnetic therapy, counselling about diet, weight loss, and other lifestyle factors, dietary supplements, and other alternate therapies like homeopathy.

According to Dr. Andrew Weil, chiropractic spinal manipulation has now had about three decades of very active research, and hundreds of studies have been published in peer-reviewed medical journals examining its clinical usefulness.

He believes that chiropractic theory, stressing the importance of the spine on general mind and body health, and the accompanying manipulative techniques, may be of benefit in the treatment of several conditions, particularly for back and neck pain. "A chiropractor who looks beyond the spine can be a useful resource for restoring and preserving health. For a specific complaint, feeling better is the sign of successful treatment. Excellence in chiropractic practice includes recommending lifestyle changes, including home-based exercises, stress-reduction techniques and sound dietary advice that may include the prudent use of supplements. Treatment should leave you feeling more competent to care for yourself, and most of all, it should result in your feeling better promptly."

Dr. Jussawalla who, in a manner of speaking, pioneered it all in India, firmly believed that different parts of the body and their functioning was controlled by different spinal centres.

His methods were simple: For the upper body -- eyes, ears, throat, lungs and arms -- adjustments were made in the cervical spine. For the centre of the body -- stomach, kidney, intestines, liver, bowels, pancreas and spleen -- the adjustments were made in the dorsal spine. For the lower body -- legs, bladder, rectum, ovaries and uterus – the adjustment took place in the lumbar spine. Chiropractic concerns itself with the abnormalities in the spinal tissues and the correction of these abnormalities.

The Basis

Chiropractic is founded on the theory that vertebrae may become subluxated which means that a slight displacement of their opposing articular surfaces may occur. As a consequence of this subluxation, there is an impingement on the nerves which pass through the intervertebral foramen corresponding to the vertebrae involved in the displacement.

The pressure upon the nerve blocks the production of impulses at this point, and the organ supplied by those nerves does not receive its full quota of innervation. Since the functional activity and organic integrity of all parts depend upon their innervation, withdrawal of all or a portion of this nerve supply constitutes a predisposing cause of disease.

For years, healers were of the opinion that displacements of the vertebrae, in the absence of fracture, are practically impossible.

There are three chief reasons why subluxation of the vertebrae has been regarded as impossible by those who have not investigated this subject:

(a) The fact that the vertebrae are surrounded and held in position by numerous ligaments, the natural tendency of which is to bind the vertebrae so firmly in place that any movement beyond that essential to the normal mobility of the spine as a whole is impossible;

(b) The configuration and placement of the articular processes;

(c) failure to discriminate between a subluxation and a dislocation. But on studying the joints of the spine it is obvious that the spine is constructed for the horizontal and not the vertical position. The spine is used as a column while it was constructed as a beam. When the word subluxation of vertebrae is used it is meant to convey the idea.

One should discriminate between the terms 'subluxation' and 'dislocation'. Subluxation means a slight shifting of a vertebra from its position. There has been a shift in the position of one of the surface areas of the two vertebrae which still oppose each other. It is freely conceded that complete disarticulation of a vertebra is practically impossible except as a coincident to fracture. Chiropractic, however does not deal with luxation but with subluxation, now easily referred to as 'slipped disc'.

Subluxations can also easily be palpated by those trained for this work. It can readily be demonstrated that conditions which existed before the adjustment of a vertebra supposedly displaced do not remain afterwards. Finally, the most valuable evidence of all in support of the existence of subluxations is the fact that, following adjustment of a subluxated vertebra all abnormal conditions disappear. This was another healing modality which Dr. Jussawalla used with enormous success.

It may be in context here to mention the Trager Approach, also known as Trager Work and psychophysical integration therapy. It was developed by Milton Trager, M.D. to treat his own chronic back pain, the result of a congenital spinal deformity. Trager Approach is based on the premise that discomfort, pain and reduced function are physical symptoms of accumulated tension resulting from accidents, weak posture, fear, emotional blockages and daily stress.

It focusses on reducing these unnatural patterns of movement and eliminating neuromuscular tension by using gentle, rhythmic rocking motions. The method is effective for back and neck pain, joint irritation and soft tissue discomfort. It can be a useful adjunct in improving athletic performance, flexibility, or problems with balance. It has also been successfully used to facilitate rehabilitation from physical injuries. Emotional imbalances can also be relieved by the Trager Approach.

Chapter 11

Osteopathy: Treating the Musculoskeletal Framework

I clearly saw the skeleton underneath
all this show of personality
what is left of a man
and all his pride but bones?

-- Jack Kerouac

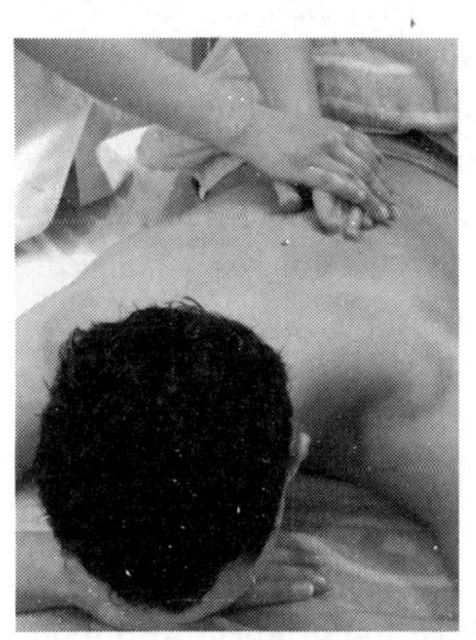

Osteopathy is a form of drug-free non-invasive manual medicine that focuses on total body health by treating and strengthening the musculoskeletal framework, which includes the joints, muscles and spine. It works on the body's nervous, circulatory and lymphatic systems. Osteopaths use manual techniques to balance all the systems of the body and not just the affected area.

Dr. Andrew Taylor Still established the practice of Osteopathy in the late 1800s in the United States of America with the aim of using manual 'hands-on' techniques to improve circulation and correct altered biomechanics without the use of drugs.

It was named "osteopathy," reasoning that "the bone, osteon, was the starting point to ascertain the cause of pathological conditions." The osteopathic medical philosophy is defined as the concept of health care that embraces the concept of the unity of the living organism's structure (anatomy) and function (physiology).

According to Osteopathy:

- The human being is an integrated unit of mind, body, and spirit

- ❑ The body possesses self-regulatory mechanisms, having the inherent capacity to defend, repair, and remodel itself.
- ❑ Structure and function of the body are reciprocally interrelated.

In Osteopathy, all parts of the body function together in an integrated manner. If one part of the body is restricted, then the rest of the body must adapt and compensate for this leading to inflammation, pain, stiffness and other health conditions.

When the body is free of restrictions in movement, Osteopathic treatment assists the body with pain minimisation, reduced stress and greater mobility providing the body with the opportunity to heal itself. Oteopaths use a broad range of gentle hands-on techniques including soft tissue stretching, deep tactile pressure, and mobilisation or manipulation of joints.

They respect the body's natural ability as a self-regulating mechanism and only intervene when pain or discomfort is present. The benefits of osteopathy are the general improvement in mobility and structural stability of the body. As a result, other systems of the body such as the circulatory, nervous and lymphatic systems function more effectively. Combined with good dietary and exercise prescription a patient's well-being is enhanced.

Osteopaths are trained to manually locate points of restriction or excessive strain in various parts of the body. Using a finely tuned sense of touch or palpation, the osteopath will assess the spine, joints, muscles and tendons. An osteopath may call for blood tests or X-rays to confirm findings, or review existing diagnostic results where available. All treatment programs are highly individualised.

Osteopathy has been effective for headaches; back, neck, and heel/ foot pain; sciatica; shin splints; tennis elbow and repetitive strain injury; asthma; arthritis; digestive problems; carpal tunnel syndrome; whiplash and postural problems. Sports injuries are also treated.

Preventive, Palliative & Curative

Dr. Jussawalla underscores the fact that Osteopathy premises that the body is a vital and physical mechanism subject to derangements, structural alternations and functional changes as a result of violence on the mechanical plane, as well as disturbances on the psychic and biochemic planes. Osteopathy believes in preventive, palliative and curative measures.

He adds that, according to the principles of Osteopathy, disease is caused by abnormal changes in the tissues of ligaments, muscles and organs as well as in the position and mobility of the bones. It holds that the structural integrity of the body mechanism is the most important factor in restoring and maintaining the well-being of the living organism. Its chief therapeutic measure is the adjustment of the body tissues and body structures.

The body is regulated through the nerves. Nerves control the action of the stomach, the heart, the lungs, and every part of the body. Through the nerves nature gives each of these parts the ability to keep itself strong and healthy.

Through the blood every part of the body receives new material for building and repairing itself as well as oxygen for the vital chemical processes. Through the lymphatic system the nerves direct the elimination of impurities and keep the body free from their harmful effects.

Where nerve action is impaired nature cannot carry out her duties and the body is handicapped by inadequate means for shielding itself. This is the great truth which osteopathy gave science.

Before a bodily part becomes sick its resistance must have been lowered by some interference in the proper working of the marvellous, intricate body machinery. Osteopathy's method is to look for the cause, find that interference, and remove it. Then nature begins her own effective campaign against the ailment. On this truth rests the Osteopathic method of treatment by the adjustment of structure.

Chapter 12

Chiropractic and Osteopathy: A Comparison

The part can never be well unless the whole is well.

-- Plato

Now that we have explained Chiropractic and Osteopathy, let us examine the differences. The main points of difference, says Dr. Jussawalla, are manifest in the manner of application of the sciences, and the results of application. Both sciences have the same end in mind and there are many similarities. But what is the essential difference between the two?

The Chiropractor makes the spine the special and only locality of effecting results essential to the cure of abnormal or diseased conditions. The chiropractic philosophy is defined as an adjustment of 'luxated or subluxated vertebrae', which causes all the physical ills to which mankind is subject.

Acting on this hypothesis, the practitioner aims to return these vertebrae to their normal state in the belief that when this is accomplished disease necessarily subsides as its cause is removed. The normal state is then re-established and health is restored.

The claim of the Chiropractor is that 'impinged or unduly pressed spinal nerves', resulting from spinal luxation or subluxations, is the cause of the diseased condition and that adjustments of these nerves remove the cause, and a restoration follows as naturally as night follows the day.

Chiropractors claim that the entire body is supplied with energy emanating from the spine, and that these nerves control every tissue and function of the body, and that when these spinal nerves are free from pressure or interference, the body is in a condition denominated normal or healthy.

Spinal Adjustments

The adjustment of the spine is characteristic of Chiropractic and differs from all other methods. It is a sudden movement and if done at the exact point where the adjustment is required, results follow instantaneously.

All health conditions are diagnosed by 'palpation' which is the deviation of the spinous process from its supposed normal condition. When all the processes are in 'line', the patient is in a state of health.

The science of Osteopathy consists of the physical manipulation of the patient to improve blood circulation and other fluids of the body, the removal of nerve pressure wherever found, the adjustment of the bones, reducing dislocations, relaxing the muscular system and using the limbs when thought necessary to accomplish the purpose.

The means employed by Osteopaths are not confined to any special part of the body. Whatever is necessary to be adjusted is resorted to by the Osteopath. It could be the massage of a muscle, the treatment of the spine, the articulation of a joint, the use of a limb, the stretching of a muscle or the spine, or a general going over of the entire body.

The manipulation of muscles, which includes pulling, stretching and any and all sorts of manipulations, frees the system from what is supposed to cause the disease.

The time taken to treat a patient is markedly different. Osteopaths require 15 minutes to an hour, and the Chiropractor from one to five minutes, palpating and adjusting the spine. That is all he has to do.

Parts of Drugless Science

There is no question of one science being superior to the other, asserts Dr. Jussawalla. They both serve very useful purposes in the field of drugless science. Osteopathic movements may be comparatively more gentle (as far as the spine is concerned) and the patient naturally feels better about this, not being in fear of pain or injury.

On the other hand, the results from osteopathy, perhaps, are not as quickly discernible as from chiropractic. Osteopathy is an older science. Before Chiropractic came into vogue, it probably was merely an improved and extended study of Swedish movements and massage or corrective movements.

It later embraced treatment of the vertebrae by adjustments which are peculiarly Osteopathic. The means to the end in both cases are very different and that should be recognised, insists Dr. Jussawalla. "They are not the same science. The two sciences can be blended and used to advantage in many cases. The health care professional would profit by being proficient in both systems as healing efforts and results would be better."

The science of Osteopathy and Chiropractic are practised independently of Nature Cure science. So if a naturopathic physician desires to include and practise osteopathy and chiropractic as a valuable adjunct to other Nature Cure methods, he should get qualified for the purpose. Dr. Jussawalla rooted for stringent quality control in alternate health care studies which he wanted to popularise all over India.

Spinal manipulation, both Osteopathic and Chiropractic, is used to a great extent in Nature Cure work. But Dr. Jussawalla maintained that although Osteopathy and Chiropractic exist as separate healing mechanisms, they are effective when combined with other forms of natural treatment.

But it must be emphasised here that though nature cure practitioners may use Osteopathy and Chiropractic, Osteopaths and Chiropractors are not primarily nature cure practitioners. Just as a masseur is not a nature cure practitioner because massage is used in natural treatment!

Success of Bone-Setters

In India, bone setters have been treating strains, sprains, fractures, dislocations and subluxations of the spine since time immemorial. These bone-setters usually have the 'art' or 'science', whatever you may term it, handed down from father to son for generations.

Dr. Jussawalla admitted that long before the function of the intravertebral disc was fully known, the general medical practitioner, who was as ignorant about 'slipped disc' as he was about poliomyelitis, treated slipped disc cases as lumbago, sciatica, and backache. "But osteopaths, chiropractors and bonesetters practised manipulations and mechanical adjustments long before this to treat 'out of alignment' or a 'misplaced vertebra' now known as 'slipped disc'.

Their success was often much greater than that of general practitioners who used to treat their patients with anti-rheumatic pills and pain-killers." These days, of course, disc problems are directed to appropriate specialists --- neuro or orthopaedic surgeons or Osteopaths and Chiropractors.

Chapter 13

Vibrotherapy: The Healthy Wake-Up Call

Healthy citizens are the greatest asset any country can have.

-- Winston Churchill

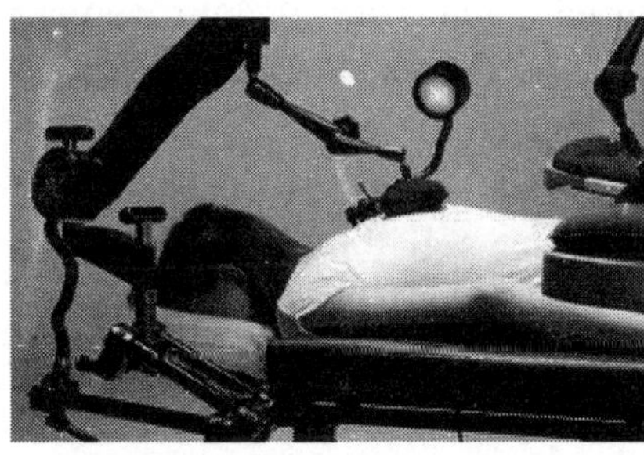

This is another method of 'non-violent medicine' used by Dr. Jussawalla. Vibration therapy or Vibrotherapy is a form of therapy that uses whole-body-vibration to enhance physical health and well-being. It has been in vogue for decades and is widely accepted in physiotherapy, rehabilitation and sports medicine.

Vibrotherapy was first used in the Russian space programme to assist astronauts to increase their muscle strength and enhance their bone density while in space. Interestingly, after Vibrotherapy they found that they could stay up to 420 days in space with little or no gravity while their American colleagues had to return to earth after 120 days.

Vibrotherapy has many benefits. It helps to fight osteoporosis and also helps with muscle strength, weight loss, lymphatic circulation, bone density and hormone levels. The whole body vibration therapy helps people with physically debilitating conditions such as scoliosis, arthritis, multiple sclerosis, spinal stenosis, stroke, *Parkinson's disease,* back pain and obesity.

The vibrations have a positive impact on hormone balance and help reduce stress as the entire muscular system is stimulated. Studies have shown that vibration therapy enhances blood distribution, which is critical in regenerating damaged tissues as well as in the circulatory system's ability to deliver vital nutrients and hormones throughout the body.

Vibrant & Resilient Cells

Whole body vibration therapy accelerates the body's natural healing process. It increases cellular oxygen circulation, stimulates cellular nutrient uptake, enhances cellular fluid movement and assists cellular waste removal.

As a result, new cells are more vibrant and resilient. The vibrations also increase the production of regenerative cells and repair hormones, improve blood circulation in skin and muscles, strengthen bone tissue, improve lymph drainage and increase the basal metabolic rate.

All this results in more strength, more speed, more stamina, rapid recovery of muscles and tissue, increased flexibility, mobility and coordination, anti-cellulitis, collagen improvement, and fat reduction. There is improvement in muscle strength, balance, flexibility, stamina, range of motion, bone density, blood circulation and lymph drainage. Pain, fatigue, stress, blood pressure, fat and cellulite are reduced.

Vibrotherapy uses vibrations which are passed through a vibrating platform to the body. The Vibrogym delivers a series of pulses or stimuli to the nervous system that produces muscle stimulus. It is this stimulus that exercises the muscles. Almost all the body's muscles are exercised in Whole Body Vibration Therapy. In contrast, conventional physiotherapies only stimulate 40-60 per cent of a person's muscles. The deeper lying muscles such as the postural muscles particularly benefit from whole body vibration training.

Vibration has been applied principally to chronic as well as acute conditions. It has been a valuable adjunct to various other forms of treatment as it aids physiological processes and therefore assists in a perfectly natural way the restoration of disturbed function.

Whether it is applied to nerve centres or to their peripheries, to lymphatics or to producing circulation changes, the vibration results in either stimulation or inhibition depending upon the type of vibrator, the time factor, and the manner in which the operator adapts the technique to the personal requirements of the patient. Of course, it goes without saying that in all forms of natural healing, the total co-operation of the patient is required. He should have faith in his doctor and the method employed.

Chapter 14

Orificial Therapy: Bringing about Nerve Balance

"Deho Devalaya" – Body is the temple, scriptures teach us. Realise that the human body is not just a mass of flesh and bone. The human body is a sacred instrument equipped with reason and emotion, capable of being used for deliverance from grief and evil; you have earned it after long ages of struggle. Honour it as such, keep it in good condition, so that it might serve that high purpose. Maintain it even more carefully than your brick homes and never let go of the conviction that it is an instrument and nothing more.

-- Satya Sai Baba

Orificial therapy is another healing modality employed by Dr. Jussawalla. He states that, "It is a system of treating human ailments that recognises the orifices of the body as being peculiarly subject to various pathological alterations, the symptoms of which owing to the prolific or specialised nerve supply to these parts are disproportionate to the extent of the lesion." It seeks to normalise the structures through digital, mechanical and electrical measures.

According to Dr. Jussawalla, every tube in the body is controlled by the sympathetic nervous system. In orificial therapeutics, the central aim is to cure the sympathetic nerve terminal at the outlets. The nerve supply of orifices is from the voluntary and involuntary nervous system, predisposing them to belligerent conditions, and tending to a state of imbalance.

If both orifices of a canal are normal, then the canal itself is more than likely to be normal. But a lesion at the orifice of any tube exerts a pernicious influence of considerable magnitude in preventing normal function of the part or by reflex action, the function of other parts.

Orificial therapy, therefore, is a method based on the theory that many morbid or abnormal conditions are due to reflexes originating at the orifices, such as the mouth, nostrils, ears and eyes in the upper part of the body, and the lower orifices, such as the anus or rectum, vagina, urethra and uterus (cervix).

It seeks to normalise the structures through digital, mechanical and electrical measures. Orificial therapy aims to relieve and avoid impingement of sympathetic nerve terminals. This way, the bloodstream is improved, the capillaries flushed, and the entire body benefits.

Chapter 15

Spondylotherapy: Stimulating The Spine for Relief

Physical fitness is not only one of the most important keys to a healthy body, it is the basis of dynamic and creative intellectual activity.

--John F. Kennedy

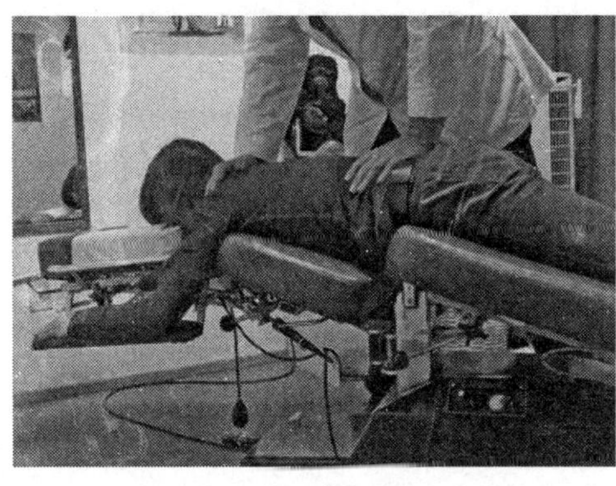

The medical dictionary defines spondylotherapy as a therapeutic approach in which the practitioner places the middle finger on the spinous process while using the other hand to strike the finger with blows that rapidly rebound. Typically, the practitioner applies one or two cycles per second. This approach is generally applied to at least three vertebrae adjacent to each other. It is also called percussion technique.

Spondylotherapy, a branch of drugless science, may be considered a therapeutic agency by itself, explains Dr. Jussawalla. Apart from the therapeutics of the spine in which emphasis is laid on the correction of bony lesions, the removal of impingement of special nerves and the straightening of curvatures, it is a system which is strictly a spinal treatment.

It consists of stimulating one or more of the spinal nerve centres by means of concussion (light hammering), deep pressure or electricity, creating an effect upon peripheral organs and tissues. By spondylotherapy every organ is either contracted or dilated.

Spinal Reflex

The practice of spondylotherapy includes what is known as a reflex. A spinal reflex is a change in the tone, size or functional activity of an organ or blood vessel that follows the stimulation of the spinal tissues. This is because a motor impulse may be produced by some disturbance of a tissue or part supplied by the sensory nerves which are closely associated in the spinal cord.

The theory of spondylotherapy therefore is that the spinal segments are stimulated and the effects are produced in the organs or parts which are directly influenced by the nerves proceeding from that particular segment or from the various vertebral regions concerned. *Spondylotherapy* does not take into consideration subluxations and for this reason should not be considered as a part of chiropractic, but as an adjunct to it.

The various methods of spinal stimulation are -- pressure, concussion and electricity.

- ❑ Pressure should be applied on both sides of the spinous processes. The tips of the thumbs may be used, or some blunt instrument. The fingers should be placed behind the laminae or behind or just below the transverse processes of the vertebra. For stimulation, the pressure should be heavy enough to produce a feeling of pain and tenderness and should not be continued for more than thirty seconds. When pressure is used for the relief of spinal or visceral pain or tenderness, less force is used and the treatment is continued from three to five minutes.
- ❑ Concussion may be administered by the hand or with a wooden mallet. The blows should be on the tips of the spinous processes and it should be with the clenched fists of the hand. It is important that the vertebra to be treated be located first.

For hand concussion, the second finger of the left hand should be placed on the tip of the spinous process and it should be struck with the clenched fist of the other hand. When a mallet is used, a small block of soft rubber should be kept on the spinous processes to protect the tissues from injury.

> "There is no single method of treatment for various problems," adds Dr. Jussawalla. "All or some of the various drugless agencies should be combined and used as required. Chiropractic has many merits and should be used in such cases as we require it, but to employ it for every sort of human ailment is not logical. *Spondylotherapy, at best, should be only an adjunctive method.*"

Chapter 16

Psychotherapy: Addressing The Mind

All that we are arises with our thoughts. With our thoughts, we create the world.

– The Buddha

In today's complex existence, psychotherapy has become an integral healing methodology. But it was also used decades ago by Dr. Jussawalla.

Psychotherapy refers to the therapeutic interaction or treatment between a trained professional and a client, patient, family, couple, or group. The problems addressed are psychological in nature.

Psychotherapy aims to increase the individual's sense of well-being and employs a range of techniques based on experiential relationship building, dialogue, communication and behaviour change. Psychotherapy works with the mind, with perceptions and emotions; it works on how we view ourselves and the world we live in.

According to the Oxford English Dictionary, psychotherapy first meant 'hypnotherapy' instead of 'psychotherapy'. The original meaning, 'the treatment of disease by psychic (i.e., hypnotic) methods', was first recorded in 1853 as 'Psychotherapeia, or the remedial influence of mind'.

The modern meaning, 'the treatment of disorders of the mind or personality by psychological or psychophysiological methods', was first used in 1892 by Frederik van Eeden translating 'Suggestive Psycho-therapy' for his French 'Psychothérapie Suggestive'.

There are several systems of psychotherapy detailed here and culled from several sources. A broader understanding of the subject will help.

- Psychoanalytic is the first practice to be called psychotherapy. It encourages the verbalisation of the patient's thoughts, including free associations, fantasies and dreams. From this the analyst formulates the nature of the unconscious conflicts which are causing symptoms and character problems.
- Behaviour therapy/applied analysis focusses on changing maladaptive patterns of behaviour to improve emotional responses, cognitions, and interactions with others.
- Cognitive behavioural seeks to identify maladaptive cognition, appraisal, beliefs and reactions with the aim of influencing destructive negative emotions and problematic dysfunctional behaviour.
- Psychodynamic is a form of depth psychology, whose focus is to reveal the unconscious content of a client's psyche in an effort to alleviate psychic tension. Although its roots are in psychoanalysis, psychodynamic therapy tends to be briefer and less intensive than traditional psychoanalysis.
- Existential is based on the existential belief that human beings are alone in the world. This isolation leads to feelings of meaninglessness, which can be overcome only by creating one's own values and meanings. *Existential therapy* is philosophically associated with phenomenology.
- Humanistic emerged in reaction to both *behaviourism* and *psychoanalysis* and is therefore known as the *Third Force in the development of psychology.* It is explicitly concerned with the human context of the development of the individual with an emphasis on subjective meaning, a rejection of determinism, and a concern for positive growth. It believes in an inherent human capacity to maximise potential.
- *Brief therapy* is an umbrella term for a variety of approaches to psychotherapy. It differs from other schools of therapy in that it emphasises a focus on a specific problem, and direct intervention. It is solution-based rather than problem-oriented. It is less concerned with how a problem arose than with the current factors sustaining it and preventing change.

- Systemic seeks to address people not at an individual level but as people in relationship, dealing with the interactions of groups, their patterns and dynamics which can include *family therapy* and *marriage counselling*). Community psychology is a type of *systemic psychology.*
- Transpersonal addresses the client in the context of a spiritual understanding of consciousness.
- Body Psychotherapy addresses problems of the mind as being closely correlated with bodily phenomena, including a person's sexuality, musculature, breathing habits, physiology, etc. This therapy may involve massage and other body exercises as well as talking.

Power of Meditation

Meditation may not be directly under the purview of psychotherapy, but it is gaining currency as a useful method to still the mind. Meditation is broadly classified into concentration, mindfulness and contemplation. The fundamental premise is that the state of mind determines thc quality of one's life, and the best method is to make friends with it and be freed from reactive conditioning.

Meditation is said to liberate the person in a multi-tiered way. It helps balance the left and right brain hemispheres and calm a stressed mind. *Meditation* also activates the *multi-sensory perception* and improves awareness.

Interestingly, we all know that cellular movement is crucial for brain health, that serotonin levels in the brain increase as we maintain a fit body, and that *as one gains weight, the brain declines in health.* But research has also shown brain health is much better when one is successful in life and achieves set goals. In short, the brain controls life, and the other way around too!

The great Zen master Eihei Dogen wrote in the 13th century, "*To study the Self is to forget the Self.*" Meditation is of particular relevance in today's stress ridden times as it allows adherents, through the simple act of awareness, to disengage from long-standing beliefs in a fixed identity.

When we follow our breath, we are simply breathing, nothing more, and our thoughts cease to be the foundation of our identity. Our awareness expands and on a macro level, we begin to identify with the cosmos. This way, the ego is killed and we hopefully assume responsibility for a larger family – the planet itself!

In Nature Cure, which has always been open to a new understanding of traditional healing methods, the tendency has been to use the science of psychology merely to correct bodily ailments and mental errors. The treatment of psychosomatic cases is to guide the reciprocal influences of mind and body.

> According to Dr. Jussawalla, "Psychology should be employed more as an integrating factor than as an analytical factor. Most psychological disorders can be traced to a failure in the individual to experience the joy of living.
>
> This is, of course, general in most people, and endless time is spent, both by practitioners and patients, in contrary means to combat the results of this failure. As naturopathy attempts to deal with the causes rather than with symptoms in the physical structure, the mental and emotional side of life is important as well."

I have only outlined a few psychotherapeutic approaches or schools of thought that are in vogue; but there are many more.

DIFFERENT SCHOOLS OF PSYCHOANALYSIS

The undisciplined man doesn't wrong himself alone. He sets fire to the whole world.

--Rumi

Psychotherapy has been practised through the ages. *Psychoanalysis* was perhaps the first specific school of psychotherapy, developed by Sigmund Freud and others through the early 20th century. Trained as a neurologist, Freud began focussing on problems that appeared to have no discernible organic basis, and theorised that they had psychological causes originating in childhood experiences and the unconscious mind.

Techniques such as dream interpretation, free association, transference and analysis of the identity, ego and superego were developed. Many theorists, including Anna Freud, Alfred Adler, Carl Jung, Karen Horney, Otto Rank, Erik Erikson, Melanie Klein, and Heinz Kohut, built upon Freud's fundamental ideas and often formed their own differentiating systems of psychotherapy. These were all later categorised as *psychodynamic*.

Behaviourism developed in the 1920s, and *behaviour modification* as a therapy became popular in the 1950s and 1960s. Notable contributors were *Joseph Wolpe* in South Africa, M.B. Shipiro and Hans Eysenck in Britain, and John B. Watson and B.F. Skinner in the United States. *Behavioural therapy* approaches relied on principles of operant conditioning, classical conditioning and social learning theory to bring about therapeutic change in observable symptoms. The approach became commonly used for phobias.

Some therapeutic approaches also developed out of the European school of existential philosophy. Concerned mainly with the individual's ability to develop and preserve a sense of meaning and purpose throughout life, major contributors to the field in the US (e.g., Irvin Yalom, Rollo May) and Europe (Viktor Frankl, Ludwig Binswanger, Medard Boss, R.D.Laing, Emmy van Deurzen) and later in the 1960s and 1970s both in the United Kingdom and in Canada, Eugene Heimler attempted to create therapies sensitive to common 'life crises' springing from the essential bleakness of human self-awareness.

The Theory of Human Needs

A related body of thought in *psychotherapy* started in the *1950s* with *Carl Rogers*. Based on existentialism and the works of Abraham Maslow and his hierarchy of human needs, Rogers brought person-centred psychotherapy into mainstream focus. The primary requirement of Rogers is that the client should be in receipt of three core 'conditions' from his counsellor or therapist: unconditional positive regard, congruence (authenticity/genuineness/transparency), and empathic understanding.

Fritz and Laura Perls created Gestalt therapy, Marshall Rosenberg founded Non-violent Communication, and Eric Berne came up with Transactional Analysis. These fields of psychotherapy would later become what is known as *humanistic psychotherapy.*

During the 1950s, Albert Ellis originated Rational Emotive Behaviour Therapy (REBT). A few years later, psychiatrist Aaron T. Beck developed a form of psychotherapy known as *cognitive therapy.* Both included relatively short, structured and present-focussed therapy aimed at identifying and changing a person's beliefs, appraisals and reaction-patterns, by contrast with the more long-lasting insight-based approach of psychodynamic or humanistic therapies. Cognitive and behavioural therapy approaches were combined and grouped under the umbrella-term Cognitive Behavioural Therapy (CBT) in the 1970s.

A "third wave" of cognitive and behavioural therapies developed, including Acceptance and Commitment Therapy and Dialectical Behaviour therapy, which expanded the concepts to other disorders and/or added novel components and mindfulness exercises. Counselling methods developed, including *solution-focussed therapy* and *systemic coaching*

During the 1960s and 1970s, *Eugene Heimler*, after training in the new discipline of psychiatric social work, developed the *Heimler method of Human Social Functioning,* a methodology based on the principle that frustration is the potential to human flourishing. Positive Psychotherapy (PPT), since 1968, based on the positive image of man, is the name of the method of the psychotherapeutic modality developed by Nossrat Peseschkian and co-workers. Prof. Peseschkian, MD, (1933–2010) was a specialist in neurology, psychiatry, psychotherapy and psychotherapeutic medicine.

Systems Therapy also developed focussing on family and group dynamics and Transpersonal Psychology which focusses on the spiritual facet of human experience. Other important orientations developed in the last three decades include Feminist Therapy, Brief Therapy, Somatic Psychology, Expressive Therapy, Applied Positive Psychology and the Human Givens approach which is building on the best of what has gone before.

Possible Drawback

One of the major criticisms levelled against psychotherapy is about its lack of effectiveness. In one study, Psychologist Hans Eysenck found that two-thirds of participants either improved or recovered on their own within two years, regardless of whether they had received psychotherapy. But in a meta-analysis that looked at 475 different studies, researchers found that psychotherapy was effective at enhancing the psychological well-being of clients. In his book, *The Great Psychotherapy Debate*, statistician and psychologist Bruce Wampold concluded that factors such as the therapist's personality as well as his or her belief in the effectiveness of the treatment played a role in the outcome of psychotherapy.

Chapter 17

Zone Therapy: Stimulating Prana

Health is a state of complete harmony of the body, mind and spirit. When one is free from physical disabilities and mental distractions, the gates of the soul open.

--B.K.S. Iyengar

Reflexology, or *zone therapy*, another healing method that is in vogue today, involves the physical act of applying pressure to the feet, hands, or ears with specific thumb, finger and hand techniques without the use of oil or lotion. Reflexologists claim that there is a system of zones and reflex areas that reflect an image of the body on the feet and hands. It is believed that areas on the foot correspond to areas of the body, and that by manipulating these, one can improve health through one's *qi* or *prana*. Reflexologists divide the body into ten equal vertical zones, five on the right and five on the left.

The *Reflexology Association of Canada* defines reflexology as: "A natural healing art based on the principle that there are reflexes in the feet, hands and ears and their referral areas within zone related areas, which correspond to every part, gland and organ of the body. Through application of pressure on these reflexes without the use of tools, crèmes or lotions, the feet being the primary area of application, reflexology relieves tension, improves circulation and helps promote the natural function of the related areas of the body." According to reflexologists, the blockage of an energy field, invisible life force, or *Qi*, can prevent healing. The basic idea is to release that life force from its confines.

Though its origins are not well documented, there are reliefs on the walls of a *Sixth Dynasty Egyptian tomb* (c. 2450 B.C.) that depict two seated men receiving massage on their hands and feet. Hieroglyphics and ancient paintings depicting this therapy have been found in Egypt and India. *Reflexology was introduced to the United States in 1913 by William H. Fitzgerald, M.D. (1872–1942), an ear, nose, and throat specialist, and Dr. Edwin Bowers.* Fitzgerald claimed that applying pressure had an anaesthetic effect on other areas of the body. Reflexology was modified in the 1930s and 1940s by Eunice D. Ingham (1889–1974), a nurse and physiotherapist. Ingham claimed that the feet and hands were especially sensitive, and mapped the entire body into 'reflexes' on the feet. 'Zone therapy' also began to be called *Reflexology.*

Science of Zone Therapy

Simply put, zone therapy divides the body by vertical lines into five zones on the left side and five zones on the right side. These zones relate to all parts of the body within each zone. The fingers and toes affect corresponding parts of the body and are the primary areas of treatment. *Zone therapy* works more directly on nerve endings that are connected with organs along the zones. *This therapy is a very effective technique for pain release.*

The emphasis is on the hands and feet, especially the fingers and toes because nerve endings in these areas are near the surface and thus more accessible. The procedure is to press down using a circular, rolling motion. The practitioner begins with a light probe, looking for the tender spots. If no tenderness is found, more pressure is applied gently.

Pressure is applied on the upper and lower surfaces as well as the sides of the fingers and toes. All tender spots are massaged. Each tender spot is stimulated for a maximum of 30 seconds and pressure is slowly increased. For maximum effect, pressure is applied for 30 seconds to four minutes, depending on the severity of the tenderness. Any tenderness is an indication of some degree of congestion in the associated zone.

Precise Stimulation

Pinching the thumb and index finger together are the best instruments for fine in-depth stimulation. Pressure may also be applied with a blunt point applicator like a pencil with a rubber eraser. Clothespins may be used to apply strong, steady pressure. Pocket combs can be used along a wide area, clenching the fist to press the teeth of the comb against the inner surfaces of the fingers.

Practitioners insist that *foot-zone therapy* is precise. The practitioner observes the foot and interprets the 'messages' it conveys through discolouration, texture and tenderness. When a signal point is triggered within a certain zone, a message goes to the tissue or organ effected, through a reflex arc to the spinal cord and then to the brain. Discomfort is experienced in the areas of imbalance.

Zone therapy stimulates every organ and renews the cell system. It is a holistic approach which recognises that all of the body's cells and organs make up a complex and interactive organism. Zone balance works with the body's own innate intelligence, and only allows the body to do what it can when it can.

Early Detection

The most important benefit of *foot-zone therapy* is that it can detect and treat health imbalances long before they manifest in a serious disease. As medical science has repeatedly explained, imbalances or the early stages of ill-health occur long before the symptoms are manifested. Detectable imbalances precede observable symptoms. Medically this is called *sub-clinical illness*. It simply means that an illness or medical problem is not detectable yet. But by the time it is detected the problem is usually well advanced. With zone therapy, there is early detection.

Zone therapy encourages the body's natural healing capability by stimulating blood circulation, hormone balance, lymph flow, digestion, assimilation, elimination and function of the autonomic nervous system. Cell systems are renewed, there is more life energy and the body is brought into balance.

Dr. Jussawalla adds, "The relief of pain and often the cure of various disorders by pressure applied directly below the seat of the trouble or at some point on a finger, toe, knee, elbow or ear remote from the seat of trouble, but in the same zone, aids in the healing process. The body is divided arbitrarily into ten longitudinal zones, running from the tips of the toes to the tips of the corresponding fingers, and even to the corresponding zones of the head.

> "Zone-therapy relieves pain by what has been called 'nerve block', a condition in which the nerves affected become less capable of forwarding the impulse of pain to the headquarters of sensation. This process allows the patient to relax and recuperate to enable the organic forces to overcome the local difficulty. Thanks to all this new knowledge, several cases of chronic disorders that have resisted most other known forms of treatment have been cured or greatly relieved." He also reiterates that since none of the remedial agents or sciences of treatment is broad enough in its scope to be efficacious as a cure for every disease and condition, the naturopathic physician selects and uses the particular one best suited to the needs of the case in hand with a "combination of other suitable measures for their cumulative effect or because one may be effective when aided by another."

Chapter 18

Exercise And Nature Cure

Life is like riding a bicycle. To keep your balance, you must keep moving.

– Albert Einstein

Better to play football than read the Gita.

– Swami Vivekananda

However much one eulogies the benefits of exercise, it may still be insufficient. Exercise, or even simple everyday movement, is paramount to keep fit. "The first law of life is activity," says Dr. Jussawalla. "Either use or lose. If any part of the body is allowed to remain idle, it will soon become atrophied or smaller in size and inferior in substance. *This applies to the brain and muscle.* In the evolution of the human race, man had to exercise to survive. He had to be able to run from an enemy; hunt for his food, climb trees and mountains and cross rivers; every moment of life was purchased with physical effort. In short, the physical struggle to stay alive was exercise enough.

"Apart from dietetics, exercise, active or passive, is the most valuable therapeutic agent," he points out. "All our activity must have a definite purpose apart from productive labour and recreational play. It may be classified into two main groups -- exercise for development and exercise for eliminating disease and regaining health."

Dr. Jussawalla explains that when a body is clogged with waste material as a result of too much food and lack of physical activity, there is a feeling of sluggishness and fatigue. This tired feeling or condition cannot be overcome by rest and sleep. **"Exercise in such conditions must have one sole purpose -- to increase the individual's vitality. Exercise promotes**

blood circulation. More heat is generated, more air taken into the system oxygenating the blood stream, and the eliminating organs become more active. In the process, metabolism is increased."

In diseased conditions, exercise should be done with as small an expenditure of nerve energy as possible. A sick cell has no vitality to carry on development and growth and its whole force is used to eliminate the sick, morbid elements. Muscular exercise has a remarkably stimulating and rejuvenating influence on the system. But it must be remembered that health and strength are not synonymous.

Dr. Jussawalla was a firm believer in exercise. "Exercise is one of the most powerful preventive medicines in staving off the disabilities of middle and old age, as well as being an important therapeutic tool in repairing the ravages of diseases. Not only is it necessary for the maintenance of health and the building up of a shapely and capable body, it also has, in many instances, a specific curative value. There are a number of deformities, sometimes congenital, sometimes acquired through faulty postures, and sometimes the aftermath of disease, for which exercise, in conjunction with curative measures, has to be specially prescribed."

Contemporary Research

As some one who has exercised all his life, I would like to dwell on the benefits of exercise. Simple, regular, everyday physical activity can completely overhaul a person's life. One doesn't have to be an Olympic athlete to live a full life.

In fact, pushing oneself too hard and engaging in the most extreme contact sports can be harmful. Even extreme endurance cardio, such as marathon running, can damage the heart. Exercise should be viewed as a drug that needs to be taken in the ideal dosage for optimal benefit. Too little, and you won't get any benefit. Too much, and you could do harm. So a moderate everyday dose is ideal. Science now suggests that the best fitness regimen is actually one that mimics the movements of our hunter-gatherer ancestors, which included short bursts of high-intensity activities.

New research insists that little exercise and poor eating habits are the bane of modern man. Studies are now revealing that exercise can boost intelligence and mental acuity. Regular exercise has been shown to improve even IQ levels. Staying active and exercising offers unique benefits for brain health. It has been observed that exercise even helps the brain grow as one gets older. It doesn't have to shrink, as generally believed.

Studies have shown that exercise can lower the risk of breast cancer and can also boost survival rates for women who have been diagnosed with the disease. **According to researchers, women who exercised 10 to 19 hours per week or two hours a day for five days could reduce their breast cancer risk by 30 per cent. Any amount of exercise at any level of intensity helps lower the risk of estrogen-receptor-positive breast cancer, the most common type.**

Even women who begin exercising later in life can lower their breast cancer risk by 20 per cent; all that is needed is a brisk, half-hour walk five days a week. A study published in the *Journal of the American Medical Association* found that women who walked as little as an hour a week at a pace of 2 to 2.9 miles per hour had cancer survival rates 20 per cent higher than women who exercised less or not at all. Better yet, the women in this study who walked three to five hours a week had a 50 per cent lower risk of death from breast cancer than those who participated in little or no exercise.

Exercise & the Brain

"Exercise is the single best thing you can do for your brain in terms of mood, memory, and learning," says Harvard Medical School psychiatrist John Ratey, author of the book, *Spark: The Revolutionary New Science of Exercise and the Brain*. **"Even 10 minutes of activity changes your brain."** In studies, published in *The Archives of Internal Medicine*, two geriatricians, Dr. Marco Pahor of the University of Florida and Dr. Jeff Williamson of Winston-Salem, N.C., pointed to "The power of higher levels of physical activity to aid in the prevention of late-life disability owing to either cognitive impairment or physical impairment, separately or together."

They add, "Physical inactivity is one of the strongest predictors of unsuccessful aging for older adults and is perhaps the root cause of many unnecessary and premature admissions to long-term care. It is well established that higher quantities of physical activity have beneficial effects on numerous age-related conditions such as osteoarthritis, falls and hip fracture, cardiovascular disease, respiratory diseases, cancer, diabetes mellitus, osteoporosis, low fitness and obesity, and decreased functional capacity."

Exercise tends to improve the ability of different parts of the brain to work together. It was discovered that men who exercised just after learning a new motor skills task performed more accurately and with greater agility than men who exercised prior to the learning, or not at all. Research shows exercise may help strengthen memory, build new brain cells and brain cell connections, and even increase IQ and productivity at work

Senior citizens or the elderly are also greatly benefited by mild exercise as it activates hippocampal neurons in the brain which helps in the creation of new brain cells. Short periods of intense exercise increase testosterone levels which benefits brain health. There is increased blood flow to the brain as well as stress reduction. Exercise simply helps the brain grow.

There is a new hypothesis that it is thanks to exercise that the human brain has outgrown those of other, far larger, mammals. Researchers are now suggesting that the increases in aerobic capacity and physical activity that occurred during human evolution may have directly influenced the human brain. They examined data that found animals bred to be proficient endurance runners developed high levels of substances that promote tissue growth and health, including Brain-Derived Neurotrophic Factor (BDNF), which activates brain stem cells to convert into new neurons.

Weight-bearing & Aerobic Exercise

Regular exercise reduces osteoporosis and fragility. Weight-bearing aerobic activities like brisk walking and weight training to increase muscle strength can reduce or even reverse bone loss.

In one study, German researchers who randomly assigned women 65 and older to either an 18-month exercise regimen or a wellness programme demonstrated that exercise significantly increased bone density and reduced the risk of falls. And at any age, even in people over 100, weight training improves the size and quality of muscles, thus increasing the ability to function independently.

Aerobic exercise has long been established as an invaluable protector of the heart and blood vessels. It increases the heart's ability to work hard, lowers blood pressure and raises levels of HDL-cholesterol, which cleans the arteries. As a result, active individuals of all ages have lower rates of heart attacks and strokes. Aerobic training has also been found to be equally important for maintaining brain and cognitive health. Aerobic fitness improves the ability to coordinate multiple tasks and stay focused for extended periods.

Moderate activity has also been shown to lower the risk of developing diabetes even in women of normal weight. A 16-year study of initially healthy female nurses found that those who were sedentary had twice the risk of developing diabetes, and those who were both sedentary and obese had 16 times the risk when compared with normal-weight women who were active.

Exercise & Dementia

As the population continues to age, perhaps the greatest health benefit of regular physical activity will turn out to be its ability to prevent or delay the loss of cognitive functions. A new study of healthy men and women older than 55 found that those who were physically active three or more times a week were least likely to become cognitively impaired or to suffer from dementia.

As little as 30 minutes of exercise three times a week may cut the risk of dementia in seniors by 40 per cent. This physical activity can also help ward off the age-related decline in thinking skills by 60 per cent, according to a new study published online November 1, 2012, by the journal *Stroke*.

European researchers followed 639 seniors in their 60s and 70s for three years and checked up on them annually. At the beginning and end of the study, all of the participants underwent MRI (magnetic resonance imaging) tests to look for changes in the brain that can indicate cognitive decline. When the study ended, 90 participants had signs of dementia, including 54 with vascular dementia stemming from impaired blood flow to the brain; another 34 had developed Alzheimer's disease, and 147 exhibited a decline in thinking ability but not dementia.

Those who had reported performing regular physical activity were much less likely to have developed signs or symptoms of compromised thinking. The exercise effect (from gym classes, walking or biking) held true regardless of age, education, brain changes and previous history of stroke or diabetes. In addition to regular physical activity, exercising the mind also helps. Crossword puzzles, mind games, and challenging reading or educational classes help keep the brain agile and strong.

An Australian study published in *The Journal of the American Medical Association* randomly assigned 170 volunteers who reported memory problems to a six-month programme of physical activity or health education. A year-and-a-half later, the exercise group showed "a modest improvement in cognition." Various other studies have confirmed the value of exercise in helping older people maintain useful short-term memory.

Short periods of exercise are known to protect the chromosomal caps, called telomeres, against stress-induced damage. Researchers believe that the length and health of the telomeres -- which are pieces of DNA at the end of each chromosome -- is linked to cellular aging. In an experiment, 63 women were divided into two groups. One group exercised vigorously for 33 minutes a day and the other group was sedentary. Units of stress were measured by a 10 unit perceived exertion scale.

In the sedentary group, just one unit of stress increased the risk of damaging telomeres 15 fold. The same amount of stress didn't affect the exercise group. According to Elissa Epel, PhD, who performed the study, "Even a moderate amount of vigorous exercise appears to provide a critical amount of protection to the telomeres." Health and fitness expert Dr. John Douillard concludes, "Even short, high intensity exercises for less than 12 minutes a day is beneficial. Your chromosomes will thank you!"

Exercise & Cancer

According to Dr. Mercola, an esteemed voice in the world of healing, exercise should be part of standard cancer care. Studies have shown that exercising during and after cancer treatment can reduce the risk of dying from cancer, reduce the risk of cancer recurrence, boost energy, and minimise the side effects of conventional cancer treatment. Previous research has shown that breast and colon cancer patients who exercise regularly have half the recurrence rate of non exercisers.

Exercise helps normalise insulin levels, lowers estrogen and testosterone levels, and improves the circulation of immune cells in the blood. A Norwegian study pointed out that even high-intensity interval training can be a safe choice for patients recovering from heart attacks or heart surgery. Exercise is considered safe both during and after most types of cancer treatment. Doctors are now advising patients to avoid inactivity and return to daily chores as soon as they can after surgery or even during adjuvant cancer treatments.

Recent research indicates that having a healthy heart and lungs may be one of the most important factors for academic excellence in middle school students. Studies have shown that children who exercised regularly nearly doubled their reading scores. Thirty minutes on a treadmill allowed students to solve problems up to 10 per cent more effectively.

Even plain and simple walking helps. Even walking backwards "which helps use muscles and movements that you probably rarely use, making it an ideal way to change up your exercise routine for greater fitness gains," says Dr. Mercola. "When you walk backwards, it puts less strain and requires less range of motion from your knee joints, which is useful for people with knee problems or injuries. Backward walking may help relieve lower back pain, improve hamstring flexibility, burn more fat and calories in less time than traditional walking, improve balance and even sharpen your thinking skills and vision."

The evidence on the benefits of exercise are too numerous to enumerate here. So let's give the last word on the subject to the prestigious Mayo Clinic --- *Want to feel better, have more energy and perhaps even live longer? Look no further than exercise.*

Yoga as Exercise

On a slightly different plane -- which we won't go into detail at this stage -- yoga and meditation are also very useful in maintaining good health. Regular yoga has been shown to cure and reverse several lifestyle diseases.

Several scientific studies have categorically proved that yoga can reduce levels of cortisol, the so-called stress hormone.

According to George Brainard, M.D., a professor of neurology at Thomas Jefferson Medical College, "I was very surprised that a single set of yoga poses could make a significant change in cortisol. We have seen enough promise to consider studying it in challenging situations like chronically ill patients who have abnormally high levels of cortisol, such as those who suffer from depression, type 2 diabetes, Cushing's disease, and high blood pressure."

Studies have shown that practicing yoga --even for the very first time -- can normalise cortisol levels that are either too high or too low. Vijayendra Pratap, Ph.D., President of the Yoga Research Society in Philadelphia says, "My hypothesis is that yoga brings the body to balance." Jennifer Johnston, yoga director and research clinician at the Mind Body Medical Institute in Boston believes that "the deep breathing we do in yoga elicits something called 'the relaxation response,' which invokes the restorative functions of the body. Researchers from Boston

University School of Medicine (BUSM), New York Medical College (NYMC), and the Columbia College of Physicians and Surgeons (CCPS) are in agreement that yoga may be effective in treating patients with stress-related psychological and medical conditions such as depression, anxiety, high blood pressure and cardiac disease.

A further lease to good health is extended consciousness. During *Yoga Nidra* meditation, for example, it was discovered that there was increased endogenous dopamine release in the ventral striatum in the brain (considered a reward centre). *Yoga Nidra* is characterised by a depressed level of desire for action, associated with decreased blood flow in prefrontal, cerebellar and subcortical regions of the brain.

But, as I said, we won't go into that now. It will need another book.

In summation, there is simply no substitute to exercise. It reverses the detrimental effects of stress, boosts levels of soothing brain chemicals like serotonin, dopamine, and norepinephrine, and even works on a cellular level to reverse the toll of free radicals on the aging process. Exercise is an antidepressant and improves learning by increasing the level of brain chemicals called growth factors that help make new brain cells.

On an external level, it builds self-esteem and improves body image. High-intensity exercise can leave you with euphoria. A new study by researchers at Northwestern University's Feinberg School of Medicine in Chicago has found that exercise lowers the activity of bone-morphogenetic protein or BMP which slows the production of new brain cells. At the same time, it increases Noggin, a brain protein that acts as a BMP antagonist. According to the *New York Times*, "The more Noggin in your brain, the less BMP activity exists and the more stem cell divisions and neurogenesis (production of new brain cells) you experience."

Need I say any more?

What Dr. Jussawalla expounded decades ago when scientific research was in its infancy has now been fully comprehended and has become a global movement!

Chapter 19

Massage: Manipulating Body Tissues

A healthy body is a guest-chamber for the soul; a sick body is a prison.

--Francis Bacon

Massage, also globally acknowledged today as a healing methodology, is an integral part of nature cure. According to Dr. Jussawalla, "Therapeutically, scientific massage ranks among the best and most valuable resources of medical practice with a practically unlimited scope of action." Massage is a term used to signify a group of systematic and scientific manipulations of bodily tissues which are best performed with the hands. A good massage affects the nerves, the muscular systems and the general circulation.

The sense of touch has long been an accepted medium for social bonding. It has also been linked to healing and many traditions refer to it as a form of energetic healing. In Ayurveda, the sense of light touch directly corresponds to the element of air and to the energy called *Prana* or *Vayu*, or "life force." The *Sushruta Samhita*, one of the main Ayurvedic texts, states: "*Vayu*, (which is directly linked to light touch) which courses through the body, is self-begotten in origin and regarded as identical to eternal life or God itself."

In Ayurveda, each of the five senses is understood to be an avenue of consciousness and a vehicle to elicit a self-healing response. Ayurvedic massage uses the element of touch as a means of moving *prana*; the *marma* point therapy is the massage of special points of concentrated life force on the body.

Massage brings balance to the body and mind and enhances self-awareness. Light touch, in particular, which helps move *prana* is considered an effective tool of self-awareness and a trigger for a potent healing response. The advantages of massage are numerous. Massage helps decrease cortisol, a disease-producing and degenerative stress hormone. It also increases dopamine and norepinephrine, which boost the mood and well-being. Massage has also been found to boost immunity and killer T cells in AIDS patients.

In a recent study published in *Alternative Therapies*, 95 subjects had their blood levels evaluated for the following chemicals before and after a 15-minute massage: Oxytocin: the primary target, and a bonding and anti-anxiety hormone ACTH (adrenocorticotropin): a hormone that increases with stress and decreases with relaxation. The primary target of this study was to evaluate the release of oxytocin following a massage. Oxytocin has been known to increase when one feels trust and/or empathy. It is the "giving hormone," released during acts of appreciation, gratitude and profound emotional connections.

Labouring mothers secrete large amounts of oxytocin at birth, which triggers an inexplicable oxytocin surge in the baby which helps trigger a bond with the mother. Research also shows that oxytocin extends life in cancer patients, reduces cravings for sweets, reduces anxiety and depression, increases sexual potency and desire, reduces cortisol, and boosts immunity. It was found that oxytocin levels increased by 17 per cent for the group that received massage. The control group who just rested showed a 9 per cent decrease in oxytocin. ACTH (adrenocorticotropin) – which increases with stress – increased by 30 per cent for the group who rested without receiving massage. Interestingly, it decreased by 20 per cent for those who were in the massage group.

Passive Exercises

Massage has been used as a method of treatment for numerous conditions and has also been combined with electrical or light therapy. "It is often a useful adjunct to treatment by exercise. Consequently, massage is also termed a passive form of exercise," says Dr. Jussawalla. **"Massage softens and relaxes parts which have been hardened and congested and forces out of the tissues stagnant and impure blood and brings in new arterial blood laden with oxygen and food materials, thus ensuring rapid combustion and perfect elimination. Massage is an art. Rightly used, it**

can be one of the most important therapeutic agencies; wrongly used, it may produce infinite harm, even to the extent of preventing recovery. Massage is not simply an ordinary touch for contact of the hand with the body. But it is a skilled or professional touch. It is a touch applied with intelligence, with control, and with physiological effects."

In massage, a therapist manipulates muscles and other soft tissues of the body to improve health and well-being. Varieties of massage range from gentle stroking and kneading of muscles and other soft tissues to deeper manual techniques. Massage helps relieve muscle tension, reduce stress, and particularly influences the activity of the musculoskeletal, circulatory, lymphatic, and nervous systems. It is believed to support healing, boost energy, reduce recovery time after an injury, ease pain, and enhance mood. It is useful for many musculoskeletal problems, such as low back pain, osteoarthritis, fibromyalgia, and sprains and strains. Massage may also relieve depression in people with chronic fatigue syndrome, ease chronic constipation, decrease swelling, and alleviate sleep disorders. It may also relieve chronic back pain more effectively than other treatments. Clinical studies show that massage may be an effective treatment for children with autism, attention deficit hyperactivity disorder (ADHD), bulimia, rheumatoid arthritis and several other ailments.

Lymphatic massage, also called lymphatic drainage or manual lymph drainage, is a technique developed in Germany for the treatment of lymphedema, an accumulation of fluid that can occur after lymph nodes are removed during surgery, most often a mastectomy for breast cancer. It has been found that up to 25 per cent of breast cancer patients whose surgery includes removal of lymph nodes in the area of the armpit eventually develop lymphedema. A lymphatic massage session for women who develop lymphedema starts with light massage on the surface of the skin of the neck. The therapist gently rubs, strokes, taps or pushes the skin in directions that follow the structure of the lymphatic system so that accumulated lymph fluid can drain through proper channels. Lymphatic drainage is gentle, not painful, and doesn't have a stimulating effect. It is a valuable adjunct to conventional therapy too.

Origin

Massage has been practiced as a healing therapy for centuries in nearly every culture around the world. The word "massage" comes from the Greek root "masso," which means "to touch". Massage therapists use a variety of gliding, kneading and cross-fibre friction strokes to work the muscle tissue. The use of massage for healing dates back 4,000 years in Chinese medical literature and continues to be an important part of Traditional Chinese Medicine (TCM). A contemporary form of massage, known as Swedish massage, was introduced to the United States in the 1850s. By the end of the 19th century, a significant number of American doctors were practicing this manual technique. Today, massage is very popular all over the world.

There are nearly 100 different massage and body work techniques.

The most common ones are:

- ❑ Aromatherapy massage: Essential oils from plants are massaged into the skin to enhance the healing and relaxing effects of massage.
- ❑ Craniosacral massage: Gentle pressure is applied to the head and spine to correct imbalances and restore the flow of cerebrospinal fluid in these areas.
- ❑ Lymphatic massage: Light, rhythmic strokes are used to improve the flow of lymph throughout the body. Manual lymphatic drainage (MLD) focuses on draining excess lymph.
- ❑ Myofascial release: Gentle pressure and body positioning are used to relax and stretch the muscles, fascia (connective tissue), and related structures.
- ❑ On site/chair massage: On site massage therapists use a portable chair to deliver brief, upper body massages to fully clothed people in offices and other public places.
- ❑ Polarity therapy: A form of energy healing, polarity therapy stimulates and balances the flow of energy within the body to enhance health and well being.
- ❑ Reflexology: Specialised thumb and finger techniques are applied to the hands and feet.
- ❑ Rolfing: Pressure is applied to the fascia (connective tissue) to stretch it, lengthen it, and make it more flexible. The goal of this technique is to realign the body so that it conserves energy, releases tension, and functions better.
- ❑ Shiatsu: Gentle finger and hand pressure are applied to specific points on the body to relieve pain and enhance the flow of energy through the body's energy pathways called meridians. Shiatsu is widely used in TCM.

- Sports massage: Often used on professional athletes to enhance performance and prevent and treat sports related injuries.
- Swedish massage: A variety of strokes and **pressure** techniques are used to enhance the flow of blood to the **heart,** remove waste products from the tissues, stretch ligaments and tendons, and ease physical and emotional tension.
- Trigger point massage: Pressure is applied to "trigger points" (tender areas where the muscles have been damaged) to alleviate muscle spasms and pain.
- Integrative touch: A gentle form of massage therapy that uses gentle, non-circulatory techniques. It is designed to meet the needs of patients who are hospitalised or in hospice care.
- Compassionate touch: Combines one-on-one focused attention, intentional touch, and sensitive massage with communication to enhance the quality of life for elderly, ill, or dying patients.

Chi Nei Tsang (CNT) is a centuries-old variety of healing touch therapy from China which focuses on deep, gentle abdominal massage. This is said to help the internal abdominal organs to work more efficiently which could improve physical and emotional health. The words Chi Nei Tsang translate to "working the energy of the internal organs" or "internal organs *chi* transformation." According to CNT unresolved emotional issues are stored in the digestive system and poor "emotional digestion" is one of the main reasons for ill health. CNT was first used a thousand years ago by Taoist monks in their monasteries to help detoxify, strengthen and refine their bodies.

Acupuncture:Inserting Needles

Dr. Jussawalla didn't use acupuncture but it may be relevant to add a bit about acupuncture here since it has joined mainstream alternate therapies in recent times as a valuable addition.

Acupuncture is a system for inserting very fine needles into specific body locations to alleviate pain. It is a complete medical protocol focused on correcting imbalances of energy in the body. From its inception in China more than 2,500 years ago, acupuncture has been used traditionally to prevent, diagnose and treat disease, as well as to improve general health. Acupuncture modifies the flow of energy (known as *qi* or *chi*) throughout the body. Research published in *Nature Neuroscience* demonstrated that the effects of needling include influencing the activity of adenosine, an amino acid which becomes active in the skin after an injury to ease pain. This may explain in part why pain relief is often experienced with acupuncture. Acupuncture was popularised in the U.S. during the early 1970s after President Nixon opened relations with China.

Acupuncture can be used for a wide variety of conditions, from emotional disorders to digestive complaints. It is beneficial for pain syndromes due to an injury or associated with chronic degenerative diseases like rheumatoid arthritis. It also helps in treating neurological problems like migraines or Parkinson's disease or even with stroke victims. Respiratory conditions, including sinusitis and asthma have been relieved with acupuncture, as have many gynaecologic disorders and infertility. Acupuncture has also proved beneficial for reducing fatigue and addictions, and for promoting overall well-being.

Acupuncture is often performed along with dietary interventions. It is frequently used in conjunction with "cupping," an Asian technique designed to increase blood flow to a particular area of concern by using heated glass cups to create suction and promote blood flow to the surface of the skin. Acupuncture is used effectively with massage, chiropractic or osteopathic manipulation, as well as different movement therapies such as tai chi and qigong.

India uses acupuncture these days, but it has a legendary tradition of massage carried through generations. Almost every Indian is familiar with massage (*maalish*)!

Chapter 20

When is Traction Needed?

I have no regrets. I've got my health.

--Naomi Campbell

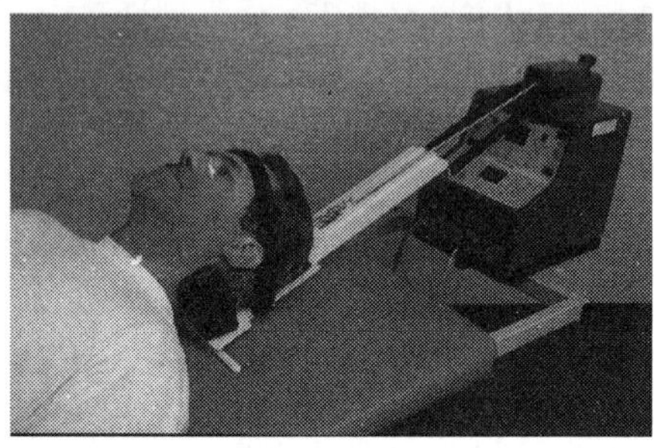

The spinal column is more than merely the vertical, central axis of the body that supports the remainder of the framework. The systems of spinal manipulation have popularised knowledge about the spinal column, and most people are aware of the fact that down through the body's centre runs the spinal cord, and that from this, through numerous openings, the spinal nerves pass to supply all the structures below the skull," says Dr.Jussawalla.

"There are 23 intervertebral discs, one between each of two movable vertebrae. These discs are composed of fibro-cartilage, with more or less gelatinous centres. They are all elastic and rubber-like, and serve as shock-absorbers, minimising the effects upon the spinal cord and the brain of jolts, jars and concussions.

Were it not for these discs, motion would be slow, clumsy, very limited, and no doubt more or less painful. These pads serve also to separate the vertebrae, and to maintain suitable space for the spinal nerves which pass out and also for the blood-vessels which pass through the openings between each pair of vertebrae."

He adds that through many years of improper posture, or on account of weakness, strains, jolts, jars and numerous other conditions occurring in everyday life, the connective tissue, whether composed of cartilage or ligaments, becomes more or less damaged. "This is noticed particularly in the intervertebral discs. The spinal 'windows' or openings are so large that an accident, or shrinkage from old age or other conditions, rarely permits direct pressure of the bone upon the spinal nerves and vessels. But such conditions do have a very detrimental effect upon these structures, filling out these windows and the connective tissue fibres that extend outward from them onto the sheaths covering the nerves and vessels."

Dr. Jussawalla explains that with age, the circulation of the body diminishes, less heat is produced, the walls of the blood-vessels contract, lessening the possibility of normal circulation. All the glands secrete less, all the functions associated with nutrition become weakened, elimination becomes sluggish, the suppleness of the joints and articulations gives way to stiffness allowing twists and sudden jerks and movements to irritate or produce pain, lubricating cells and tissues draw up, muscular and other tissues harden and contract, losing their tone and becoming otherwise impaired, organs shrivel up, and function barely enough to maintain life.

In short, the machinery of the body gradually wears out and life becomes an increasing burden. Many of these changes may be reasonably considered as the result of the shrinking of the spinal fibrous cushions and ligaments, inhibiting nerve-impulses from the spinal cord to the vital organs and tissues throughout the body.

Spinal Traction

Spinal traction opens up the spaces between the vertebrae and permits the discs to receive more nutrition. Because the discs are closely attached to the vertebrae immediately above and below them, traction pulls upon the fibres of these discs and directly stretches them, tending to restore them to their thickness.

Traction opens up spinal circulation channels, permitting a better flow of nourishing blood to the spinal cord causing it to generate and transmit better and stronger nerve-impulses. Traction helps to restore the normal forward-backward curves in the spine so necessary to prevent irritating jars of the spinal cord and brain; it also helps to restore normal posture and to elevate the ribs and make them more flexible -- a condition necessary for full vigour. It stretches the muscles of the entire trunk, and the blood vessels in these muscles, thus serving as a valuable exercise and as a means of securing better nutrition throughout the body.

In orthopaedic medicine, traction refers to the set of mechanisms for straightening broken bones or relieving pressure on the spine and skeletal system. There are two types of traction: skin traction and skeletal traction.

Traction is one of the arms of Nature Cure.

Chapter 21

Dietotherapy:Healing with the Right Foods

The human body is a wonderful and perfect machine. If it gets out of order, it can set itself right without medicine, provided it is given a chance to adjust itself. If we are not abstemious in our habits of food etc. or if our mind is agitated by passion, emotion or anxiety, the body cannot eliminate all the refuse and that part which remains uneliminated turns into toxins whose presence gives rise to symptoms which we call disease. Disease is an attempt of the body to get rid of toxins. If the body is helped in the process of elimination by fasting, cleansing of the bowels by enemas, baths and massages, the body could be restored to its normal health.

-- Morarji Desai
(Former Prime Minister of India and practitioner of auto-urine therapy)

The right diet is essential for good health. Exercise, yoga, and any form of medical treatment are futile without the right diet. Simply put – the wrong diet results in ill-health. *Dietotherapy is a branch of dietetics that focusses on the therapeutic uses of food and diet.* It is a scientific regulation of diet to treat disease. It is a complicated science and a work in progress with new discoveries happening all the time.

The effect of dietotherapy is determined by the quantity and composition of the food consumed (proteins, fats, carbohydrates, vitamins, minerals, trace elements), the caloric content and physical properties of the food (volume, temperature, consistency), the eating regimen (time, number, and distribution of meals), and the therapeutic value of the particular foods (for example, milk, honey).

The concept of medicinal foods has been prevalent all over the world from ancient times. In *Traditional Chinese Medicine (TCM),* the body is considered healthy when it is in a harmonious state. TCM uses many common foods as medicine, taking into account both the nature and flavour of food to achieve good health. Food can be cool, cold, warm or hot. It can be salty, sour, sweet, bitter and pungent. In TCM, disease is cured by applying the opposite nature and flavour to that of the illness. For example, illnesses with symptoms such as high fever, thirst, headache, deep-coloured urine and yellow fur on the tongue surface are said to be of a hot and excessive nature. Diseases with symptoms such as cold extremities, chills and shortness of breath are of a cold and deficient nature. In severe cases of hot illnesses, cold remedies should be used; in milder ones, cool remedies. Cold diseases, then, are treated with hot or warm remedies.

Cai Jingfeng explains in his book *Eating Your Way to Health* that food and medicine had a common origin because during prehistoric times man must have eaten plants and fruits that had a therapeutic effect on the body as well as providing nutrition. The legendary Shen Nong, who is credited with introducing agriculture to China, was said to have tasted all the plants and waters to know which was poisonous or beneficial. In the course of his experiments, he was poisoned at least 70 times. Cai cites a quotation from the *Book of Han Fei* (280-233 BC) that mentioned how people got sick after eating food that had an adverse affect on the body. There are innumerable references to food and health in ancient Chinese chronicles.

It is well established that most diseases – both mental and physical -- originate in the digestive system. Once the digestive system works properly, disease symptoms automatically resolve. It is now known that up to 85 per cent of children with autism also suffer from some kind of gastrointestinal distress, and researchers are now beginning to look for links between gut flora, autism, and irritable bowel disease. The impact of human breast milk – and not bottled or powdered milk -- on infants' gut flora provides valuable insights as it appears to promote a healthy colonisation of beneficial biofilms. For grown-ups, a healthy diet is the ideal way to maintain optimal gut flora.

It is also important that the foods eaten are organic. However, this is not easy in today's world with the abuse of insecticides and pesticides. The Environmental Working Group (EWG) in the U.S. has prepared a Shoppers Guide to Pesticides in which it lists fruits and vegetables that are the most and least likely to contain pesticide residue. According to the

EWG, eating five servings a day from this "Clean 15" list reduces your exposure to pesticides by almost 90 per cent. The list includes: Onions, Sweet corn, Pineapples, Avocado, Asparagus, Sweet peas, Mangoes, Eggplant, Cantaloupe (domestic), Kiwi, Cabbage, Watermelon, Sweet potatoes, Grapefruit and Mushrooms. Many of the products listed are easily available in India. Likewise, the EWG has listed produce with high pesticide residues. They include: Apples, Celery, Sweet bell peppers, Peaches, Strawberries, Spinach, Nectarines (imported), Grapes, Green beans, Lettuce, Cucumbers, Blueberries (domestic) and Potatoes. Kale/ collard greens may also be added to the list as they contain organophosphate insecticides, which the EWG characterises as "highly toxic."

Principles of Unani

Unani, the traditional system of medicine in India, lays stress on the importance of diet on health. It states categorically that most of the illnesses arise as a result of prolonged disorders related to diet and regimen. There are three aspects of food metabolism -- digestion, assimilation and residue -- that must be carried out efficiently for a person to remain healthy. In Unani, the food is selected according to its ability to improve the metabolic activity of the body in general and specific organs in particular. The nutritive value of the food is kept in mind including the temperament of the individual, appropriate season, age, climate, and so on. The food should be able to produce a balance among the four essential humours of the body. Foods should also be in season and preferably locally produced as it will then contain the necessary antidotes for all the bacteria and viruses in the region.

Yogic Diet

When one's food is pure, one's being becomes pure, says the Chandogya Upanishad (7.26.2) *Foods dear to those in the mode of goodness increase the duration of life, purify one's existence and give strength, health, happiness and satisfaction. Such foods are juicy, rich, wholesome, and pleasing to the heart,* adds the Bhagwad Gita (17:8). Ramana Maharishi, the saint of Arunachala, observed, '*It is within our power to adopt a Sattvic diet, and with earnest and incessant endeavouring to eradicate the ego, the cause of all misery. Food affects the mind. For the practice of any kind of yoga, vegetarianism is absolutely necessary since it makes the mind more Sattvic. However, once you have attained illumination it will make less difference what you eat, as, on a great fire, it is immaterial what fuel is added.*

The Yogic Diet is supposed to be food that is good for the soul. A vegetarian diet, it consists of fresh fruits and vegetables, beans and grains, nuts and seeds, and, in some cases, a moderate amount of dairy products. Food is traditionally classified according to its effect on the body and mind, using the three *Gunas*: *Sattva* (the quality of love, light and life), *Rajas* (the quality of activity and passion, lacking stability) and *Tamas* (the quality of darkness and inertia, dragging us into ignorance and attachment).

Sattvic food promotes clarity and calmness of mind and is favourable for spiritual growth. It includes most fruits, nuts, seeds, vegetables, particularly green leafy vegetables, whole grains, honey, pure water and – sometimes – milk. The emphasis is on pesticide-free, organic foods. *Rajasic* food feeds the body, but promotes activity and restlessness. It includes spicy foods, stimulants like coffee and tea, eggs, garlic, onion, meat, fish and chocolate, as well as most processed food. Eating too fast or with a disturbed mind is also considered *Rajasic*. A little *Rajasic* food can be *Sattvic* and includes hot spices that help digestion. *Tamasic* food induces heaviness of the body and dullness of the mind. It includes alcohol and food that is stale or overripe. Overeating is also considered *Tamasic*. The traditional dictum is to fill half the stomach with food, one quarter with water, leaving the last quarter empty. The nature of food changes with cooking. Grains become *Sattvic* after cooking. Honey becomes *Tamasic* with cooking. The nature of a food also changes when combined with other foods and spices, or if it is stored for a long time.

Foods can also have different vibrational energy. Foods that represent the colours of the *chakras* strengthen that particular area. For example, orange foods such as squash and yams are healing for the root *chakra* and can strengthen the reproductive organs. Black foods nourish and strengthen the kidneys and when they are functioning optimally the body takes on a loving, confident energy.

Ayurvedic Diet

According to Ayurveda, when we are balanced we desire foods that are good for us. But if our mind, body, or spirit is out of sync, our connection to our body's inner intelligence goes awry. Ayurvedic texts emphasise *ahara* or proper diet, as vital for promoting health and happiness. Ayurveda creates health by enlivening the body's inner intelligence to create harmony.

Ayurveda maintains that there is no one single diet or food that is healthy for all individuals. There is no blanket rule. According to Ayurveda there are six major tastes we need in our diet every day -- sweet, sour, salty, pungent, bitter, and astringent. Each of these tastes has specific health-giving effects. By including all six, we will be nourished. But when we consistently eat only a few of the tastes, there are health problems and also cravings for unhealthy foods. For instance, fast food contains mostly sweet, sour, and salty tastes. If we eat a steady diet of fast food, we can develop a craving for sweets. Adding more pungent, bitter, and astringent tastes can help tame desires for sugary foods.

The six tastes also affect the *doshas*. Different foods cause specific *doshas* either to increase or decrease. The *doshas* increase and decrease on the principle of "like attracts like." If there is a predominance of *vata*, there will be a tendency to accumulate more *vata*. Foods that decrease a *dosha* are said to pacify that *dosha*, and foods that increase it aggravate it. Sweet, sour, and salty foods pacify *vata*. Sweet, pungent and bitter foods decrease *pitta*. Pungent, bitter, and astringent foods pacify *kapha*.

Vata types need foods that calm their tendency toward anxiety and over activity. Heavy, cooked foods served warm are the most soothing. Dairy products, sweeteners, and foods cooked or served with fats and oils pacify *vata*. Rice and wheat are excellent grains for *vata* types. Juicy fruits and vegetables, heavy fruits (such as avocados and bananas), sweet and sour veggies etc help pacify *vata*. Avoid hot, spicy foods.

Fiery *pitta* needs to be cooled down and so needs foods at cool temperatures. *Pittas* thrive on reduced amounts of fats, oils, and salt. Sweet, completely ripe fruits and all vegetables except garlic, tomatoes, radishes and chilies are *pitta*-pacifying. Coconuts, pomegranates, grilled vegetable salad, and rice pudding all reduce *pitta*.

Sluggish, cool *kapha* needs to be stimulated and warmed up. Light, dry, warm foods reduce *kapha*. There should be minimal amounts of fats and oils. Grains such as barley, buckwheat, and rye are the best for *kapha* types. *Kapha* types can eat all spices and herbs but need to be cautious with salt. Pumpkin and sunflower seeds and most beans suit them.

The assimilation of food is also important. Food is the substance through which we bring nature's intelligence into our bodies. The digestive fire is called *agni* and when it is strong, our body fully assimilates nutrients and eliminates what it doesn't need.

A fully functioning digestive system uses the food we eat to produce a biochemical called *ojas*, a fluid substance that nourishes the mind and body and maintains the balance of all bodily systems. If the digestive fire is weak, the incompletely digested portion of the meal forms a sticky, toxic substance called *ama* which blocks the flow of the body's inner intelligence. It settles in areas of the body that are out of balance and can become calcium deposits in the joints, plaque in the arteries, and cysts and tumours. *Ama* is indicated by a coated tongue, bad breath, depression, etc.

Ayurveda also recommends drinking plenty of water at room temperature. There are other rules too: Dinner should be had around sunset, food should be freshly prepared, and seasonal, organic fruits and vegetables used. Ginger and black pepper help kindle *agni*. Ayurveda also says that *agni* goes to work as soon as the food hits the tongue. Dishes that make the taste buds sing kindle *agni* and enliven your body's inner intelligence. According to the ancient Ayurvedic text *Sushrita Samhita*, "*He whose doshas are in balance, whose appetite is good...whose body, mind, and senses remain full of bliss, is called a healthy person.*"

Different Types of Diets

Today, there are diets and there are diets. An apparently simple thing like a diet is not so simple after all and is dependent on a host of factors, theories and ideologies. For one, there is the *Body Type* diet. According to Dr. John Berardi, a leading expert in the field of fitness and nutritional science and consultant for the University of Texas Longhorns, the three main body types are *ectomorphs, mesomorphs and endomorphs*. Ectomorphs are naturally thin with skinny limbs; mesomorphs have athletic, muscular builds; and endomorphs have naturally broader and thicker builds. Understanding the physiological characteristics of each body type allows for specific tailoring of the diet.

It is impossible to detail all the diets in vogue but let me mention a few to underscore the complexities involved. Some diets focus on carbohydrates, others on portion control, and so on. There is also 'intuitive eating' in which people decide when and what to eat based on physical cues, not habit or emotion. This way there are no moral judgements about food.

Then there is the

Perfect 10 Diet

The Atkins Diet

The South Beach Diet

The Zone Diet

The Jenny Craig Weight Loss Plan

The Sensa Weight Loss System

The Buddhist diet

The Edenic diet

The Hallelujiah diet

The Hindu and Jain diets

The Islamic dietary laws,

The Kosher diet

The Different Types of Vegetarianism

The Flexitarian diet (a little meat is occasionally consumed)

The Pescetarian diet (some fish)

The Plant-based diet

The Low-calorie diets

The Breatharian diet (no food is consumed, based on the belief that food is not necessary for human subsistence)

The Israeli army diet

The Blood Type Diet

The 100-Mile Diet

The Mediterranean diet

The Purple food Diet (followed by Mariah Carey and others in which they only eat purple foods like plums, grapes and eggplants three days a week because "a plum a day keeps facelifts away"),

The New Nordic Diet

The Okinawa Diet

The Three Season Diet which calls for using a different diet appropriate to the season:low fat in the spring, high carbohydrates in the summer, and high protein (fat) in the winter; one season is typically dormant - a resting season, and so on forever and ever.

I should, however, point out here that for the third year in a row, the DASH Diet Eating Plan has been named the best overall diet by *U.S. News & World Report*. The journal asks experts to rank more than 25 diet plans to help consumers make informed decisions about nutrition. "To be top-rated, a diet had to be relatively easy to follow, nutritious, safe and effective for weight loss and against diabetes and heart disease," affirms the journal.

DASH, or Dietary Approaches to Stop Hypertension, was developed by the National Institutes of Health (NIH) for people with high blood pressure. It is also effective in lowering cholesterol and reducing risk for heart disease, stroke, kidney stones and diabetes. The focus of DASH is to limit one's daily intake of sodium. The meal plan has three whole-grain products each day, four to six servings of vegetables, four to six servings of fruit, two to four servings of dairy products and several servings each of lean meats and nuts/seeds/legumes.

Colourful Foods

Foods are also chosen by colour.

Green: A great source of vitamins (including folate, one of the B vitamins) green vegetables also provide minerals and fibre. Some - including spinach, collards, kale and broccoli - contain lutein and zeaxanthin, compounds from a group of antioxidants known as carotenoids that can protect aging eyes from developing cataracts and macular degeneration. They may also help protect against blockages of the carotid arteries in the neck. Cruciferous vegetables such as broccoli, cabbage, Brussels sprouts, and kale contain antioxidants and other phytonutrients that help reduce cancer risk.

Oranges/Yellows: Sweet potatoes, carrots, mangoes, apricots and other yellow or orange fruits and vegetables are also rich in carotenoids and other antioxidants that protect the body from oxidative stress. Orange fruits and vegetables also give you vitamin C and folate, needed to reduce the risk of heart disease and prevent certain birth defects.

Reds: Tomatoes, watermelon, papaya, and pink grapefruit are among the red pigmented fruits and vegetables that contain lycopene. This powerful antioxidant helps prevent the development of heart disease and some types of cancer, particularly prostate cancer.

Blues/Purples: The deep colours in blueberries, purple grapes, red cabbage, beets, and plums come from anthocyanins, phytocompounds that protect against carcinogens and may help prevent heart disease. Blueberries are especially potent: a half cup provides antioxidant activity equivalent to five servings of peas, carrots, apples, squash or broccoli. Blueberries also give you almost three grams of fibre per half-cup serving.

Whites: Garlic and onions contain allicin, a phytochemical that may help lower cholesterol and blood pressure. Raw garlic is a potent antibiotic that is especially active against fungal infections. It has immune-stimulating properties as well as antibacterial and antiviral effects. Other phytochemicals – polyphenols – found in pears and green grapes, may reduce the risk of some types of cancer.

On a lighter note, even the good old everyday beans were a major part of the diets of many of the Mesoamerican cultures, including the Mayan and ancient Aztecs, and they're still a staple throughout Latin and South America. Beans are also a part of lore. Apollo, the Greek god of prophecy, healing and music was given beans as sacred offerings; and on one particularly special occasion the Egyptian king Ramses III offered 11,000 jars of shelled beans to the deities. Even today, some Hindu traditions continue to offer white beans to their goddesses, while in the United States, Boston enjoys an entire baked bean dish named after it. On 'Bean Day' especially (taken as January 6) beans can be added to any diet to increase longevity. Ancient lore has it that beans can also fatten the bank account when eaten with that exact intent. So, beans are not only good for the heart, but also attract money!

Also, according to Feng Shui teacher, Grandmaster Professor Lin Yun, colours can even help in the treatment of cancer. He recommends that the patient look upon an image containing the Feng Shui 'Six True Colors' (white, red, yellow, green, blue and black -- in that exact order) so that this healing colour sequence can be transmitted to all afflicted cells. This, he believes, can be empowering.

Amidst the din of all these diets, it was possibly the Ornish diet by Dr. Dean Ornish, author of *Dr. Dean Ornish's Program for Reversing Heart Disease*, which gave medical credibility to meditation and yoga as being just as important as diet and exercise in combating heart disease. "Food is deeply tied to our culture and our emotions, and we retain deep connections with the foods that were used to make us feel better when we were kids, which weren't necessarily the healthiest ones," says Mimi Guarneri, author of *The Heart Speaks: A Cardiologist Reveals the Secret Language of Healing*, and founder of the Scripps Center for Integrative Medicine, in some consolation.

Diet & Nature Cure

"Dietotherapy is both an art and a science," points out Dr. Jussawalla who emphasised the right diet for good health long before the 'fad diets' took over. **"To affect desired results intelligently, knowledge which extends into many branches of science as well as into the practice of healing**

and preparation of foods is necessary. Not only must the practitioner have knowledge of foodstuffs and its break-up into various chemical components, but he must also have a complete knowledge of physiology and pathology."

He explains in detail. **"Naturopathy gives diet a prominent place. It is the key to health. Most health problems can be traced, sooner or later, to diet. The right diet is now recognised as the most important factor in good health. Wrong eating and drinking causes disease and so diet should be in harmony with nature's laws and principles. Nearly all chronic disorders are associated in one way or another with wrong eating and one cannot expect a permanent cure until one is educated along scientific dietetic lines. A balanced diet is the strongest shield against degenerative diseases both for the diseased person and the healthy individual.** Dietology is the most difficult of the therapies as well as the least investigated."

Foods & Diseases

There is new research every day on how the foods we consume impact our bodies. No research is conclusive as science throws up new information all the time. Now a growing body of research suggests that there may be a powerful connection between the foods you eat and your risk of Alzheimer's disease and dementia, via similar pathways that cause *Type 2 diabetes.*

Researchers from the Brown University in Providence, Rhode Island, were able to induce many of the characteristic brain changes seen with Alzheimer's disease (disorientation, confusion, inability to learn and remember) by interfering with insulin signalling in their brains. Alzheimer's disease was tentatively dubbed "type 3 diabetes" in early 2005 when researchers learned that the pancreas is not the only organ that produces insulin; the brain also produces insulin, and this brain insulin is necessary for the survival of brain cells. Over-consumption of sugars and grains is the primary reason your body becomes incapable of "hearing" the proper signals from insulin and leptin, leaving both body and brain insulin-resistant.

Obesity has also been linked to wrong eating. A multi-part BBC documentary by Jacques Peretti holds the government and the food and beverage industry responsible for promoting low-fat diets, processed foods, foods loaded with sugar (especially fructose) and artificial sweeteners. Growing and eating patterns of food have changed over the last four decades resulting in the all-prevalent morbidity today. Humans are genetically programmed to seek energy-dense foods which was fine thousands of years ago when food was scarce. But this is dangerous in today's environment of readily accessible, cheap, high-calorie but nutritionally bankrupt foods. It has been discovered than even the lean and apparently healthy may have a dangerous build-up of fat around the internal organs.

The importance of the right foods has echoes at all levels. According to a former White House executive chef, Laura Bush was "adamant that in all cases if an organic product was available it was to be used in place of a non-organic product," and Mitt Romney's wife, Ann, has publicly credited a combination of organic foods and holistic medicine for turning her health around after she was diagnosed with multiple sclerosis in 1998. In a 2008 interview, **Michelle Obama is quoted as saying: "...you start reading the labels and you realise there's high-fructose corn syrup in everything... Everything that's in a bottle or a package is like poison in a way that most people don't even know..."**

Mahatma Gandhi's Principles

One of Mahatma Gandhi's favourite subjects was diet and nutrition. Throughout his life he experimented with a variety of diets. He tried meat-eating, vegetarianism, fasting, restricting salt, and even a raw food diet. While he was imprisoned for two years by the British, he spent time laying out his views on diet and traditional remedies in a book titled *Key to Health*, arguably his most popular book.

Some of his principles:

- ❑ Disease is an attempt by the body to get rid of toxins. These toxins can be eliminated by fasting, eating and drinking natural food, and cleansing of the bowels by enemas.
- ❑ Fresh green and leafy vegetables should be eaten everyday. Fresh fruits and vegetables should be eaten when they are in season and preferably raw.
- ❑ A certain amount of fat is necessary and nourishing to the body. Oil is not as nourishing as ghee (clarified butter).
- ❑ Starchy foods should be eaten when dry so as to allow for more chewing and flow of saliva.

Many of the principles that are at the core of the vegan and raw food diets today were laid out by the Mahatma. He was also convinced of the health benefits of earth, air, water, and sun.

Chapter 22

Fasting: Cleansing the System

Everyone has a doctor in him or her; we just have to help it in its work. The natural healing force within each one of us is the greatest force in getting well. Our food should be our medicine. Our medicine should be our food. But to eat when you are sick, is to feed your sickness.

--Hippocrates, M.D

460-377 B.C., Father of Western Medicine

Fasting and natural diet, though essentially unknown (in today's U.S.) as a therapy, should be the first treatment when someone discovers that she or he has a medical problem. It should not be applied only to the most advanced cases, as is present practice. Whether the patient has a cardiac condition, hypertension, autoimmune disease, fibroids, or asthma, he or she must be informed that fasting and natural, plant-based diets are a viable alternative to conventional therapy, and an effective one. The time may come when not offering this substantially more effective nutritional approach will be considered malpractice.

-- Joel Fuhrman, M.D.,

From his book, Fasting And Eating For Health: A Medical Doctor's Program for Conquering Disease

Fasting and detoxification for health is the world's oldest and most effective system. Dr. Jussawalla used this method with heart-warming results. Socrates, Plato, Gautama, Mohammed, Jesus, Moses, Abraham, Hippocrates, Paracelsus, Mahatma Gandhi, Lao Tzu, Confucius and countless others both practiced and prescribed it.

Fasting is a period of abstinence from all food or specific items. Fluids are consumed in sufficient quantity to satisfy thirst and physiologic requirements. It is believed – thanks to extensive research on the subject – that during the absence of food, the body will systematically cleanse itself of everything except vital tissue. (It should be underscored here that extensive fasting should be done under medical supervision as the human body undergoes many changes and

if there are chronic underlying health issues they may manifest with disastrous consequences).

Starvation will occur only when the body is forced to use vital tissue to survive. Although protein is being used by the body during the fast, it is generally believed that a person fasting even 40 days on water will not suffer a deficiency of protein, vitamins, minerals or fatty acids. In the breakdown of unhealthy cells, all essential substances are used and conserved in a most extraordinary manner. According to A. J. Carlson, Professor of Physiology, University of Chicago, a healthy, well-nourished man can live from 50 to 75 days without food, provided he is not exposed to harsh elements or emotional stress. Human fat is valued at 3,500 calories per pound. Each extra pound of fat will supply enough calories for one day of hard physical labour. Ten pounds of fat are equal to 35,000 calories! Most of us have sufficient reserves, capable of sustaining us for many weeks.

In a fast, a person rids his body of toxins and excesses. The body is then allowed to use its own wisdom to healthfully reorganise itself from the atomic level. As the toxic load is reduced, the functioning of every cell is enhanced.

The human body has many modes of eliminating waste: the liver, lungs, kidneys, colon, etc. When these are overloaded, the body will resort to "extra ordinary" methods of elimination: boils, mucous and other discharges, sweats, vomiting, diarrhoea, and so on. The toxic overload can also seep into the joints, vessels, muscles, organs; almost any tissue in the body.

While fasting, the body is highly conservative of its energy and resources. During this deep and profound rest, toxin intake and production are reduced to a minimum while autolysins and elimination proceed unchecked. Anabolic processes such as tissue and bone healing also proceed well.

The Process

In the body, the first stage of cleansing removes large quantities of waste matter and digestive residues. The first few days of a fast can be rough due to the quantity of waste passing into the blood stream. The tongue becomes coated and the breath foul as the body excretes waste through every opening. After the third day of the fast, there is little desire for food. The second stage is the cleansing of mucous, fat, diseased and dying cells, and the more easily removed toxins. As the fast continues, the cleansing process becomes more thorough. The last stage is the cleansing of toxins that have been accumulating in your cellular tissue from birth, and the microscopic tubes that carry vital elements to the brain.

Cleansing of the last layer is only possible through a combination of *juice fasting*, *water fasting*, and *a healthy diet high in raw foods*. It has been observed that to overcome a severe disease like cancer, it is important to continue through a series of fasts, to the point where the full scouring action of catabolism removes the disease from the tissue.

During extended fasts, the body removes dead, dying and diseased cells; unwanted fatty tissue, trans-fatty acids, hardened coating of mucus on the intestinal wall; toxic waste matter in the lymphatic system and bloodstream; toxins in the spleen, liver and kidney; mucus from the lungs and sinuses, imbedded toxins in the cellular fibres and deeper organ tissues; deposits in the microscopic tubes responsible for nourishing brain cells and excess cholesterol.

Fasting is the simplest, easiest and most effective way to find out that we do indeed have the power and freedom to heal and take control of our bodies.

Fasting also enhances mental acuity. Perhaps the most instructive testimony to the acuteness of mental powers during fasting comes from *Dr. Herbert Shelton* who supervised the fasting of more than 40,000 people over a period of 50 years. His message is that the freer the body is of toxic materials flowing through the blood and lymphatic system, the clearer is the ability to think.

Short Fasts

According to a BBC report, scientists are uncovering evidence that short periods of fasting, if properly controlled, could achieve a number of health benefits. Calorie restriction, eating well but not much, has also been shown to extend life expectancy, at least in animals. It has been repeatedly documented that mice and monkeys put on a low-calorie, nutrient-rich diet live far longer and healthier than their gorging counterparts.

Research on Alternate Day Fasting (ADF), involving eating what you want one day, then a very restricted diet (fewer than 600 calories) the next, is throwing powerful evidence in favour of fasts. According to US scientists, fasting for regular periods could help protect the brain against degenerative illnesses. Researchers at the National Institute on Ageing in Baltimore said they had found evidence which shows that periods of stopping virtually all food intake for one or two days a week could protect the brain against some of the worst effects of *Alzheimer's, Parkinson's* and *other ailments.*

According to Ori Hofmekler, author of *The Warrior Diet*, *The Anti-Estrogenic Diet*, *Maximum Muscle Minimum Fat*, and *Unlock Your Muscle Gene*, fasting has shown to improve conditions of metabolic disorders, lower the need for insulin medication, and help relieve inflammation. Body scientists acknowledge three major mechanisms by which fasting benefits your body. They say that fasting decreases the accumulation of oxidative radicals in the cell, thereby preventing oxidative damage to cellular proteins, lipids, and nucleic acids associated with ageing and disease. Fasting increases insulin sensitivity along with mitochondrial energy efficiency, and helps retard aging and disease. Fasting also induces a cellular stress response (similar to that induced by exercise) in which cells up-regulate the expression of genes that increase the capacity to cope with stress and resist disease and ageing.

Researchers from the Salk Institute report interesting findings on fasting and mice. One group of mice had access to food both day and night, while another group had access to food for only eight hours at night (the most active period for mice) which, in human terms, would mean eating only for eight hours during the day. Despite consuming the same number of calories, mice that had access to food for only eight hours stayed lean and did not develop health problems like high blood sugar or chronic inflammation. They also exhibited improved endurance motor coordination on the exercise wheel. The all-day access group, on the other hand, became obese and were plagued with health problems.

Another recent animal study published in the *International Journal of Endocrinology* showed a beneficial glycemic effect from fasting that resulted in a lower gain in body weight than in non-fasting animals. Several research studies have shown that fasting triggers a variety of health-promoting hormonal and metabolic changes similar to those that occur during exercise. Research has also confirmed that intermittent fasting normalises insulin sensitivity, which is key for optimal health as insulin resistance is a primary contributing factor to nearly all chronic disease, from diabetes to heart disease and even cancer.

Interestingly, the typical breakfast did not exist during Biblical times. In the original Hebrew text of the Bible, breakfast is called "*pat shacharit*" which meant a tiny piece of bread at dawn, nothing more. And there isn't a single mention of breakfast in the New Testament; supper was the main meal of the day (hence, the *Last Supper*). The ancient Greeks and Romans were very particular about eating their main meal at night. According to Plutarch and Cicero, only slaves and farm animals were fed breakfast and lunch, as contrary to free men and soldiers who ate one meal per day at night.

Fasting and Nature Cure

Dr. Jussawalla, who used fasting with encouraging results in nature cure, says: **"Fasting is an overhauling process; it is constructive. On the other hand, starvation is a destructive, fatal process, a slow form of suicide." He makes an interesting and valuable point, "We may gradually starve on three meals a day, consisting of foods that lack the essential organic minerals salts, and conversely we may fast our way back to health, for fasting is nature's own way of cleansing and regenerating the body and mind. Fasting, properly conducted, is not only not injurious but distinctly beneficial. As much misunderstanding is caused in regard to fasting, it must be pointed out that it is merely digestive or physiological rest during which the body is enabled to devote all its energies to eliminating the accumulation of waste poisonous matter from the system. It is not starvation in any sense of the word."**

According to him a fasting cure can be undertaken for three reasons. The first is the so-called 'conquest fast'. This means exactly what the name implies; namely, to conquer yourself, to strengthen your mind and will power and to perfect your personality. "It will be found that clarity comes into your mind as never before, for not only your conscious but also your unconscious self will undergo a complete rebirth and awakening."

Another kind of fasting is the spiritual fast for religious reasons. Many great seers and saints have been devout apostles of fasting for illumination and spiritual revelation.

The main purpose of fasting from the therapeutic point of view is, Dr. Jussawalla continues, the treatment of diseases or tendencies toward disease. "There is hardly a diseased condition in which fasting cannot be used with benefit. Although we generally understand fasting to mean abstention from solid food, a very strict fast means also going without liquid. In this way you obtain very quick results, for you live entirely on your own flesh, and all surplus of carbon, mucus, acid and other harmful elements of the system are burned up. In other words, your body, if properly taken care of, will cleanse itself."

Natural and Positive Method

Fasting requires an unusual measure of self-mastery, will power and personality. It is, of all methods of nature cure, the most natural and positive, and a real short-cut to health; one that will create normal functioning of the various bodily organs.

Fasting is difficult only for the first three days, he explains. After that the body will have adjusted itself to the changed conditions. The most effective way is not to gradually lessen the amount of food, but to stop eating altogether and to drink nothing but plain water. "If you use orange juice or pineapple juice, you cannot call it fasting, for this manner of fasting will be found even more difficult to carry through, because the stomach nerves are continually being stimulated. The effect of the fast is enhanced by early cleansing of the bowel. This is a regular feature of naturopathic practice and is usually carried out by enemas or colonic washes."

He explains it in detail. The practice of fasting is employed as the only possible way of cleansing the poisons of the body and its organs and tissue. "This method is probably as near to nature as anything can be, as it overhauls the whole system and gives rest to the overworked vital organs. So necessary has this method of cleansing out the system been to the life and safety of the body itself, and so reluctant have people been to practise it, that every religion on earth, in all probability, has incorporated in its requirements the practice of fasting. No theology has existed without it, and the practice of fasting has been employed for thousands of years."

When fasting is continued beyond the stage of elimination of poisons, or when it ceases to be a cleanser, it begins to do harm as it leads to starvation. "Fasting is a double-edged sword. Long fasts should never be conducted without the supervision of an experienced Nature Cure physician," cautions Dr. Jussawalla. Before I end, I simply cannot resist this new finding. Research says that when combined with high intensity exercise, intermittent fasting can be a winning strategy to raise one's fitness to the next level. Restricting carbohydrates can help burn calories more efficiently and increase muscle oxidative potential even in highly trained athletes!

Chapter 23

When Should One Fast?

Effective health care depends on self-care; this fact is currently heralded as if it were a discovery.

--Ivan Illich

According to Dr. Jussawalla, fasting should not be resorted to only when one is ill. "A short fast for a day or two should be undertaken systematically for the prevention of disease."

Overeating or indiscriminate eating and drinking along with a lack of exercise are an almost universal vice in this modern, 'civilised' world. People keep their bodies constantly surfeited with food, forcing every organ to work overtime. Their nerves and glandular systems are overtaxed and their reserve forces are called upon to digest and assimilate surplus food. This is the only way the poisons that result from the decomposition of food in the intestines can be eliminated. "A fast reverses all this," explains Dr. Jussawalla. "The surplus food is used up, the toxins are eliminated, organs of the body get needed rest and are able to repair themselves. **By abstaining from food, the stomach, bowels, kidneys, glands, heart, nerves and other tissues of the body rest automatically. In the process, they repair themselves. It is not merely the digestive organs which rest during a fast; the benefits extend to every part of the organism. Hence, the two chief purposes of a fast are to allow the body to 'catch up' with its elimination and to provide physiological rest."**

Besides this, those who are sick usually suffer from nervous fatigue (enervation) and are in need of rest, not of stimulation. They are suffering from redundancy of nutrition and require a fast rather than 'plenty of good nourishing food' to ostensibly get their strength back. Their organs are damaged from toxic irritation and overwork. Nothing can be of more value to them than a period of reduced activity such as fasting affords. "Instead of wasting time treating (suppressing) individual symptoms we should correct the systematic condition that causes these symptoms. Instead of forcing an already overworked organism to do more work, we can accomplish real and lasting results by giving it less work to do. Nothing will serve this purpose better than fasting under proper conditions," he adds.

It should be explained here that healing through fasting and natural aids is a complicated process and needs supervision. The healing crisis that takes place can be frightening at times. The patient may feel that he is getting worse. But he will get better after the crisis. Initially, the forward steps will be accompanied by backward steps. But with a little time and patience, the many layers of toxicity that the body has accumulated over a lifetime will clean out. In the end, naturopaths (and even mainstream physicians) conclude emphatically that there will be radiant health.

Chapter 24

Vegetarian *vs* Non-Vegetarian: The Endless Debate

The food that you eat is life. It is other forms of life that we are eating – The other forms of lives are giving up their lives to sustain our lives. If we can eat with enormous gratitude for all the living things which give up their lives to sustain our lives, then the food will behave in a very different way within you.

-- Sadguru

The Dalai Lama adds, *"I would like my people to reduce their intake of meat and meat products. Good health and good eating habits go together. Research shows that food that does not involve killing makes you emotionally stronger."* Richard Wagner, the great German Composer of Operas tells of his reason for becoming a vegetarian: "*It was the result of the profound metaphysical insight of the Brahmin when he pointed to a manifold appearance of the animal world and said: 'This is thyself'. This woke in me the consciousness that in sacrificing one of our own fellow creatures we mangled and devoured ourselves. In truth, we have developed heartless blindness to things that lay before our oldest ancestors in all their naked horror.*" Rabindranath Tagore became a vegetarian when "*Once, looking out of the window, I saw a chicken crying and trying to escape from the man who was running after it. Since that day I became a vegetarian.*"

The vegetarian versus the non-vegetarian debate is a long one. Vegetarianism itself means different things to different people. From the dietetic point of view vegetarians in India are mostly lacto-vegetarians or those who do not eat the flesh of animals but who use a plentiful supply of milk and milk products, vegetables, fruits, nuts, pulses and cereals. Some also include eggs in their diet. There are others like the Jains who take no food which grows underground -- like potatoes, carrots, turnips and the like.

"The slaughter of animals obstructs the way to heaven," say the Dharma Sutras. The history of vegetarianism in India began in the Vedic period, sometime between 4000 and 1500 b.c.e. "The concept of the transmigration of souls first dimly appears in the Rig Veda," explains Colin Spencer in *Vegetarianism: A History*. "In the totemistic culture of the pre-Indus civilisation, there was already a sense of oneness with creation," he adds. A fervent belief in this idea, he contends, would give rise to vegetarianism. In subsequent ancient texts, including the Upanishads, the idea of rebirth emerged as a central point. In these writings, according to Kerry Walters and Lisa Portmess, editors of *Religious Vegetarianism*, "Gods take animal form, human beings have had past animal lives, and animals have had past human lives." All creatures harboured the Divine. A cow alone, notes Spencer, held 330 million gods and goddesses. To kill one set you back 86 transmigrations of the soul.

In the *Laws of Manu*, written between 200 b.c.e. and 100 c.e., dietary guidelines became explicit, say Walters and Portmess. Manu starkly states, "He who permits the slaughter of an animal, he who cuts it up, he who kills it, he who buys or sells meat, he who cooks it, he who serves it up, and he who eats it, must all be considered as the slayers of the animal." The Bhagawad Gita, written sometime between the fourth and first centuries b.c.e., added to the vegetarian argument with its practical dietary guidelines on *Sattvic*, *Rajasic* and *Tamasic* foods.

But, interestingly, along with this call for vegetarianism, animal sacrifice persisted. The Vedas that extolled the virtues of the natural world also emphasised the need for animal sacrifice to the gods. According to Edwin Bryant, professor of Hinduism at Rutgers University, the uneasy coexistence between India's emerging inclination toward vegetarianism and its history of animal sacrifice continued over hundreds of years. But later, the Jainas and the Buddhists says Bryant, "could scorn the whole sacrificial culture and preach an unencumbered *ahimsa*." This concept of ahimsa or non-violence, championed by Mahavira in the sixth century, has emerged at the core of the vegetarian argument in modern times.

Much later, Swami Vivekananda, writing a hundred years ago, said, "The amoeba and I are the same. The difference is only one of degree;

and from the standpoint of the highest life, all differences vanish." Swami Prabhupada, scholar and founder of the International Society for Krishna Consciousness (ISKCON), offered a more stark pronouncement: "If you want to eat animals, then God will give you the body of a tiger in your next life so that you can eat flesh very freely." Even the great yoga guru B.K.S. Iyengar feels that a vegetarian diet is "a necessity" to the practice of yoga. But there are yogis who eat meat.... and the great vegetarian versus non-vegetarian debate continues.

"Sophisticated prejudice against a vegetarian diet is born of preconceived notions which have no foundation," stated Dr. Jussawalla. "Our misfortune is that vegetarianism has become a mere habit among many in India. It has not emerged from understanding the dietary needs of the body and there is considerable ignorance." What is important, he continued, "is to encourage a balanced diet and the right quality of food over quantity. Cutting down on excess will help health and food scarcity. The vegetarian world has proved that life based on a vegetarian diet is not only possible but is worthwhile and can be maintained through generations."

Auto-Intoxication

From the Nature Cure point of view, the underlying cause of most diseases is auto-intoxication or self-poisoning or poisoning from within, he asserted. As meat increases the toxaemic condition, a vegetarian balanced diet is preferred. "Physiologically speaking, a well-adjusted vegetarian diet, besides providing a balanced menu, is absolutely free from the effete matter resulting from the metabolic activity of the animal abounding in its flesh. It therefore obviates the extra burden which is thrown upon the excretory mechanism of the flesh-eater who is compelled to dispose off such noxious residues from his system. These, retained in the body due to defective excretion, sets up various disorders which cause self-imposed suffering. One of the most convincing reasons why flesh should be left out of the diet is the fact that it is often a carrier of germs. Diseases of many kinds are on the increase in the animal kingdom, making flesh foods more and more unsafe as a source of food supply," says Dr. Jusawalla. Additionally, "Fear, anger and tension poison the blood. Imagine the plight of animals dragged to the slaughter-house. Vegetarianism is a way of life which has various aspects -- aesthetic, ethical, moral, spiritual and humanitarian, apart from the dietetic and health point of view."

Dr. Jussawalla, who was not born vegetarian but gave up eating meat later in life as a part of his spiritual evolution, explains that the problem with vegetarianism is a complicated one. "We must, of course, realise that the entire world can never become vegetarian," he admits. "Geographical and climatic conditions are often such that, for the most part, cultivation of vegetable crops is not possible, so one chooses one's food for reasons of habit, economy and other external circumstances. An Eskimo living in the Arctic would find vegetarianism difficult! But where nature provides man with fruit, grains, vegetables and other products of the soil, there can be no excuse for man's maintaining his own life by destroying other living beings." But it is important to mention here that to maintain good health much more is needed than the mere avoidance of meat. An imbalanced vegetarian diet and unwholesome cooking methods could be more harmful!

According to him the true meaning and significance of vegetarianism is not fully understood. "It is looked upon as something connected merely with dietetics rather than as a great movement inspiring humanity towards a purer and saner state of being and a full realisation of the true purpose of life. While the ethical and moral aspects are of the first importance, we have scientific and medical arguments which reinforce them and make the case for vegetarianism much stronger. It is the question of man's well-being in every way -- physical, mental, moral, spiritual, aesthetic, social, and economic. Man is more than meat. It is the spirit in man with which we are concerned. Vegetarianism in its broader aspects is a superior way of life. A Zoroaster or a Buddha could not possibly partake of flesh as food. Similarly, a Karma Yogi or an enlightened soul will never take to flesh food." This is probably what Leo Tolstoy meant when he said, '*A vegetarian diet is the acid test of humanitarianism*'. But Tolstoy also added, '*the moral progress of humanity is always slow*'."

Destruction of Life

As the years passed, Dr. Jussawalla grew increasingly passionate about vegetarianism. He saw the spiritual changes within him and also how a simple vegetarian diet impacted his patients favourably. "The very fact of eating meat implies the destruction of life which constitutes the gravest offence one can commit against morality, because the life of the animal is also divine," he stated in one of his books. He continued, "The idea of feeding on dead and decomposing flesh offends aesthetic taste. Meat and poultry are kept in refrigerators for many days and even months before they reach the kitchen, green and livid-looking and sending forth suspicious odours which have to be doctored with chemicals and spices. Even the artificial fattening processes, to which the animals are subjected in order to increase their weight and consequent market value, are fraught with deleterious effects upon meat products, after their slaughter. It is a well-recognised fact that, in most instances, a superabundance of flesh on the human animal (obesity) is synonymous with systemic poisons and incipient diseases. Why should we expect better results from this unnatural and inhuman, though unquestionably 'profitable', stuffing treatment inflicted upon cattle, pigs, chickens and so on, just prior to their conversion into food for man?"

According to him, and we all agree wholeheartedly, animals have a premonition of danger and death. **"They have to be beaten quite savagely in order to get them into the slaughter house and they are filled with terror and horror at the stench of blood. In abattoirs, a dumb creature is strangled or has its throat cut while fully conscious; then there is blood-letting, skinning, disembowelling, and dissecting. The whole process is done while the animal is still warm and hardly through its death throes. No person with any compassion or feeling could possibly endure the agonised cries and the brutal killing of victims. The processes of slaughter and of eating flesh on the way to decomposition are revolting and barbaric."** But he is quick to add that, "A person who is a vegetarian is not necessarily a superior person. He can be very cruel and even a heartless brute apart from being indifferent to the suffering and cruelties of dumb animals."

Dr. Jussawalla was a visionary. Several decades before the world woke up to the environmental crises facing mankind, he realised that we, as a race, were in for a freefall if we continued with the untrammelled hegemony of the planet. Today, the amount of greenhouse gases released in the atmosphere to produce half a pound (227g) of hamburger is equivalent to driving a 3,000 pound (1.3 ton) car for almost 10 miles (16km). Meat production contributes between 14 and 22 per cent of the 36 billion tons of greenhouse gases produced in the world each year. "Realise that man breeds his 'meat animals' to excess for business and selfish motives and brings on to the earth far more than nature normally would. One should not overlook the fact that an animal especially bred for its flesh needs a much bigger area of land for its food than a human being. It takes quite a stretch of land to raise a few head of cattle, and the soil becomes depleted. That same acreage which is used as pasture to fatten animals, the meat of which could feed a few people -- if cultivated -- with millet, peas, lentils, barley, nuts, etc., would be able to feed not only numerous families but would, at the same time, produce high-quality and nourishing food."

Worse, food animals are also being stuffed with antibiotics. As I write this, the Government Accountability Project (GAP) in the USA has filed a lawsuit against the FDA after the agency refused to release data on the amount of antibiotics sold for use in food animals. The US uses nearly 30 million pounds of antibiotics annually in food production. Livestock antibiotic use accounts for 80 per cent of the total antibiotics sold annually. It is believed that antibiotics such as penicillins and tetracyclines are routinely added to animal feed in order to make the animals grow faster. As a result, there is a rampant development of antibiotic-resistant bacteria. The only option now, according to Dr. Mercola who is opposing the practice, is to purchase antibiotic-free meats raised on high-quality organic farms.

Revolting & Unscientific

Dr. Jussawalla vehemently attacked the Indian government for its stand on meat when it issued a report stating that 'Meat is virtually important to the Indian population because their diet is deficient in first-class proteins and those could easily be obtained from meat.' **"This is a most revolting and unscientific statement based on insufficient, inefficient and inaccurate information," he retorted. "What are 'first class' and 'second class' proteins? Just because it occurs to someone to distinguish proteins and divide them into classes, it does not necessarily follow that meat is the only food that would supply the so-called 'first-class protein'.** The stock argument of non-vegetarians when thinking and talking about vegetarianism is that one cannot be healthy without including meat in their diet. In some mystical and mysterious way meat is supposed to be the food that can build virile health and provide the individual with a full supply of rich red blood. My advice to vegetarians in this connection is that they should not be misguided and led away by such illusions and delusions."

He argued that the consumption of meat is not a prerequisite either for physical or intellectual vigour, strength and energy. **"The fact that the strongest of animals, the elephant, the bison and hippopotamus, and the fastest of animals, the horse and the deer, thrive exclusively on a vegetable diet and that many of the profoundest thinkers and philosophers of the world, both in the East and in the West, have also**

been abstainers from meat may be cited as relevant illustrations. Vegetarian athletes, ranging from Greek marathon runners to modern swimmers, weight-lifters, wrestlers, and long distance runners and cyclists have demonstrated that the peak of physical fitness can be achieved without slaughter-house products. Whoever hides behind it and sometimes we vegetarians do -- the health argument is a spurious one. Some vegetarians are strong, some weak, as are meat-eaters. Some live long, some die prematurely. It is the reverence for life which distinguishes one from the other."

It also requires a resolve of steel to stick to one's convictions. Dr. Jussawalla narrated the instance of Kasturba (Gandhiji's wife). She had been very ill and the doctors insisted that nothing could save her barring non-vegetarian broth. **She said to Gandhiji, 'I would rather die in your arms that pollute my body with such abominations' and she whispered 'take me away at once'. Gandhiji thought about it and said that it was for her to decide how to die. So Kasturba was taken away and everybody thought, including the doctors, that she would never survive the journey. Well, she did not die. Gandhiji was impressed by her resolve and paid glowing tributes to her courage, her spirit and her faith in his autobiography.**

With a growing global consciousness for better health and more spiritual sustenance in the face of challenging times, vegetarianism has been in the forefront in the drive for wholesome foods. This includes the growing of fruits and vegetables by organic methods (composting) and not by taking recourse to chemical fertilisers and poisonous sprays and insecticides; whole-grain bread without toxic 'improvers', and unprocessed foods preferred over demineralised and devitalised foods reduced to zero nutrition by milling, refining, canning, preserving and colouring with chemicals.

Non-vegetarianism & Cancers

The conventional medical establishment is also slowly coming around to the superiority of a vegetarian diet. According to Dr. Andrew Weil, **an interesting new study found that avoiding meat, fish and poultry leads to more frequent reports of positive mood.** The researchers from Benedictine University in Illinois and Arizona State University noted that, in general, vegetarians report better mood than omnivores (those whose diets include meat, fish and poultry).

In the latest study, published February 14, 2012 in *Nutrition Journal*, the investigators noted that high intakes of arachidonic acid (a long-chain omega-6 fatty acid found in fatty red meat, egg yolks and organ meat) can promote brain changes that disturb mood, and wanted to explore how changing the fatty acid profile in the diet might impact mood. They recruited 39 volunteers for a two week trial. The participants were divided into three groups. Those in the "omnivore" group continued to follow their usual diets and to eat meat, fish or poultry at least once a day; those in the second group were told to avoid meat and poultry and to have at least three to four servings of fish per week (they were also allowed to eat eggs); and those in the third group avoided all animal derived foods, except dairy, for the duration of the study.

At the end of the two weeks, the researchers tested all of the participants with standard questionnaires designed to measure stress and mood and found that those on the vegetarian diet showed a decline in stress and tension and reported better moods than those in the other two groups. The researchers suggested that these positive changes could have been due to a reduction in the intake of arachidonic acid as well as to the effects of antioxidants in fruits and vegetables that may have boosted mood via a reduction of oxidative stress.

There is more evidence supporting a vegetarian diet. **According to Harvard researchers, people who eat less red meat may live longer than those who regularly eat burgers, steaks, and processed foods like bacon, hot dogs, and sausage. The research found that people who ate the most red meat were more likely to die of cancer or heart disease, compared to people who reported eating the fewest daily servings of beef, pork, and lamb. Researchers estimate that a single daily 3-ounce serving of unprocessed red meat raises the risk of dying of heart disease by about 18 per cent and raises the risk of dying of cancer by 10 per cent.**

Processed meats appear to be even more hazardous. A single daily serving of processed meats like bacon (two slices), sausage, or hot dogs (1 piece), raised the risk of dying of heart disease by 21 per cent and dying of cancer by 16 per cent. "Processed red meat is definitely more harmful than fresh or unprocessed red meat," says researcher An Pan, PhD, a research fellow in the department of nutrition at the Harvard School of Public Health, in Boston. While red meat is high in protein, it is also high in heme iron which can be helpful for those who suffer from anaemia.

But red meat is also high in saturated fat and cholesterol. Processed meats like bacon and salami are often high in sodium, which is known to raise blood pressure. They also contain preservatives like nitrites, which have been linked to pancreatic, kidney, and bladder cancers. And when meat is cooked at high temperatures, by grilling or broiling, chemicals linked to cancer are generated.

Without a doubt, the findings point to the possible benefits of a vegetarian diet. The researchers noted that their findings warrant further investigation.

The last definitive word on the subject can probably be reserved for Dr. Michael Brown and Dr. Josef Goldstein, heart specialists from the USA and winners of the Nobel Prize for Medicine who admitted that, "All flesharian food cause many diseases such as constipation, piles, gall bladder stones, colon cancer, indigestion, ulcers and kidney failure." What greater indictment of flesh based foods can conventional medicine give?

Chapter 25

Herbs in Nature Cure

Water, air and cleanliness are the chief articles in my pharmacopoeia.

--Napoleon

Natural foods are those which nature gives us in abundance. They are foods that have not deteriorated through manipulation, foods that can be eaten directly from the soil without being spoilt by chemicals, prolonged cooking or preservatives. Herbs and roots are rich in mineral salts, vitamins and many other substances which help clean the blood, build tissues, prevent organic ailments, and keep the digestive and eliminating organs in order. Often used in salads and teas, these herbs and roots contribute greatly to the maintenance of a healthy body.

From time immemorial, herbs have been used as food and medicine. It is only now that chemical preparations from laboratories are being used as curative remedies diverting people from the good, old-fashioned, time-tested natural remedies. But the pendulum is fast swinging; and herbs, roots and seeds are regaining favour.

Nutritive Salts

"Herbs and plant juices are particularly effective because they contain a wealth of nutritive salts. More importantly, the human system is best able to receive and easily digest these nutritive salts when contained in plant juices," says Dr. Jussawalla. "Man in his search for food tried herbs and plants and probably indirectly stumbled upon their healing powers. This knowledge he imparted to future generations. In the early ages the 'medicine' man and later the religious leaders attributed the curative effects of herbs to supernatural forces, and surrounded the gathering and making of herbal medicines with superstitions and religious practices and ceremonies. They also ascribed the healing virtues of herbs, roots and barks to the influence of stars and planets under which they grow."

Over time, the curative properties of herbs, roots and barks have been identified and well-documented. Colours and their healing powers were also researched. Red, for instance, was used for blood disorders, while yellow for conditions of the liver.

Certain plants bearing a resemblance to organs of the body were selected as cures for the organs they resembled. Animals also greatly contributed to the knowledge of herbs, roots, and barks. Primitive medicine men watched animals chewing on herbs and experimented with these herbs on humans. In certain cases, herbs when taken internally in varying quantities produce symptoms of well-recognised maladies. When these are administered curatively in non-toxic doses they restore good health.

Primitive man appreciated the value of herbs, roots and plants through trial and error without knowing the science behind their remedial properties. Only in recent times, through chemical analysis and food research, has it become known that herbs and roots are exceedingly rich in nutritive minerals, tissue salts and vitamins.

"The most important fact in this connection is that these nutritive minerals and tissue salts are in an organic state and can be easily received and digested by the human system," adds Dr. Jussawalla. "They abound in the most valuable elements like iron, lime, sodium, magnesium, iodine, phosphorus, silicon and the other elements of which our bodies are composed. The salts in the herbs help purify the blood by lessening the accumulated acids, they help feed starved nerves, tone up weakened organs, and cleanse the entire system."

Edible & Medicinal

Herbs are classified as edible and medicinal. In the edible category belong the well-known herbs like parsley, mint, slippery elm, lemon grass, etc. The medicinal herbs are those which are effective in their physiological action and are characterised as laxatives, sweat-producing, depuratives, etc. But it should be remembered that many edible herbs possess medicinal properties and many medicinal herbs are edible as well. Herbs have been used both internally and externally to combat disease.

To provide a few examples, ginseng and ashwagandha are rejuvenating agents; asparagus, alfalfa and parsley help promote good health, spirulina has more protein content than meat, and parsley is said to be a rich source of vitamins A and D and potassium. Garlic helps with cold, cough, sinusitis, bronchitis, diarrhoea, auto-intoxication and high blood pressure. Wheatgrass is effective in vitamin-mineral deficiency. Tea made from fenugreek seeds is reputed to be equal to quinine for reducing fevers; it soothes inflamed stomach and intestines, and cleanses the stomach, bowels, kidneys, and the respiratory tract of excess mucus. Tulsi is considered holy. It has several medicinal properties and destroys gas and phlegm. The best idea is to choose organic fruits and vegetables whenever possible. They are not just better for the environment but contain more antioxidants too. Organic plants must fight off pests and diseases naturally and undergo more environmental stress. This makes them produce more valuable phytonutrients.

Even the normally dismissed prickly pear cactus (*Opuntia spp*), called nopal in Spanish, a plant native to Mexico and the American southwest, and widely cultivated in many part of the world, especially the Mediterranean regions, has medicinal value. It has been observed that prickly pear extract helps as a supplement to help control blood sugar levels in those with diabetes or pre-diabetes. In Mexico, prickly pear is widely used for preventing hangovers. In a research study it was found that volunteers who took a prickly pear extract five hours before consuming five to seven alcoholic drinks had significantly less nausea, dry mouth and loss of appetite the following day compared to those who took a placebo. The researchers believe that the benefits were related to prickly pear's strong anti-inflammatory effects. The juice contains betalains, a rare class of antioxidants that is responsible for the rich colour of beets and red Swiss chard. Prickly pear juice also contains vitamin C. Research also suggests that prickly pear may also help control cholesterol levels. The humble prickly pear has other uses too. The heated cactus pads serve as poultices for rheumatism, and the fruit of the plant is consumed as treatment for diarrhoea, asthma and gonorrhoea. Mexicans also consume prickly pear to address high blood pressure, gastric acidity, ulcers, fatigue, shortness of breath, glaucoma, and liver disorders.

Visual & Medical Appeal

Incidentally, many of the holiday herbs, apart from lending visual and symbolic appeal, have medicinal benefits too. For example, pine (*Pinus* species) appears in cough syrups. This expectorant and antioxidant helps lung-related complaints such as asthma and respiratory infections. Dr. Alfred Vogel, the late Swiss herbalist, used pine syrup in his popular cough formulas. Pine tea added to a bath relieves sore muscles, while pine sap in a salve benefits eczema and psoriasis and draws out splinters. Gold figured as a valuable gift in the age of the three wise men, but what about frankincense and myrrh?

In the Middle East, people burned these resins to help purify the air, especially in public places of worship, where airborne disease presented a particular health threat. Myrrh (*Commiphora myrrha*), a plant native to the Red Sea region, served as a disinfectant, destroying bacteria and stimulating white blood cell production. Small amounts of the resin, usually used in tincture form, also treats gum infections, candida, impetigo, lung infections, and arthritis.

In traditional European and Ayurvedic medicine, the pale-coloured resin of frankincense (*Boswellia carteri*) taken internally helped treat dysentery, fevers, vomiting, and menstrual cramps. Topical applications improve arthritis, athletic injuries, bruises, acne, and tumours. Mistletoe (*Viscum album* in Europe and *Phoradendron serotinum* in America) were recorded as far back as 200 B.C. in the winter celebrations of the Druids, who gathered sprigs of the plant and hung them in their homes for good fortune. Herbalists today use small amounts of the herb to lower blood pressure, promote menstrual flow, and as a diuretic.

In the anthroposophical medicine of the Austrian philosopher and educator Rudolph Steiner (1861-1925), mistletoe even factors as a cancer treatment in a formula called Iscar that works as an immuno-modulator. Interestingly, rose petals are edible and may contain bioflavonoids and antioxidants, such as vitamin A, B3, C, and E. The bitter white base is removed and the petals are used in drinks, desserts and jams. Rose petals can give food a lovely flavour and aroma. The darker the colour of the petals, the greater the flavour. Several species of flowers like basil, chamomile, chrysanthemum, dandelion, pansy, and sunflowers are also edible. Just ensure that they are originally grown!

Herbal medicine, also known as herbalism or botanical medicine, is a medical system based on the use of plants or plant extracts that may be eaten or applied to the skin. Since ancient times, herbal medicine has been used by many different cultures throughout the world to treat illness and to assist bodily functions. Even doctors in today's conventional stream in the western world use herbal remedies in the form of extracts, tinctures, capsules and tablets as well as teas.

Herbal medicine has been used to treat or alleviate virtually every possible medical condition. In India, the spice turmeric in curry dishes is one reason for the elderly to have one of the lowest rates of Alzheimer's disease in the world. Some of the most popular herbal remedies and the conditions for which they are used include aloe used topically for minor burns, sunburns, skin irritation or inflammation; arnica used topically for bruises, sprains, sore muscles and joints; chamomile tea ingested for upset stomach, heartburn, indigestion and colic; ginseng for men and women, ingested to improve general health and stamina; echinacea ingested for colds, flu, sore throat; garlic ingested to possibly reduce cholesterol and blood pressure, treat fungal infections and colds; ginger ingested for nausea and motion sickness and as an anti-inflammatory; mullein ingested for chest congestion and dry, bronchial coughs; passionflower ingested for non-sedating relaxation; peppermint tea ingested for indigestion, nausea and other digestive problems; peppermint oil (in enteric-coated capsules) ingested for irritable bowel syndrome and other chronic intestinal ailments, and so on.

The list is long, which only goes to show that herbal remedies are safe, effective and widely used. It is proven that herbs may help fight heart disease and other chronic diseases, as well as premature aging. Certain herbs and spices help with maintaining a healthy body weight by increasing metabolism, shrinking fat tissue and suppressing appetite. Ginseng, cayenne pepper, black pepper, cinnamon, turmeric, cardomam, cumin, mustard and ginger help with weight loss. Additionally, they are good antioxidants.

Chapter 26

Medicines in Nature Cure

If diet is wrong, medicine is of no use.
If diet is correct, medicine is of no need.

---Ancient Ayurvedic Proverb

"It is generally believed that medicine is inconsistent with the philosophy of nature cure," says Dr. Jussawalla. "In order to avoid this misunderstanding and misinterpretation, let us understand clearly what we mean by medicine and its scope from the nature cure point of view."

He explains the scope of medicines in nature cure in detail. The common meaning of the word 'medicine' is 'any substance used in the treatment of disease'. Diseases are either caused or aggravated by a deficiency of positive alkaline mineral elements in blood and tissues. To bring the body to its desired state of good health, the nature cure practitioner provides it with the necessary mineral substances in a well-balanced nature cure diet.

But if these 'natural' foods are grown in mineral-starved soil, they may be deficient in mineral elements. Any consequent deficiency in the body is met by herbal tissue remedies and vito-chemical foods. In some cases, it becomes necessary to resort to herbal medication, tissue cell salts and vito-chemical foods.

"Medicines, therefore, are in conformity with the constructive principles in nature cure in so far as they, in themselves, are not injurious or destructive to the human organism, and in so far as they act as tissue foods and promote the neutralisation and elimination of morbid matters and poisons," states Dr. Jussawalla. "Many of those who have adopted natural methods of living and of treating disease have acquired an actual horror of the word 'medicine'. Besides, many people who have lost faith in the orthodox methods of treatment have swung to the other extreme. Both extreme attitudes are not justified."

According to Dr. Jussawalla, it is difficult to draw a sharp line of distinction between remedial medicines and drugs. "Nature cure is not inclined to the use of drugs in so far as they are poisonous and destructive and in so far as they suppress acute diseases in healing crises which are nature's cleansing and healing efforts.

On the other hand, in so far as a 'drug' has been defined to mean 'any substance used medicinally or as a chemical ingredient in the arts', it becomes obvious that the use of a 'drug' as such is not objectionable. The objection to drugs by a nature cure physician is not based on prejudice. He realises that many medicines have a proper place in the doctor's arsenal and knows that a certain percentage of disease needs 'medicine'. The naturopathic physician has to make sure that a drug should not be used if its intrinsic danger out-weighs the symptoms except, of course, in extreme emergencies."

Nature cure has a great respect for the art of surgery when practised in a constructive manner. At the same time, a naturopathic physician should guard his patient against promiscuous and uncalled-for surgical interference. Dr. Jussawalla explains, "After the removal of the inflamed part of an organ, which is usually but a symptom of the disease, one should examine the cause or causes and give treatment accordingly to avoid further recurrence and complications. It should be remembered by every naturopathic physician that when conditions and circumstances demand surgical intervention and assistance, there is no substitute."

Chapter 27

Diagnosis in Nature Cure

Keeping your body healthy is an expression of gratitude to the whole cosmos -- the trees, the clouds, everything.

--- Thich Nhat Hanh

Is diagnosis necessary in nature cure?

"The progress of nature cure, despite its wonderful achievements, has been greatly retarded by the perpetuation of the old idea that diagnosis is not a necessity. Looking at disease from the unity viewpoint, it is thought by many that it is only necessary to intensify elimination and neutralise toxaemia and nature cure will take care of the rest. This, though true in many cases, is not always so, and the physician who has been in practice for any length of time soon comes across cases that require specific diagnosis," says Dr. Jussawalla.

Although the assumption that all diseases have a common origin in wrong living, and that a return to nature establishes equilibrium is correct in a general sense, it does not justify the negligence of determining what is wrong with a patient and to what extent an organ or organism has deteriorated. A good Nature Curist will ensure several tests to arrive at the right diagnosis.

"How shall we ascertain if a given case is beyond nature's repairing forces?" asks Dr. Jussawalla. "There is no substitute to the necessity of a thorough diagnosis. The fact that medical practitioners treat their patients symptomatically does not render diagnosis superfluous in our practice. Adopting the available diagnostic means does not necessarily mean imitating conventional medical practice. It means progress, or being true to our patients, and it also means to cease being the laughing stock of other practitioners. By being or attempting to be scrupulously correct in all our clinical activities we will win the respect and the admiration of the world."

There is no denying that even for a nature cure physician, a thorough examination of the patient gives him a much better understanding of his health condition, especially abnormal conditions, and helps with better treatment protocols. The patient is also entitled to a correct diagnosis of his case and to a rational and reliable prognosis. The patient's faith and cooperation is essential in a cure. **"So accuracy in diagnosis is a very necessary procedure," concludes Dr. Jussawalla. "With correct diagnosis and specific treatment, the risk of malpractice is also considerably avoided."**

Chapter 28

Iridology:Eyeing the Right Diagnosis

Our body is a machine for living. It is organised for that, it is nature. Let life go on unhindered and let it defend itself, it will do more than if you paralyse it by encumbering it with remedies.

--Leo Tolstoy

Do the methods of diagnosis in nature cure differ from those of modern medical practice?

"The methods used for examination and diagnosis, from the nature cure view point, are a combination of all that has proved true and efficient in all systems from the oldest to the most advanced, whether orthodox or irregular; provided it conforms to the fundamental laws of cure. This is what makes nature cure philosophy and practice the true eclectic system of treating human ailments," elucidates Dr. Jussawalla. "The progressive naturopathic physician employs diagnostic tools generally adopted in medical practice. In addition, he uses osteopathic and spinal diagnosis. This reveals causes of functional derangement which are not discoverable by other methods of examination. Furthermore, naturopaths frequently use Iridiagnosis, a method of diagnosing bodily conditions by an examination of the iris of the eye."

Iridology is the scientific analysis of patterns and structures in the iris which locates areas and stages of inflammation throughout the body. The iris is the portion of the eye showing colour. It reveals body constitution, inherent strengths and weaknesses, health levels and life transitions. Iridology (also known as iridodiagnosis or iridiagnosis) claims that patterns, colours, and other characteristics of the iris can be examined to determine information about a patient's systemic health. Practitioners match their observations to iris charts, which divide the iris into zones that correspond to specific parts of the human body.

Iridologists see the eyes as "windows" to the body's health. A complete iris analysis is believed to reveal a good constitution or a poor one, depending upon the density of the iris fibres. It also reveals the relative site of over-activity, irritation, injury or degeneration of the tissues and organs. Toxic accumulation as well as nutritional and chemical imbalances can be deciphered. Iridologists generally use equipment such as a flashlight and magnifying glass, cameras or slit-lamp microscopes to examine a patient's irises for tissue changes, as well as features such as specific pigment patterns and irregular stromal architecture.

Origin

The first explicit description of iridological principles such as homolaterality (without using the word iridology) are found in *Chiromatica Medica*, a famous work published in 1665 and reprinted in 1670 and 1691 by Philippus Meyeus. The first use of the word Augendiagnostik ("eye diagnosis," loosely translated as iridology) began with Ignaz von Peczely, a 19th-century Hungarian physician. Iridology got attention in the United States in the 1950s, when Bernard Jensen, an American chiropractor, began classes. In ancient India, Egypt and China, doctors and priests were making health-related diagnosis based on the condition of the iris.

According to A. Jackson Read in his book *Eye Signs*, "The greatest feature and main advantage of Iridology over other forms of health screening is that changes appear in the iris before the physical symptom develops, and therefore preventive action may be taken. The iris reflects the condition of the tissues (eg. inflammation, acidity, toxicity, congested lymph, hardened arteries, etc.) Iridology helps restore and maintain health through building up the patient's immunity and life force."

The International Iridology Practitioners Association (IIPA) states that iridology is "the study of the iris, or coloured part, of the eye. This structure has detailed fibres and pigmentation that reflects information about our physical and psychological make-up. It identifies inherited dispositions (how our body reacts to our environment and what symptoms are most likely to occur), risks (what areas or organ systems are more likely to have symptoms) and future challenges (where we are likely to have more problems as we age). Iridology helps identify inherited emotional patterns which can create or maintain physical symptoms, as well as identify lessons or challenges and gifts or talents available to us."

Dr. Jussawalla explains: "In the normal functioning of the body, there are no discolourations or marks in the iris. When we look into the average individual's eyes, the iris presents almost every conceivable colour, although normally there are merely two fundamental colours -- blue and brown. Bodily conditions, racial characteristics and climatic conditions have mixed many other colours, which gives us the various colours of the iris; for example, different shades of brown, greyish blue, inky blue and hybrid shades of mixed colour, such that one iris may be brown and the other blue or one iris may have one part brown and the other part blue, etc.

"The iris contains many minute pigmented cells, muscular fibres, vessels and filaments of nerves, which through the optic nerves, optic thalami, the sympathetic nervous system, and the spinal system, connect the iris with every part of the body. This enables it to receive impressions from all parts of the body, and by its delicate structure it can reproduce the changes that take place in the organs of the remotest part of the body. These changes can be recognised by the various colours deposited in the layers of fibres of the iris. Sluggishness and atrophy of nerves and other structures of the body are recognised in their respective stages, such as acute, chronic and destructive. When more destructive, the local effect is deeper; thus the impressions (holes) will be effected in the deeper layers of the iris.

"The science of iridology is of paramount importance in the diagnosis and rational treatment of disease. In nature cure diagnosis it is often noticed that diagnosis from the iris independently describes the same lesions in the eyes which the spinal therapist discovers in the spine and nerve centres and which the physician finds through his physical examination and which is confirmed by the findings in the laboratory and by radiology as well." According to him, one of the greatest benefits of iridology is that we see in the iris the changes taking place in the purification of the whole system by the elimination of morbid matter and various poisons. "Nature alone proves to us through the eyes that all substances which cannot be assimilated or be absorbed in any form and made a part of the body are injurious and, therefore, should not be taken into the system. The diagnosis from the iris is of great interest and importance not only because it gives accurate information about causes of disease which cannot be diagnosed in any other way, but also because these wonderful records confirm the fundamental principles of nature cure philosophy and practice," he concludes.

As it is often said, the eyes are the windows to the soul. In spiritual terms, healthy eyes can project and see the truth in all things. The eyes require strengthening as they have muscles within them. If these muscles become weak they start to lose strength just like any of the muscles in our bodies. The eyes are also attached to the health of the gut flora. When our gut flora is in harmony, our vision is good. If we suffer from candida, for example, the vision can deteriorate over time. Once again, we come to the original truth that the human body must be taken as a whole and looked at in a macro perspective.

Chapter 29

Astro Diagnosis:Health Based on the Stars

Tayata Om Bekanze Bekanze Maha BeKanze Radza Samudgate Soha (to eliminate the pains of diseases but also to overcome the inner sickness of attachment, hatred, jealousy, greed, desire and ignorance.)

--- Prayer of the Medicine Buddha

Are there other diagnostic methods which would be useful to a nature cure practitioner?

Dr. Jussawalla wanted the method of diagnosis known as *Nadi Vaidya* (the science of pulse or the system of diagnosis from the examination of the pulse), practised by the old school of *Vaids*, to be included in Nature Cure practice. He also, interestingly, moots the use of "astro-medical-analysis in the understanding of diseased conditions and the scientific cultivation of health."

This may come as a surprise, but Dr. Jussawalla, a man who believed in science and empirical knowledge, also believed in the power of the planets on human health. Medical astrology (traditionally known as Iatromathematics) is an ancient medical system that associates various parts of the body, diseases, and drugs with the sun, moon, and planets, along with the 12 astrological signs. **Each astrological sign is associated with different parts of the human body. After examining an individual's natal chart, a medical astrologer may give advice to the client about the areas of the body in which he or she is most likely to experience trouble.**

Five Basic Elements

According to Ayurveda, the human body consists of five basic elements -- Earth, Water, Air, Fire and Sky. The imbalance of these basic elements causes disease. It is said that not only humans but also every element, herb and vegetation in the universe represents a specific planet, *rashi* and *nakshatra*. Astro Medicine provides diagnosis, prognosis and prophylaxis. It is the method of diagnosing a disease based on the combination and permutations of the planets in the 12 houses. Its practitioners say that astro-diagnosis is scientific and a proper study of the planets will pinpoint latent tendencies and help prevent and even cure diseases.

Dr. Jussawalla expounds, "The zodiac is the broad belt of space in which the sun and planets seem to travel around the earth. It is divided into 12 segments, each of which corresponds to and sympathises with some part of the body. Thus the first segment, or division called Aries, corresponds to the head; the second, Taurus, to the neck; and so on till the twelfth and last, called Pisces, corresponds to and sympathises with the feet. Any one or more of the planets can occupy these various portions of the zodiac, depending upon where their orbital revolutions bring them at any given moment. In astro-pathology, special importance is attached to the so-called malefics. Thus, the fiery Mars can mean fevers and acute diseases, while the chronic Saturn is coldly obstructive, Uranus spasmodic, and so on."

All this can be complicated and has to be deciphered by an expert in the subject. Details have to be accurate and then interpreted correctly. From the person's date, place and time of birth, the practitioner gets a view of the fundamental astro-vital forces at work in that person's system. Weak parts or organs, constitutional tendencies, astral influences in any given period, etc., can be figured out. They can be cross-checked by a physical examination. This way the accuracy of the astro-diagnosis can be determined.

Birth Cell-Salts

According to Dr. Jussawalla, the 12 zodiac signs constitute the 12 different parts of the body and are related to the mineral salts of the body. Known as birth cell-salts they play an important role in the ailments of the individual. They are as follows:

- **Aries** — The ram, rules the head. Its chief constituent is *kali phos* (potassium phosphate).
- **Taurus** — The bull, rules the neck, throat and cerebellum. Cell salts: *natrum sulph* (sodium sulphate).
- Gemini — The twins, rules the lymphatic and respiratory systems. Cell salts: kali muriaticum (potassium chloride).

- **Cancer** — The crab, rules the solar plexus and the chest. Cell salts: *calcara flour* (calcium fluoride).
- **Leo** — The lion, rules the heart and motor nerves. Cell salts: *magnesia phos* (magnesium phosphate).
- **Virgo** — The virgin, rules the abdominal region. Cell salts: *kali sulph* (potassium sulphate).
- **Libra** — The balance, rules the urinary and sexual organs. Cell salts: *nutram phos* (sodium phosphate).
- **Scorpio** — The scorpion, rules the hips. Cell salts: *calcar sulph* (calcium sulphate).
- **Sagittarius** — The archer, rules the thighs. Cell salts: *silica* (silicic oxide).
- **Capricorn** — The goat, rules the bones and thighs up to the knee. Cell salts: *calcarphos* (calcium phosphate).
- **Aquarius** — The water bearer, rules the calves upto the ankle and nerves. Cell salts: *natrum mur* (sodium chloride or common salt).
- **Pisces** — The fish, rules the feet and blood, chiefly red blood corpuscles. Cell salts; *ferrumphos* (phosphate of iron).

"Each of these 12 cell-salts originates and develops on this earth in the vegetable kingdom and in all the animals when the sun enters each sign of the zodiac, i.e., when the earth comes between the sun and each sign of zodiac," continues Dr. Jussawalla. **"Astrology not only helps in diagnosing the physical characteristics but the character of the patient can also be known -- whether he is weak and whether he is negative or emotional."** He admits that there is nothing empirical about character reading and diagnosis through astrology. "There are many conditions hidden deep down in the forces of the body which laboratory and other fine tests are unable to reveal. Diagnosis of a disease is important but what is more important is the diagnosis of the condition of the whole body -- physical, mental, emotional and spiritual. When nature cure physicians, scientists, occult scientists and astrologers have reached a friendly understanding, health will be universally enjoyed."

Chapter 30

Health over Disease

It is a mistake to neglect the body and let it waste away. The body is the means of the 'sadhana' and should be maintained in good order. There should be no attachment to it, but no contempt or neglect either of the material part of our nature.

-- Sri Aurobindo

The naturopathic physician gives more importance to the prevention of disease rather than just curing it. For the naturopath, good health is the priority.

"A strong and healthy body is the greatest resistance against disease," affirms Dr. Jussawalla. "Health is a positive state of well-being where every part of the body and mind is in harmony and in proper functioning balance with every other part. In other words, when every organ of the body is functioning normally the state of physical well-being known as health exists. So functional balance is health, and functional imbalance is disease."

He points out that the whole universe, from the mighty sun to the tiniest atom, is controlled by law. "There is perfect order everywhere. There are laws in the mental plane. There are laws of physics, of astronomy, of mathematics. There are laws of hygiene and health which govern us. In the vast universe, man alone is the breaker of law and the violator of rules. He is the single example of lawlessness and discord. He wilfully disregards the laws of health, leads a life of dissipation and then wonders why he suffers from disease and disharmony. Persons who treat their bodies as they please and transgress rules of personal hygiene of which they should have a definite understanding are physical sinners, and they are not only committing a crime against themselves, but against their dependent and future generations."

Normally, people give very little attention to health until it is destroyed. Then they call on a doctor almost as a last resort. "The idea that they alone might be responsible for their health or disease and that responsibility for their recovery rests on them and not on the doctor is foreign to them," says Dr. Jussawalla. "But barring trauma (accidents), congenital abnormalities and surroundings uncongenial to human life, the primary cause of any and all disease is a violation of one or more health principles. It may be in eating, drinking, resting, working, breathing or exercise; or in thinking, feeling; or in moral or sexual conduct which results in certain primary or secondary manifestation of disease."

Dr. Jussawalla believes that a man reaps what he sows. The person with wrong living habits is sowing the seeds of disease. Health should be regarded as capital in the bank. By neglecting to take care of any part of the body, injury results and this is like drawing a certain amount of capital out of the bank. "Good health and physical power seldom come to a man without effort on his part. For superior health, real strength and beauty, one must first acquire knowledge necessary to perfect the body and then adhere to the rules," he says. According to him, the human race is growing weaker physically.

Each generation bequeaths to its successors the accumulated knowledge of preceding ages. There is growth in intellectual wisdom. But is man growing stronger and more healthy? "The human body is a wonderful machine made of flesh and blood. It must be fed correctly and given the particular attention needed to keep it in thorough repair. Natural health, which has the ability to resist disease, is the result of living in accordance with the natural laws that govern our being. Health is an inestimable blessing and the only way to maintain it is through care of the body."

He believes that the proper care and development of the body should be started in childhood. If the parents are in good health physically and mentally there is every chance that their children will be healthy too. People inherit good and bad health to a great extent, but a lot can be changed for the better or worse by living within and without the immutable laws of health and life. "The best heredity may be dissipated through the unwise management of our bodily powers and exceeding our bodily capabilities, or neglecting to replenish fully our body's own losses. Health squandered may never be fully restored. The waste of health is one of the most inexcusable of all wastes. Health is one of our choicest possessions. It should be highly prized and carefully guarded."

Chapter 31

Tenets for Good Health

The doctor of the future will give no medicine, but will interest her or his patients in the care of the human frame, in a proper diet, and in the cause and prevention of disease.

--Thomas Edison

Good health is the only true prophylactic against disease.

Despite the advancement of science and knowledge, disease and sickness are on the rise. Evidently, something is seriously wrong with the accepted norms of conventional living. *Health is the result of living in accordance with the natural laws that operate in the mind, emotions and body of man.* To build and maintain good health, the natural laws of life need to be observed.

They may be summarised under the heads:

- Fresh air and sunshine
- Deep breathing, regular exercise and corrective posture
- Rest, relaxation, recreation and sleep
- Proper food and regulated diet
- Right mental attitude
- External and internal cleanliness and proper elimination.

Fresh Air & Sunshine

Live, work, play and sleep in the open as much as possible and secure ample amount of fresh air when indoors, says Dr.Jussawalla. "Fresh air and sunshine are as necessary for good health as food and water. Oxygen, received from the air is necessary for every function of the organs. Besides, it also burns up 'waste material' in the body. It is impossible to have good blood and good nerves if fresh air is denied. When taking an air bath we expose the entire body to the air, bathing in the air so to speak. Air baths give the skin a chance to breathe. They keep the pores active and promote the elimination of wastes. They also have a soothing and invigorating effect upon the nervous system."

Sun, the great steriliser and life giver, is the greatest aid to health. Sunlight is an essential factor for maintaining health. The curative and health-giving action of light is stupendous. "Injurious bacilli on the skin are rendered innocuous by sunlight, but processes vastly more subtle than this take place. Although sunlight cannot manufacture vitamin A by its action on the skin, it induces changes by which the least amount of vitamin will serve to maintain growth and health.

It has been proved that sunlight induces the production of vitamins D and E by its action on the skin," notes Dr. Jussawalla. "The action of the sun on the skin is due to light rays and not heat. Therefore cold rays of the sun should be availed of as far as possible. The best time for exposure to the sun is the morning and in the evening when diffused light is present. Too much exposure to sun should be avoided. It must be borne in small doses so that it doesn't injure the skin."

Apart from the production of vitamin D, exposure to sunshine enhances mood and energy, melatonin regulation, suppression of MS symptoms, has helped in the treatment of tuberculosis long before the arrival of antibiotics, and even aids in the treatment of skin diseases. Vitamin D deficiency is common in sick children and in the poor health of the elderly. Researchers at the University of Manitoba, Canada, recently found that children with severe early childhood teeth problems had significantly lower vitamin D levels than cavity-free children. Evidently, a little sunshine goes a long way in good health.

Deep Breathing

Svatamaram Yogendra in the *Hatha Yoga Pradipika* says, "The mind is the king of senses and body, but the breath is the king of the mind."

We can live without food for many weeks; we can live without water for several days; but we cannot live without air even for a few minutes.

Breath is life. There is a rhythmic movement at the very centre of our being; a cyclic expansion and contraction that is both in our body and outside it. It is in our consciousness and yet not in it. Breath is the essence of our being. It is present in all aspects of the universe. The same rhythmic pattern of expansion and contraction is present everywhere – whether it is the alternating cycles of day and night, waking and sleeping, high and low tides, or seasonal growth and decay.

By focusing on one's breath, one can change one's state of consciousness. Many systems of meditation use breath as the main technique. The Buddhist and yogic traditions, in particular, focus on breath to reach enlightenment. The emphasis is on doing nothing other than paying attention to the rising and falling of the breath. It is believed that in the dimensionless point between inbreath and outbreath one can get a whiff of enlightenment. Breath, in the yogic tradition, is the mystery of being unfolding right in front of one's nose, connecting the individual to the universal rhythm. So important is breath that different types of breathing have been known to produce different results on the body and mind. The right technique of breathing heals, and the wrong technique can be disastrous.

The amount of carbon dioxide in the blood generally regulates one's breathing. Too little carbon dioxide can cause many problems. According to research if you release too much carbon dioxide too quickly, as you often do when you breathe mainly through your mouth, the arteries and vessels carrying blood to the cells constrict and the red blood cells could get "sticky," and the oxygen in the blood is unable to reach the cells of the brain and body in sufficient quantity. The reduced amount of oxygen going to the cells of the brain can turn on the sympathetic nervous system, specifically the "fight or flight or freeze" response, and make one tense, anxious, irritable, and depressed. This process can result in asthma, high blood pressure, heart disease, and other serious medical conditions.

Taking a deep breath is like blowing smouldering fire as it brightens the vital flame. By taking a full breath we inhale a large quantity of oxygen and by retaining it a while, we stir and purify the air which always remains in the lungs. On exhaling, we expel carbon-dioxide and other poisonous gases," explains Dr. Jussawalla. "Deep breathing is one of the methods to develop the respiratory organs. It has the additional advantage of infusing extra oxygen into the blood which means an offer of richer material to the system to consume. We also get oxygen from water and food, but these sources are less important than air. The real life-sustaining supply depends on breathing."

Proper breathing improves not just physical health, but also mental power, happiness, self-control, clear-sightedness, morals and even spiritual growth. "Man in his normal state had no need of instruction in breathing," continues Dr. Jussawalla. "Like the animals he breathed naturally and properly as nature intended him to do, but civilisation changed all that. He adopted improper methods and attitudes of walking, standing and sitting which robbed him of his birthright of natural and correct breathing."

The proper method of breathing is to take the breath through the nostrils because the organs of respiration have their only protective apparatus filter or dust catcher in the nostrils. Also, the long narrow winding nostrils are filled with warm mucus membranes which helps warm the inhaled air to prevent any damage to the delicate organs of the throat and the lungs. In mouth breathing, the entire respiratory system is unprotected.

"As a rule, the best time to take special breathing exercises is in the morning on an empty stomach. This helps start the day well. But remember never to neglect systematic breathing while walking, exercising, sitting or resting," adds Dr. Jussawalla.

Regular Exercise

Exercise is essential to life and health. "A body can be efficient as long as its muscular system is in proper tone," points out Dr. Jussawalla. This depends on the elasticity and irritability of individual muscles, and also upon its ability to expand and contract. Normal muscles alternately contract and relax. Contraction forces blood out of the muscles and relaxation forces more blood to come to them. Venous return flow depends on the intermittent pressure of this action and reaction."

Dr. Jussawalla explains the process. Vigorous exercise requires the complete coordination of the nervous, cardio-vascular and respiratory systems. The muscles derive their energy principally from the stored carbohydrates, and also from fats and proteins. They transform potential into *kinetic energy* and during the period of rest restore their *potential energy* with the *liberation of oxygen.* This oxygen comes from the oxidation of food and is brought by the blood. Very vigorous active exercise may call for five to ten times the amount of oxygen consumed during rest. The respiratory system must supply the heart which contracts more vigorously and quickly, blood pressure rises and there is marked activity of the central nervous system. The more the oxygen consumed, the greater the increase in hydrogen-ion concentration in the blood passing through the respiratory centre and greater the increase of nervous impulses through it. Consequently, there is greater coordination of nerves, muscles and circulatory and respiratory systems.

"Violent or unaccustomed exercise should never be indulged in by those with sedentary habits or by those whose hearts have been damaged by acute or chronic infections. The result may be severe injury or death. Hence, the necessity for a complete diagnosis before any exercise is prescribed," cautions Dr.Jussawalla. "There are two principal classifications of exercise: *one is exercise for education or physical training purposes,* subdivided into athletic sports and ordinary gymnastics; *the other is therapeutic exercise for the purpose of correcting various deformities, diseases or injuries of the body, also known as medical gymnastics."*

Walking

No matter what form of muscular activity you may be indulging in, walking should always be included in your routine, feels Dr. Jussawalla. "Walking is the greatest of all exercises. It is an exercise that can be taken by everybody, strong as well as weak. For maximum benefit, walk briskly with an elastic step."

It is also a good idea to walk barefoot as one needs to be earthed. The feet also have to breathe! The Taoist sage Chung Tzu said that "While most people breathe with their throats, real human beings breathe from their heels."

Correct Posture

Hold the chest up when sitting, standing and walking and as far as possible, when at work, says Dr. Jussawalla. "Man is the only animal that walks erect. He is the only animal in whom old age brings a forward bending of the spine."

There are definite physiological results of maintaining an erect spine. The mechanical arrangement of the spine is such that if it is held erect the important nerves that radiate to all parts of the body from this central 'bureau' are able to perform their functions perfectly. When there is pressure on these nerves there is bound to be imperfect functioning. The affected organs will not work normally.

An erect carriage also helps maintain the proper position of the vital organs. When the body is held erect the chest is full, round and somewhat expanded affording plenty of room for the heart and lungs. The stomach, liver and intestines tend to drop or sag below their normal position when the body bends forward and the functioning of these organs is impaired.

Dr. Jussawalla puts it in perspective: **"From cradle to grave, man is affected by the force of gravity on his posture. He must resist this force while awake and take it into consideration when he lies down to rest. Abnormal posture is serious as it affects the spine producing rotations, curvatures, kyphosis (humps) and lordosis (abnormal sways). These spinal distortions interfere with the normal motion of the body and produce occlusion of the nerve trunks emanating from between the vertebrae leading to various parts of the body. The spinal muscles are thus weakened and individual vertebrae easily become distorted resulting in serious nerve pressure, pains, disease and malfunctions in the body.** Many of these spinal distortions, especially curvatures, impact the internal organs of the body interfering with their drainage and other functions."

He adds that the distorted posture of standing for long periods with more weight on one foot "causes the longitudinal-transverse arch to become lower or more collapsed in one foot than thc other. Tracing the effects of this unequal skeletal base or foundation on organs placed higher up, we find the sacrum, the big bone at the base of the spine, tilted lower on one side than the other, corresponding to the lowest arch which causes spinal rotations and curvatures, which may balance themselves abruptly enough at certain points of the column to produce serious nerve pressures."

Sitting in a stooped or slumped position continuously for long periods also results in a hump back and rounded shoulders which is bad for the upper part of the lungs and also results in general spinal nerve occlusion. "When any organ of the body sags below its normal position its ability to function is inhibited just as one's ability to turn is affected when the feet are in a sack. When such inhibition is placed on the stomach, it empties more slowly and its contents are likely to cause gas, indigestion pains, etc. With the intestines sagged, one may have constipation, haemorrhoids, mucous colitis and many other troubles that go with poor bowel eliminations," continues Dr. Jussawalla. "Foot troubles play a major part in bad posture resulting in fallen arches, anatomical short leg due to injuries or deformity, and so on."

Rest, Relaxation, Recreation and Sleep

All these are important for good health. But the difference between rest, recreation, relaxation and sleep should be properly understood. Interestingly (also important here to break the tedium of serious reading), Thomas Edison, who was so hell bent on his work and research, got only about three-five hours of sleep at night. But he was a master napper! While working on a creative project, Edison would doze off for 25-minute stints regularly. But here's the catch -- he would focus on the solution to his creation as he drifted to sleep, holding ball bearings. As soon as he reached an alpha (hyper-creative) brain wave state, his hand would drop, crashing the ball bearings to the floor, waking him up. He would then quickly write down all the thoughts in his mind! This surely doesn't mean that the world will get more creative with naps, but napping does help even ordinary everyday souls get more creative and alert.

"Rest means the absence of effort. It is to counter-balance work in a physiological sense, whereas recreation is a change of effort. Recreation equalises the output of energy by exercising physical or mental energies which have not been at work. In other words, recreation is an activity which calls into action parts of the body or brain not ordinarily used, or which uses parts previously active in a different manner," says Dr. Jussawalla. "Recreation refreshes by a change of activity. Relaxation is muscular limpness. Relaxation is as necessary for health as exercise is. Sleep is only conditional or partial rest of the human machine."

When one rests, the body repairs itself. But it is activity that creates a demand for rest. Muscles are also not built during exercise; they are built during periods of rest after activity when muscular relaxation takes place. When one rests both mentally and physically complete relaxation takes place. The muscles work more efficiently and there is relief from fatigue as there is venous blood circulation throughout the body. "The best method is to practise 'The Dead Pose' called *Shavasana* in yoga. When we lie down to rest in a waking condition our muscles remain slightly contracted. Even this slight contraction is overcome in *Shavasana*."

Sleep

Sleep, air, water and food are universally recognised as the essentials of life but very few people appreciate the importance of sound, healthy, regular, timely and refreshing sleep. "The purpose of sleep is to repair the body. Every nerve centre, every cell, is a storage battery. Work discharges the battery and during sleep the battery is recharged," says Dr. Jussawalla. He warns against sleep or the state of unconsciousness produced by drugs. "The subconscious which works while we sleep is essential to good and refreshing sleep. There should be regular sleeping patterns for sound sleep to occur."

Proper Food and Regulated Diet

"Life begins with feeding and ceases when it stops," says Dr. Jussawalla simply. "The function of food is like the function of gasoline in an automobile. The food burns in the body and serves the purpose of fuel. It gives heat to the body, builds tissues, and also furnishes lubrication for the smooth functioning of the whole body."

The body is built on the food we consume and so the knowledge of body chemistry or the composition of matter is a great aid in the study of nutrition. The human body is a chemical composition of 16 primary elements found in the air and in the earth. The elements in the air are the four gases: oxygen, carbon, hydrogen and nitrogen. The earth furnishes the minerals: calcium, phosphorus, sulphur, potassium, magnesium, chlorine, sodium, iron, iodine, fluorine, silicon and manganese. "Each of these 16 elements fills a particular place in the body and has a definite part to play in its construction and maintenance. This is somewhat similar to the way in which the various elements and materials are used in building a machine or a house," he adds.

Right Foods

Additionally, the body requires carbohydrates, fats, proteins, vitamins and cellulose found in different foods.

Fat is the building block of the brain. In fact, the brain is made of 60 per cent saturated fat! Fat is also where most of one's energy comes from. Fat provides endurance as opposed to the quick fix energy that comes from carbohydrates. Plant based saturated fat is found in coconut oil.

Fats are also found in nuts, seeds, avocados and olives. The cooking medium can be coconut oil, butter, olive oil or grape seed oil. Everything else is too delicate and turns into free radicals when cooked. It must be remembered that 'low fat' items can have chemical additives and have lost vitamins in processing. They act as a nutrient vacuum and suck valuable vitamins and minerals from the body.

The brain needs glucose for energy. **When we eat refined grains like white bread, white rice or sugar the body leeches vitamins and minerals from the bones and other areas of the body and use it for digestion.** A healthy diet is crucial for brain health. It needs to be fed at the cellular level. The ideal foods are mineral rich nourishment from fermented cruciferous vegetables, wild and organic leafy greens, fresh pressed juices, fermented drinks, medicinal teas, super herbs, tonics and foods. The right oil should also be used as the cooking medium. The oil should not be contaminated with metals and have fillers. It should be non-rancid. This will help decalcify the pineal gland, which is not only our line to the ether but our power area for psychic and intuitive abilities.

The focus should be on whole grains and sweeteners like raw honey. Raw honey sourced locally carries an amazing source of vitamins, minerals and enzymes.

Proteins build the neurotransmitters in the brain. Protein from vegetable sources needs to be consumed in wide variety to ensure that all the amino acids are present. Consuming a variety of legumes complimented with some grains is ideal.

Chlorella is a whole food vitamin supplement which provides a variety of vitamins and minerals and can also help support the liver in its ability to detoxify. Minerals like calcium, magnesium, zinc and iron amongst many others are also very important. Seaweeds are a great source of all the minerals the body needs. Zinc deficiency can be combated with pumpkin seeds.

Carbohydrates, Proteins and the Rest...

- ❑ Carbohydrates provide the body with starches, dextrins and sugar. They are composed largely of carbon, hydrogen and oxygen. The principal sugars which the body utilises are cane sugar, malt sugar, milk sugar and dextrose. Starch is the principal carbohydrate food. It is found in all cereals. It is found also in ripe bananas, in certain nuts and in most vegetables in varying degree. They abound mostly in those vegetables which are roots or tubules, such as, potatoes, beets, etc. Starches provide animal heat to the body and provide the energy for work. If carbohydrates are consumed in excess, it is usually stored in the body in the form of fat or in the liver in the form of sugars. This is a sort of residue on which the body draws during a fast or starvation. Reduction in weight is made possible by limiting the amount of carbohydrates consumed.

- Proteins provide the body with nitrogen, sulphur and phosphorus which together with certain other substances constitutes the living structures of the body -- the nerves, muscles, glands, etc. Examples of proteins in foods are the white of the eggs, the lean of meat, the curd of milk and the gluten of wheat. Protein is a very essential element in our diet, yet the real danger is the excessive use of proteins. Unlike carbohydrates which are stored by the body, excess protein cannot be stored and needs to be eliminated. The body needs to eliminate excess protein and this burdens the elimination process. A high protein diet putrefies in the intestines, giving rise to gases, poisons and toxins.
- Fats are derived from animal and vegetables sources. Every animal produces a fat peculiar to itself. As fat is consumed, it is deposited in the tissues in the same form in which it was eaten. There is animal and vegetable fat. It has been proved scientifically that man can live for months on a fatless-diet. So fat in the diet is not essential for life. Fat, however, is a very desirable food element. One of the most important vitamins, the growth-promoting one, is associated with fats. It is found in abundance in butter and in many vegetable oils. Fat produces a certain satiety and is an important part of our diet. But it must be remembered that consuming excess fat results in flesh and intestinal putrefaction. It may also give rise to a condition known as acidosis.
- Vitamins are invisible food elements which have been established scientifically, although their chemical composition is still not fully determined. Vitamins are necessary for growth; they are an essential constituent of nerve tissue. If one's diet lacks in vitamins, degeneration and paralysis sets in because the vitamin constituent of the nerve tissue is lost. Vitamins abound in the bran of cereals, green and root vegetables and especially in orange, lemon and grapefruit. Practically all green vegetables contain vitamins in

different degrees. A varied diet always helps supply different nutrients. Boiling, drying, sterilisation and pasteurisation destroy the vitamins in food. Therefore, it helps to consume organically grown and well cleaned raw and uncooked vegetables and fruits for good health.

- Cellulose is strictly speaking not a food element. It forms the framework and fibres of plants, the walls of vegetable cells and coverings of seeds. It is not acted upon by the digestive fluids, although it is digested by the ferments of certain bacteria which sometimes flourish in great numbers in the colon. The chief value of cellulose is in fact that it is perfectly harmless and is a laxative. The following foods contain cellulose in considerable quantity: whole wheat, cracked rolled wheat, whole wheat bread, asparagus, beans, brussel sprouts, cabbage, raw carrots, steamed cauliflower, raw celery, raw cucumbers, lettuce, onions, parsnips, dried peas, baked potatoes, pumpkin, spinach, prunes, apples, plums, cherries, grapes, raspberries, blackberries, huckleberries, strawberries and cranberries.
- Right mental attitude is very important for good health. Often, even when the diet is all wrong and circumstances are not too favourable, the right mental attitude helps keeps the body in good health. The mind and the gut are the two prime areas of trouble where health is concerned. When both are out of sync the body is in deep trouble. Which is why many healing processes, address both the body and the mind.

It is important to be calm and content and avoid depressing or exhausting emotions. It is not enough to build the body. The mind also has to be trained. We have over 40,000 thoughts a day the mind is constantly working; it is like a restless monkey on a thin stick. Thinking is not confined to the brain. The whole body participates in it. Emotions can wreak havoc on the body. Joy, sorrow, anger, fear and other emotional states may exalt or depress bodily functions as quickly and as powerfully as the most potent drugs or the most active physical agents.

Certain emotions poison the body. Hate, envy, scorn, jealousy and fear actually create poisons, not just psychological poisons, but powerful toxic substances which poison the life stream, the blood; the body is weakened and all life processes are disturbed.

The mind and body are not separate. Their relationship is so intimate that if either of them got out of order the whole system suffers. We feel and think with our bodies and the sensations arising in the body express themselves in thoughts or feelings. The great illusion is that the mind can be cultivated at the expense of the body. But the two are so closely interwoven and interdependent that any effort to develop one at the expense of the other is self-defeating. It must be underscored that the highly developed human mind is dependent on the body and vice versa. Reason, intelligence and mind rule, yet success cannot be achieved by the mind alone as the mind cannot exist or function without the body.

Mental health is vital. Dr. Jussawalla insists that **"The life of the body must be first developed to pave the way for the greater life of the mind. This is the natural order of development. The belief that new mechanical sources of power and energy have made unnecessary the physical development of man is erroneous. Man's mental dynamo is charged from his physical health. When the wheels of his physical being slow down, the electrical energy of his mind will correspondingly weaken and decay. Physical weaklings are incapable of directing the machinery of civilisation. If you neglect your body your whole life becomes a failure.** It is our duty to be strong and healthy if we are desirous of securing happiness -- mental, moral and emotional."

Spirituality also helps. Gratitude is a fundamental component of most spiritual paths, and research suggests that it has important health implications, too, including better sleep, fewer physical ailments, and a greater ability to cope with stressful situations. "Gratitude elevates, it energises, it inspires, it transforms," says Robert Emmons, a University of California, Davis, psychology professor who has helped champion the study of gratitude as a factor in mental and physical health. A series of studies he conducted found that people who kept weekly written records of gratitude slept longer, exercised more frequently, had fewer health complaints, and generally felt better about their lives when compared with those who were asked to record only their complaints. Practicing conscious gratitude has also been linked with positive mental health. Todd Kashdan, associate professor of psychology at Virginia's George Mason University, found that when veterans with posttraumatic stress disorder kept gratitude journals, they experienced a greater sense of overall well-being in their lives.

The power of sacred words is also recognised as a healing tool. Mantras are believed to contain a vibrational power that can lift people to higher spiritual states. In Hinduism, it is believed that consciousness congeals into matter progressively, moving from sound to the sacred syllable *Om* to ordinary language, and from there to the entire manifest universe. Therefore, it is believed that reciting mantras can carry people back to the very source of Being.

Scientists have also discovered that mantra and rosary recitation have physiological benefits for the heart. In a study, **Italian researchers discovered that prayer and mantra slow the breath rate to an optimal six breaths per minute which is markedly better than the average person's breath rate of 16 to 20 breaths per minute.** According to Mehmet C. Oz, M.D., a cardiac surgeon at New York Presbyterian Hospital and the director of the Heart Institute at Columbia University, "When your internal metronome slows, you get a variety of beneficial effects and you also lessen the risk of catastrophic events like heart attacks and strokes." Aditionally, it is found that vocal recitations engage the breath rhythms that, in turn, influence the heart rhythms via the central nervous system and induce a feeling of calm and well-being.

It has been said, 'Eliminate fear, conquer worry, avoid anger, omit depression, shun hate, study cheerfulness, cultivate hope, develop courage, exhibit confidence, assure success, live simply, maintain buoyance, control self, think health'. The great dictum, *mens sana in corpore sano* -- a sound mind in a sound body -- should be the watchword for everybody.

Internal & External Cleanliness and Proper Elimination

Personal hygiene and general sanitation are essential for good health. "Personal hygiene does not apply to merely washing of the outside skin or in putting on clean clothes, but also in the care of the teeth, the hair, the nose, the eyes, the hands, the feet. All should receive care if we are to be really healthy," says Dr. Jussawalla. "Health is cleanliness. Filth breeds disease."

Dr. Jussawalla considers cleanliness one of the main defences against disease. "The human body is kept bathed in an ever flowing stream of living blood. Due to impurities or abnormalities in the blood because of toxic conditions in the body there is discomfort or absence of ease which we call dis-ease or ill-health. Self-poisoning or auto-intoxication is poisoning from within. It is the intestinal form of auto-intoxication that is of the greatest importance because it takes in the range, every organ and tissue of the human body."

Colon Care

It must be remembered that the colon serves the body as a waste receptacle or sewer. Like every sewer it must be flushed regularly. The first important step in keeping the colon clean and healthy is by regulating the diet. Focus on wholesome and natural foods. "The colon's normal mode of functioning, its natural rhythm, or periodicity, must be considered and given priority. Thousands of men and women think they are in good health because their bowels move once a day. But their bowels may be incomplete, they may suffer from a foul breath, have coated tongues and many other indications of auto-intoxication. Constipation is rightly called the mother of all diseases and should be avoided. Of course, not by taking purgatives but by observing the laws of health," adds Dr. Jussawalla. "Avoidance of excess in all matters is conducive to health and prevention of disease. In short, high thinking and plain living is the key to natural health."

Chapter 32

Auto-Intoxication in Nature Cure

People who don't know how to keep themselves healthy ought to have the decency to get themselves buried, and not waste time about it.

-- Hernrik Ibsen

Great emphasis has been laid on auto-intoxication by nature cure physicians in treating diseases. Auto-intoxication means 'self-poisoning', or poisoning from within. The medical term is 'toxaemia' which means poisons in the blood. "There is no subject in clinical medicine from which the condition of toxaemia can be eliminated, particularly as a productive cause of symptoms of all sorts. It may be safely said, therefore, that autointoxication is the underlying cause of practically all diseases to which the body is said to be heir," says Dr. Jussawalla with some finality.

Clinically, it is the intestinal form of auto-intoxication that is important. Intestinal toxaemia or intestinal sub-infection is probably the biggest subject in medicine today. This type of toxaemia takes in its range every organ and tissue of the human body; many diseases, both medical and surgical, can rightfully be attributed to a toxic condition having its origin in the intestinal tract, particularly in the colon.

This will be understood in greater detail soon with the launch of The American Gut project, one of the most important natural health projects of the 21st century. The project will identify the parameters for the ideal gut flora, and how diet and other lifestyle factors affect it. The medical profession has understood that microbes in the gut play a crucial role in health. It is proved that probiotics, along with a host of other gut microorganisms, are crucial to health. Gut microbes have been found to influence a number of diseases, obesity, mental health and even gene expression. The best way to optimise gut flora is to consume fermented foods and avoid anything that promotes the growth of pathogenic bacteria like antibiotics and meats from animals fed antibiotics; processed foods; chlorinated and fluoridated water; antibacterial soap and agricultural chemicals.

"When we look for the root of the infection we at once follow the popular trend and think only of diseased tonsils, teeth, appendix or the gall bladder, but rarely is the colon thought of. Many people suffering from intestinal toxaemia have few, if any, pronounced symptoms referable to the intestinal tract. But they complain of one or more ailments from headache to premature degeneration of the body," points out Dr. Jussawalla.

"But if excessive putrefaction of the intestines continues for any length of time it is liable to produce a variety of symptoms, more or less well defined, such as headache, vertigo, auto-toxaemia, nausea, a general feeling of fatigue, loss of appetite, insomnia, melancholia, mental depression, loss of weight, unavoidable sweating, especially around the head, periodic attacks of indigestion or ptomaine poisoning, rheumatism, skin eruptions, allergies and so on. The haemolytic toxins from the intestinal tract are absorbed in the blood resulting in the breaking down of general health."

Nature Cure makes it a point to address Auto-intoxication.

Chapter 33

Nature Cure and Disease

"It is through your body that you realize you are a spark of divinity."

– B.K.S. Iyengar

Disease is an outward expression or manifestation of the penalty mankind pays for having offended nature. Nature Cure philosophy asserts that disease is brought on by the violation of nature's laws of cause and effect. As it is said, 'We are not punished for our sins but by our sins'. In disease, there is a primary and a secondary cause. The first recognises the individual's environment and his use of it. The second is the accumulation of foreign matter in the primary causes.

"The primary cause of disease barring accidental or surgical injury to the human organism and surroundings hostile to human life, is violation of nature's laws which brings about lowered vitality, and which results in abnormal composition of blood and lymph and accumulation of waste matter, morbid materials and poisons," says Dr. Jussawalla. "*Health or disease, in the final analysis, is resident in the cell.* In all our considerations of the processes of health, disease and cure, we have to deal primarily with the individual cell.

"The vibratory activity of the cell may be lowered through the decline of vitality brought about in a natural way by advancing age or in an artificial way through wrong thinking and feeling, wrong habits of living, overwork, unnatural stimulation and excesses of various kinds."

As we have stated earlier, mental and emotional conditions exert a powerful influence upon the inflow and distribution of vital force in the body. Fear, worry, anxiety and all kindred emotions create conditions similar to that of freezing. These destructive vibrations congeal the tissues, contract the minute channels of life and thereby paralyse the vital activities.

"Emotional conditions of impatience, irritability, anger, fury, wrath, etc., have a heating, corroding effect upon the brain and nerve substance and consume it like burning fire. Self-pity has been called the consumption of the soul or psychic phthisis," notes Dr. Jussawalla. While destructive emotional vibrations obstruct the normal distribution of life forces through the body, constructive emotions of faith, hope, cheerfulness, happiness, love and altruism exert a relaxing, harmonising and vitalising influence. The body tissues are energised and the floodgates of the vital energies are opened. There is buoyant health and happiness. So powerful is the mind! It is evident that the body works in a holistic manner.

The question that begs to be answered in this context is this: If acute disease represents nature's healing efforts, why are there failures? "The possible answers are several," explains Dr. Jussawalla. "The vitality may be too low, the injury or morbid encumbrances too great, harmful or inadequate treatments may have been given to deplete nature. In short, there must be enough inherent vitality remaining in the patient for the body to react towards a cure."

According to Nature Cure, the recent increase in chronic diseases like morbid and malignant growths, diabetes and heart trouble is the price being paid for poisonous drugs, drastic and violent treatments, and the suppression and prevention by unnatural means of nature's healing efforts.

"In Nature Cure there is unity of disease and treatment. What affects one part affects the whole, no matter what you call the disease. The body is a complete entity and must be treated as such," says Dr. Jussawalla. The natural healer may vary his methods of applying natural treatment, and there are differing views and methods too. But the basic principles of nature cure are eternal: man is dependent on natural food and natural elements for healthy existence.

"All kinds of diseases can be treated independently by Nature Cure except where surgical interference becomes necessary or the case is beyond repair," continues Dr. Jussawalla. "The natural system for treating disease is based on a return to the fundamentals of nature by employing various methods to eliminate the poisonous products in the system, to regulate the diet and to raise the vitality of the patient to a proper standard of health. Naturopathy is a constructive method of treatment which aims to remove the basic cause of disease."

Chapter 34

The Control of Epidemics

I tell you, the old-fashioned doctor who treated all diseases has completely disappeared, now there are only specialists, and they advertise all the time in the newspapers. If your nose hurts, they send you to Paris: there's a European specialist there, he treats noses. You go to Paris, he examines your nose: I can treat only your right nostril, he says, I don't treat left nostrils, it's not my specialty, but after me, go to Vienna, there's a separate specialist there who will finish treating your left nostril.

-- Fyodor Dostoyevsky, The Brothers Karamazov

Germs exist. They are everywhere. There is no denying the fact. But from the Nature Cure point of view, they do not begin the trouble. Dr. Jussawalla explains, "No infectious disease can be caught unless there is a soil in which the germ can flourish. Germs in themselves do not cause disease. They appear in the same way as flies do when garbage is lying about. It is the same with the human body. **If there is any filth in the system, germs will appear. Besides, particular germs find their own particular morbid soil in which to live and grow.**"

According to various scientific studies, 90 per cent of the genetic material in your body is not yours. It is from the nearly 100 trillion bacteria, fungi, viruses and other microorganisms that compose your microflora. Your microflora influence your genetic expression, your immune system, weight, mental health, memory, and your risk of numerous chronic and acute diseases, from diabetes to cancer. Science has also proved that destroying your gut flora with antibiotics and poor diet is a primary factor in rising disease rates. According to recent research, intestinal inflammation may play a crucial role in the development of certain cancers. Avoiding antibiotics (including those from conventionally-raised meats and rBGH-laced milk), adhering to a low-sugar diet, along with plenty of unpasteurised fermented foods and/or a high-quality probiotic supplement, are crucial elements for restoring and maintaining both your gut's inner ecosystem and your overall health.

Disease Germs

Nature Cure does not deny the existence of microbes or 'disease germs' as they are called. Nature Cure postulates the idea that the activity of germs, bacteria, bacillae, microbes, is related not to the primary cause of disease, but to its later stages. According to Antoine Bechamp, a contemporary of Pasteur, the microzyma are infinitesimal cell bodies from which all human body cells are elaborated. Depending on the soil upon which these microzyma feed, we get either healthy normal cells or germs. If there is an excess of toxic waste in the system, germs are naturally evolved from the microzyma to feed upon the systemic debris. When the toxic accumulation disappears as a result of the germ activity, the germs automatically disappear leaving only normal microzyma ready to be elaborated into normal body cells again.

It is found in modern bacteriological research that germs can alter in character according to the nature of the soil upon which they are fed. One type of germ can turn into another as the soil it feeds on is changed. It is thus clear that the germs depend on the toxic background in the system and not upon outside factors. "Infection from outside sources should always be considered supplementary to a pre-existent state of toxaemia. Full vital resistance and freedom from toxins means natural immunity from infection or, in other words, health," says Dr.Jussawalla. "The discovery of microzyma confirms the claims of Nature Cure philosophy which states clearly that bacteria and parasites cannot cause and instigate inflammation and other disease processes unless they find their own particular morbid soil in which to feed, grow and multiply."

In the germ theory of disease, a germ is blamed for the disease. So every effort is made to kill the germ. But not many accept the fact that germs exist in healthy as well as unhealthy individuals. Germs exist in all of us even if they do not produce any disease.

They can produce disease only in a suitable environment. To cause disease germs need to find their way into a body that is sufficiently exhausted or toxic to permit their growth. **"It is, therefore, the condition of the body that makes the disease possible and not the disease that creates the primary condition in the body," asserts Dr. Jussawalla. "Germs do not cause disease. They are the result of disease. A clean body supplies an unhealthy medium for germs. An unclean body, one choked with waste materials and poisons, forms a perfect medium for germ propagation."**

This raises an interesting question. If disease arises within the organism, how are epidemics explained? Nature Cure therapists believe that epidemics flourish where insanitary and impoverished conditions prevail. "The fact that the majority of people in a certain locality are addicted to the same unnatural habits of living and of treating their ailments produces in most of them the same kind of morbid soil, and this favours the development of diseased microzyma into similar forms of bacteria and the corresponding inflammatory processes," explains Dr. Jussawalla.

But he also adds, "Certain atmospheric and astrological conditions, which we do not fully understand, also have much to do with the periodic appearance of epidemic diseases." But the bottomline remains: immunity to disease can be acquired only by the general observance of nature's laws. If the fundamental laws of healthy living are observed bacteria will not find congenial soil for development.

Nature Cure does not disregard modern scientific knowledge. Nor does it deny the existence of 'disease germs', as they are called. The crux of the message is that germs only multiply in bodies heavily encumbered with and weakened by wrong food, drink and drug poison, and morbid-taints from disease products such as sera, anti-toxins, vaccines, etc. The danger from any infectious disease lies as much in internal filth as it lies in external uncleanliness.

According to Nature Cure, the only rational way to eradicate epidemics and zymotic diseases is in securing hygienic and sanitary conditions, personal as well as general. The emphasis is on preventive measures and on educating people to become more health-conscious.

To avoid epidemics that take a heavy toll of life, the masses should be taught the laws of health and hygiene. They should be taught to take care of the body and to pay special attention to food, cleanliness, clothing, work, rest, morals, and so on. Public sanitation, the management of sewers, the safeguarding of milk, water and food supply, etc. are vital. "More time and money should be spent on improving and checking conditions that will prevent the outbreak of epidemics rather than on methods of combating the disease germs with the administration of countless vaccines and drugs which are not only unnecessary but definitely injurious," concludes Dr. Jussawalla.

Chapter 35

Nature Cure and Vaccination

We chat together; he gives me prescriptions; I never follow them so I get well.

-- Molière

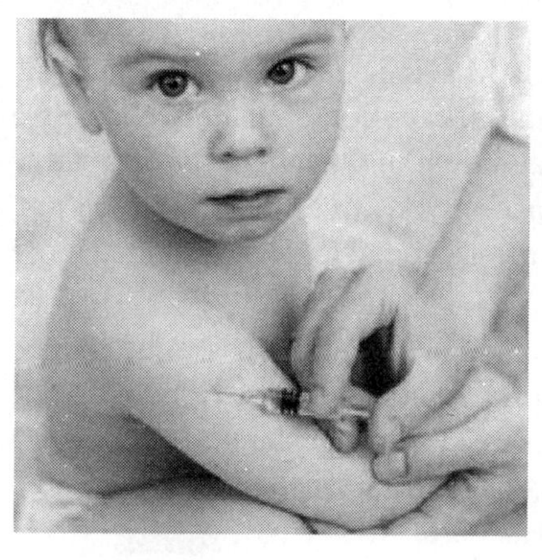

Vaccination has come in for a lot of flak in recent times. Decades ago, there were waves of vaccinations when entire populations were vaccinated. A lot of studies were then conducted on the efficacy and safety of vaccines and many startling results cropped up.

Let's look at recent evidence. Data collected from Canada and Hong Kong in 2009-2010 showed that people who received the seasonal flu vaccine in 2008 had twice the risk of getting the H1N1 "swine flu," compared to those who hadn't received a flu shot. The initial findings were largely discounted, but new research confirms the link between the flu vaccination and an increased risk of more serious bouts of pandemic illness.

There are major differences between naturally-acquired immunity and *vaccine-induced immunity.* With vaccination, you are creating an antibody in the hope of creating resistance to that particular disease. But ongoing research has confirmed that unvaccinated children naturally build up more antibodies against a wider variety of flu virus strains than vaccinated children. It is argued that vaccines can never protect 100 per cent because they provide only temporary, typically inferior immunity compared to what the body would receive from naturally contracting and recovering from a disease.

The media is rife with reports that polio has been eradicated in India, thanks to a massive oral polio vaccination drive encompassing nearly 170 million children. However, sadly, the vaccine uses a live virus that is linked to vaccine-induced polio paralysis. A paper published in the *Indian Journal of Medical Ethics* found 47,500 cases of so-called non-polio acute flaccid paralysis (NPAFP), a polio-like condition that is clinically indistinguishable from polio paralysis but twice as deadly. It has been linked to the oral polio vaccine. It has also been estimated that up to 180 Indian children develop vaccine-associated polio paralysis (VAPP) each year.

Valid Criticism?

Critics of vaccination point out that vaccines alone don't eradicate disease. Polio spreads largely through faeces-contaminated water. So the prime concern should be better sanitation and availability of potable water in Third World and developing nations. An investment in education, cleanliness and healthy immune-supporting food would have yielded more enduring results.

There are ethical issues too. Compulsory vaccination has to be judged from different viewpoints. Every person has an inalienable right to decide for himself whether or not he or she desires to be vaccinated. But if he is a conscientious objector, he should lead a hygienic and healthy life mandated by nature cure philosophy and principles.

Critics argue that healthy people should not be compelled to be vaccinated. They insist that the change in ideas can come not from the ignorant masses but from the authorities who enforce the compulsion on so-called scientific and medical grounds without actually investigating the matter. The smallpox vaccinations, they add, are causing side-effects that range from brain damage, post-vaccinal encephalitis, foetus infections, skin rashes, blood diseases, even cancer and heart disease.

But we do not live in an ideal world. Vast tracts of the populace all over the globe are deprived of proper hygienic and sanitary conditions, both externally and internally. Poverty, ignorance and unhealthy living conditions breed disease. At one level, vaccinations may be considered necessary. But unless conditions improve on the ground, there is no alternative to mass immunisation and early childhood vaccination.

Those opposing vaccinations ask for a programme of medical tests for natural immunity against diphtheria, scarlet fever, whooping cough and other illnesses. They say that children can be tested for tuberculosis in general and when they display low immunity they should be closely watched, tested and perhaps X-rayed at intervals instead of introducing BCG vaccine (tuberculosis) as a routine and then discovering a high susceptibility to a vaccine causing severe tuberculosis, tubercular encephalitis and other complications.

There are many changes in the offing now, many views both for and against vaccination, and the issue needs to be carefully studied. As I said earlier, the reality on the ground is very different from the ideal conditions we talk about. The larger good of the targeted populace will have to be taken into consideration. There are many instances too when vaccines may be mandatory. International travel from and to endemic areas of infection is a case in point. It may be mandatory to be vaccinated as a precaution. Some of the vaccinations and immunisations which travellers undergo before visiting countries are either legally compulsory or advisable. So the question to vaccinate or not is a difficult one because there is conclusive evidence that vaccination can harm the human body, and the alternative -- a return to a natural lifestyle – is not an easy one.

Dangers of Vaccines

Doctors and scientists around the world have done a lot of research for decades to figure out how brain cells work and what goes wrong when disease happens. One of the great enigmas is the connection between vaccinations and certain brain disorders such as Autism, Parkinson's disease, Alzheimer's, dementia etc.

It is well known that free radicals, found everywhere in the environment, cause damage to the human body. Now science has strong evidence that free radicals are formed by the mercury derived from vaccines. Mercury, it is believed, causes free radicals to be generated in large numbers within the brain leading to autism, spectrum disorders, neurodegeneration and other disorders. All of these diseases share another common event – over-activation of a portion of the immune system.

Before we go further, let us understand what vaccines are and what they contain. Basically, vaccines contain either killed viruses or bacteria, germ components, toxic extracts or live organisms that have been made less virulent through a process called attenuation. To stimulate an enhanced immune reaction against these organisms, manufacturers added powerful immune-stimulating substances like squalene, aluminum, lipopolysacchride, etc. These are called immune adjuvants.

The process of vaccination usually requires repeated injections of the vaccine over a set period of time. The combination of adjuvants plus the intended organism triggers an immune response by the body. It is similar to that occurring with natural infections except for one major difference: almost none of these diseases enter the body by injection. Most enter by way of the mucous membranes of the nose, mouth, pulmonary passages or GI tract. For example, polio is known to enter the body through the GI tract. The membranes lining these passages contain a different immune system than that which is activated by direct injection. This system is called the IgA immune system. It is the first line of defence and helps reduce the need for intense activation of the body's immune system. Often, the IgA system can completely head off an attack. So, in short, critics insist that injecting organisms to induce immunity can be considered abnormal.

To prevent vaccine failure -- which has happened -- manufacturers are making the vaccines more potent. They do this by making the immune adjuvants more powerful or adding more of them. The problem with this approach is that in the very young, the nutritionally deficient and the aged, over-stimulating the immune system can have an opposite effect -- it can paralyse the immune system. Another problem with modern vaccines is that the immune stimulation continues over a prolonged period of time because the immune adjuvants remain in the tissues, constantly stimulating immune-activating cells. With most natural infections the immune activation occurs rapidly, and once the infection is under control, it drops precipitously to prevent excessive damage to normal cells in the body.

Vaccination & the Brain

According to Dr. Weil, who has aggressively opposed vaccination, no one has considered the effect of repeated vaccinations on the brain. This was based on a mistaken conclusion that the brain was protected from immune activation by its special protective gateway called the blood-brain barrier. More recent studies have shown that immune cells can enter the brain directly. More importantly, the brain's own special immune system can be activated by vaccination.

The brain has a special immune system that operates through a unique type of cell called a microglia. These tiny cells are scattered throughout the brain, lying dormant waiting to be activated. The activation of the body's immune system by vaccination is a most important stimuli for activation of brain microglia.

Numerous studies have shown that when the body's immune system is activated, the brain's immune cells are also activated. The more powerfully the body's immune system is stimulated, the more intense is the brain's reaction. Prolonged activation of the body's immune system produces prolonged activation of the brain's immune system, and that is the great danger.

The brain's immune system cells, once activated, begin to move about the nervous system, secreting numerous immune chemicals (called cytokines and chemokines) and pouring out an enormous amount of free radicals in an effort to kill invading organisms. But the problem is that there are no invading organisms. The brain has been tricked by the vaccine into believing there are.

Destructive Chemicals

Unlike the body's immune system, the microglia also secrete two other chemicals that are very destructive of brain cells and their connecting processes. These chemicals, glutamate and quinolinic acid, are called excitotoxins. They also dramatically increase free radical generation in the brain. Studies of patients have shown that levels of these two excitotoxins can rise to very dangerous levels in the brain following viral and bacterial infections of the brain. High quinolinic acid levels in the brain are thought to be the cause of the dementia seen with HIV infection.

These days many vaccines are given close together and over a long period. So the brain's immune system is constantly activated. This means that the brain will be exposed to large amounts of the excitotoxins as well as the immune cytokines over the same period.

Studies on all of these disorders, even in autism, have shown high levels of immune cytokines and excitotoxins in the nervous system. These destructive chemicals, as well as the free radicals they generate, are diffused throughout the nervous system doing damage, a process called bystander injury. "It's sort of like throwing a bomb in a crowd. Not only will some be killed directly by the blast but those far out into the radius of the explosion will be killed by shrapnel," says Dr. Weil. "Normally, the brain's immune system, like the body's, activates quickly and then promptly shuts off to minimise the bystander damage. Vaccination won't let the microglia shut down. In the developing brain, this can lead to language problems, behavioural dysfunction and even dementia. In the adult, it can lead to one of the more common neurodegenerative diseases, such as Parkinson's disease, Alzheimer's dementia or Lou Gehrig's disease (ALS)."

A recent study by the world-renowned immunologist Dr. H. Hugh Fudenberg found that adults vaccinated yearly for five years in a row with the flu vaccine had a 10-fold increased risk of developing Alzheimer's disease. He attributes this to the mercury and aluminium in the vaccine. Interestingly, both these metals have been shown to activate microglia and increase excitotoxicity in the brain. The side effects include confusion, language difficulties, disorientation, seizures, memory problems, somnolence, low-grade fevers, irritability, mood alterations, combativeness, difficulty concentrating and a host of other behavioural problems.

In the child, brain immune over-activation has been shown to be particularly damaging to the amygdala and other limbic structures of the brain. Studies in autistic children have shown that a state of immune attack on the brain is occurring. Similar findings are seen with neurodegenerative diseases. It must be appreciated that this autoimmunity was triggered by the vaccinations and by organisms contaminating the vaccinations. "Once started, the immune reaction cannot stop, thus triggering all the destructive reactions," continues Dr. Weil.

Live Viruses

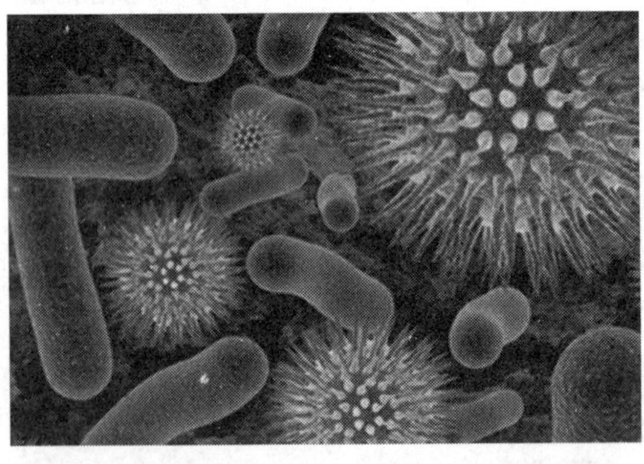

Another even more common problem is the use of live viruses in vaccines. These attenuated, non-disease-causing viruses are injected in the hope of stimulating the body to produce an immune attack. But there are two problems here. First, studies have shown, these viruses escape the immune system and take up residence in the body for a lifetime.

A recent autopsy study of elderly individuals found that 20 per cent of the brains contained live measles viruses and 45 per cent of the other organs contained live measles viruses. Similar findings have been described in autistic children and the measles virus is identical genetically to the one used in the vaccine. The second problem is that most of these viruses were found to be highly mutated. In fact, different mutations were found among viruses in various organs in the same individual.

These attenuated viruses undergo mutation brought on by the presence of free radicals in the tissues and organs and they can mutate into virulent, disease-causing organisms. Studies have confirmed that a large percentage of Alzheimer's disease patients have live viruses in their brain as compared to normal individuals.

Once these live viruses are injected, they cannot be removed. Because the viruses stay in the body, they will be under constant free radical exposure, which can increase during times of stress, illness, exercise and with aging. It is the free radicals that cause the virus to mutate. The viruses can exist in the brain, or any organ, either silently and slowly producing destruction of the brain or spinal cord or producing sudden disease once the virus mutates to a highly lethal form.

Many studies have shown conclusively that vaccinating children can lead to severe injury to the brain by numerous mechanisms. "Because the child's brain is undergoing a period of rapid growth from the third trimester of pregnancy until two years of age, his or her brain is at considerable risk.

We have also seen that live-virus vaccines and contaminated vaccines hold a special risk in that the viruses tend to persist in a substantial number of individuals and that free radicals can cause the latent viruses to transform by genetic mutation into disease-causing organisms later in life. It is vital that a person scheduled for vaccination allows no more than one vaccine every six months, allowing the immune system time to recover.

Live-virus vaccines should be avoided," continues Dr. Weil. "Finally, it is vital that anyone undergoing vaccination should start nutritional supplementation and adhere to a healthy diet before vaccination occurs. Vaccine complications are far fewer in individuals with good nutrition." Several medical practitioners also believe that some of the diseases such as chickenpox, measles, and the flu, may actually have an important place in childhood development. They feel that these diseases may actually help the child's immune system, nervous system and brain mature.

Polarised Debate

Of late, the vaccine debate in the Unites States is sharply polarised. While health officials insist that vaccines are the best way to protect the health of individuals and the public, critics are calling for a safer and more effective public health policy. "As a result, the number of doses of vaccines included in the childhood vaccination schedule has tripled over the past 30 years, increasing from 23 doses of 7 different vaccines to 69 doses of 16 different vaccines. At the same time there has been a rise in the numbers of vaccinations given to children, we've also seen a significant rise in the numbers of children suffering with chronic disease and disabilities," says Dr. Mercola who is well known for his rational anti-views. According to *Judicial Watch*, 26 children died after receiving the HPV vaccine between September 1, 2010 and September 15, 2011. Other serious side effects reported in the same period included paralysis, speech problems, memory loss, blindness, pancreatitis, ovarian cysts, and Guillain-Barre syndrome. "Rigidly maintaining the assumption that an ever increasing number of vaccines must be mandated 'for the greater good' is a dangerous assumption that fails to take into account the possibility that one-size-fits-all mass vaccination policies may be contributing to the rise in chronic disease and disability among children," says Dr.Mercola. There is a new twist to vaccines now. Genetically modified (GM) vaccines are already being produced; some are even on the U.S. Centers for Disease Control and Prevention's (CDC) recommended vaccine schedule. Like with GM foods, there is little knowledge about their long-term effects. "The use of foreign DNA in various forms has the potential to cause a great deal of trouble, not only because there is the potential for it to recombine with our own DNA, but also there is the potential for it to turn the DNA 'switches', the epigenetic parts of the DNA, on and off," adds Dr. Mercola. But the crux of the matter here may be the fact that the global vaccine market is expected to register revenues in excess of US$ 34 Billion by 2012; the global market for seasonal influenza vaccine alone is $3.6 billion.

Naturopathy & Vaccination

Without a doubt, naturopathy and vaccination do not see eye to eye. Naturopathy attributes illness to the violation of natural laws. Benedict Lust, who brought naturopathy to the United States, says in the *Universal Directory of Naturopathy*, published way back in 1918: The contemporary fashion of healing disease is that of serums, inoculations and vaccines, which, instead of being an improvement on the fake medicines of former ages are of no value in the cure of disease, but on the contrary introduce lesions into the human body of the most distressing and deadly import. To understand how revolting these products are, let us just refer to the vaccine matter which is supposed to be an efficient preventive of smallpox. Who would be fool enough to swallow the putrid pus and corruption scraped from the foulest sores of smallpox that has been implanted in the body of a calf? Even if any one would be fool enough to drink so atrocious a substance, its danger might be neutralised by the digestive juices of the intestinal tract. But it is a far greater danger to the organism when inoculated into the blood and tissues directly, where no digestive substances can possibly neutralise its poison.

Evidently, naturopathy and vaccinations have very little in common. When vaccination can apparently harm the body so disastrously, why does medical opinion strongly favour vaccination? "A doctor's training begins in youth and the doctrines of the older professionals are firmly implanted in the students. But the medical profession has two opinions on the subjects. Those who are anti-vaccination have evidenced tragic experiences in their practice which led them to study both sides of the question. The others find their professional status bound up with the belief in vaccination. They cannot break away from it without jeopardising their career," says Dr. Jussawalla.

He joins hands with those against vaccinations (we must remember here that his opinion on vaccination, though relevant today, was made decades ago). Dr. Jussawalla points out that the only countries which still have smallpox epidemics are those which have compulsory vaccination such as Italy, Egypt, Mexico and India while smallpox declined rapidly in the countries where vaccination was abandoned and conditions of sanitation, hygiene and nutrition were improved. "We gather from the book *Sanitary Measures in India* that 10 years of statistics afford no evidence that vaccination affects the usual epidemic course of the disease.

We come to the conclusion that the common factor in any country where smallpox is virulent is the poverty of a great mass of the people and the filthy conditions in which a considerable section of them are forced to live. When people who have been vaccinated get smallpox, they are told that their vaccination could not have been properly done or that the lymph was not active or that the marks were too faint or that the operation was too old or too new. It is a case of 'heads I win, tails you lose'."

Denouncing Vaccinations

On December 8, 1985, as a member of the governing body of the Central Council for Research in Yoga and Naturopathy, Dr. Jussawalla sent a strongly worded letter to the Union Health Minister denouncing compulsory vaccinations. He underscored the ethical viewpoint that every person has an inalienable right to decide for himself whether or not he desires to be vaccinated. He may be a conscientious objector, leading a healthy, hygienic life. He added that the conscientious objection to vaccination should be respected as there was evidence that the unnecessary small-pox vaccinations were causing illness and even death. "The side effects range from brain damage, post-vaccinal encephalitis, foetus infections, skin rashes and blood diseases, and even dangerous diseases like cancer and heart diseases for which vaccines and sera are principally responsible," he explained.

Many studies now are highlighting the inter-relatedness of humans with the environment. It is being clearly established that most epidemics, such as AIDS, Ebola, West Nile, SARS, and Lyme disease, just to name a few, are a direct result of man's failure to live in harmony with nature. A new project called Predict, funded by the United States Agency for International Development (USAID), aims to determine where new diseases are likely to emerge, based on how the landscape is altered by human activities. The project will also study forest, wildlife and livestock management to prevent the spread of pandemic disease. The idea is to understand how leaving nature intact can offer built-in protection against such emergencies.

Chapter 36

Contemporary Global Voices

Earth My Body,
Water My Blood,
Air My Breath,
Fire My Spirit.

--- From the book, Songs For Earthlings

The global voices advocating the right food and lifestyle in a bid to get away from conventional medicine are getting louder by the day. Well-known voices include Dr. Deepak Chopra, Dr. Manu Kalia and Christopher Kilham, the medicine Hunter who scours the Amazon for natural medicines. Back home, we have Baba Ramdev, the controversial yoga guru, Rishi Prabhakar, Dr. Pratap Chauhan, Dr. Pankaj Naram, Dr. Shashikant Patwardhan, Prof. Dr. Subhash Ranade and several others who are insisting on a return to nature and a life free from disease.

The *return-to-nature buzz* grew more strident in modern India some three decades ago after Dr. Ann Wigmore coughed out startling revelations of her cancer cure thanks largely to the curative and restorative powers of wheatgrass. Founder of the Hippocrates Health Institute in Florida, she said: "The easiest way to add living enzymes to the digestive tract is to eat ripe fruits, uncooked organically grown vegetables, sprouts and wheatgrass."

Dr. Vijaya Venkat, Kavita Mukhi and Jehangir Palkhivala, among others, then stirred the urban consciousness to a return to nature. Dr. Anton Jayasuriya and his alternative healing movement spurred the process, and the organic movement, in a sense, was born. Aloe Vera, wheatgrass, alfa alfa, sunflower seeds, spirulina, stevia and other organically grown foods are now commonplace on grocery store shelves. Auroville and other spiritual centres are also growing organic foods and exporting them with some success.

Healthy Cleansing Routine

There are also people like *Dodhisattva* who opens her soul to the world in *Aloha! Sacred Backyard Blog*. "If one is eating foods that are not serving the organs they can become swollen or unhealthy causing pressure on the spine," she says. "A healthy cleansing routine can assist this to harmonize. There also can be stored emotions throughout the body. A protocol that encompasses the cellular principles can encourage rejuvenation. Radical Forgiveness of one's past is of paramount importance when it comes to emotional traumas."

Dodhisattva, who also believes in physical activity and even gym work, affirms that after a good solid workout it is important to refuel the body with bio-available nutrition from carbohydrates and then protein. The body wants glucose soon after a workout and then protein to repair the ripped muscle tissues. "Bio-available nutrition is key here so that less work is required by the digestive tract and nourishment can penetrate the cell wall with ease."

She advocates about 30 minutes of a foot soak in filtered warm/hot water with magnesium flakes. Keeping the lymphatic system moving and flowing is key to releasing the toxins from the body. Rebounding, hot/cold showers, skin brushing and walking help bring back balance. Other important tools to utilise when incorporating strength training could be deep breathing, tai chi and restorative yoga. These internal exercises calm the mind and body, alkalise the blood and revive the organ system.

"As the body builds muscle and stays alkaline through out the process with green juices, super foods/herbs and bio-available nutrition such as cultured yogurt made from sprouted almonds and coconut meat or a sprouted organic brown rice protein we can deliver the cells amino acids for repair and build the body structure," she adds. "When we are lean, clean and serene, radiant, strong and vibrant with an abundance of energy we are experiencing cellular integrity."

Strength Training

An advocate of strength training which she believes is an important cog in any longevity strategy, *Dodhisattva* says that without muscle the body relies on the soft tissue, cartilage and bones for structural alignment. This can be dangerous because the body will begin to deteriorate more rapidly via calcification and spinal dis-alignment. "Other reasons for spinal dis-alignment can be emotional and nutritional or environmental as we strive to look at it from a balanced prospective."

She insists that the whole point is to be "more proactive, empowered and assertive while staying in alignment and integrity with your innocence, purpose and strong auric field. It is imperative to follow inner guidance, stay connected to a higher self and follow the peaceful answers that come from within. When you are living your *Dharma* your *Karma* is fulfilled."

When the body is in an acidic condition it loses magnesium reserves and the adrenals becomes stressed. With a balanced approach to cellular movement your body will experience great levels of energy, focus, adaptability and elasticity at any age.

Chapter 37

'Expand Levels of Self-Awareness'

Our bodies are our gardens – our wills are our gardeners.

-- William Shakespeare

Anyone who stops learning is old, whether at twenty or eighty. Anyone who keeps learning stays young. The greatest thing in life is to keep your mind young.

-- Henry Ford

According to Deepak Chopra, there has been a revolution in recent times in how we perceive the body. "What appears to be an object, a three-dimensional anatomical structure, is actually a process, a constant flow of energy and information. In this very moment, your body is changing as it reshuffles and exchanges its atoms and molecules with the rest of the universe – and you're doing it faster than you can change your clothes. In fact, the body you're using right now as you read this article is not the same body you woke up with or even the same body that you had a few minutes ago.

"The fifty trillion cells in your body are constantly talking to each other as they keep your heart beating, digest your food, eliminate toxins, protect you from infection and disease, and carry out the countless other functions that keep you alive. While these processes may seem out of your conscious control, hundreds of studies have shown that nothing holds more power over the body than the mind. To think is to practice brain chemistry.

Every thought, feeling, and emotion creates a molecule known as a neuropeptide. Neuropeptides travel throughout your body and hook onto receptor sites of cells and neurons. Your brain takes in the information, converts it into chemicals, and lets your whole body know if there's trouble in the world or cause for celebration. Your body is directly influenced as these molecules course through the bloodstream, delivering the energetic effect of whatever your brain is thinking and feeling."

He believes that one of the keys to harnessing this potentially unlimited power of the mind is to expand one's level of self-awareness. "When you expand your awareness, your energy flows freely. You're more flexible, balanced, and creative. You view yourself and the world with more compassion and understanding. You have more energy and are open to new possibilities. At this level of awareness, you have all the power you could possibly need to create a new reality -- a reality of vibrant health and wellbeing."

Chapter 38

'Observe Nature, Listen to Your Body'

Medicine being a compendium of the successive and contradictory mistakes of medical practitioners, when we summon the wisest of them to our aid, the chances are that we may be relying on a scientific truth the error of which will be recognised in a few years' time.

-- Marcel Proust

According to Nancy and Joseph Gill, the peripatetic couple who travel the world and live on natural produce, "Health is freedom. Disease and illness rob you of your freedom... and your money. Being healthy feels great, and it gives you the freedom to live your life the way you want, and the energy to do all of the things that you want to do, and the vitality to have all of the fun that you want to have, and to really enjoy your life, to your fullest potential."

Both of them have been living on natural foods for years and enjoy sharing their research and ideas on health. "It is a work in progress. We are always learning. Self-responsibility is essential. Everyone can be healthier. It is up to each one of us. Don't turn your power over to your doctor to heal you! Choices have consequences. It is not the length of life which is important to us but the quality. I quote:

"Simplicity is the key. Observe Nature. Listen to our body. We get thirsty for a reason. Water is one of the most essential ingredients to good health.

Drink three to four litres or more of purified water each day. Our bodies are 80 per cent water and need to be hydrated to function properly and to flush out impurities.

Junk Negativity

"Clean out our lives and possessions of all clutter. Clear our lives of negative stressful elements, people, or situations. Use only a few organic products on your body and in your surroundings. Reduce time in environments polluted with smoking, noise and exhaust. Like our bodies, our minds need to be flushed out and our spirit opened.

> *"The essential element to vibrant health is to clear our minds, open our hearts and connect now to the "Source", "Prana", "God's Love", "Qi/Chi Energy", "Nature", "Universe", "Allah", or "Great Spirit"; following whatever path we choose. Take the quiet time necessary each day. Forgive and move on. Have an attitude of gratitude. Say "Thank you God" for our many talents and blessings. Live in the NOW. With this all is possible!*
>
> *"Breathe deeply. Exercise in the fresh air daily. Stretch - use it or lose it. Enjoy the sun for 15 minutes each day. Replace negative, destructive thoughts with positive ones; or no thoughts at all - just observe what is going on around you for a time. Turn off the television. Turn off the fear. Clear out our heads and bowels. Get enough sleep. Love yourself more. Help those around us, sharing our talents and love in a healthy, balanced way. Lighten up and laugh more. We all need to look at these reminders regularly.*
>
> *"If you want to know what your mind was like in the past, look at your body now. If you want to know what your body will be like in the future, look at your mind now."*
>
> **-- Ancient Ayurvedic Saying**

"Go back to basics. Eat foods as close to the way nature produces them; at least 75 per cent raw, nothing from a package and no junk food. No animal or dairy products. Avoid expensive vitamins or supplements. Instead get everything you need from the local market or grow it yourself. Organic if available. Our bodies absorb whatever abuse we throw at them for years on end until, as we get older, it's time to "pay the piper." Your body needs high powered fuel to stay healthy. Make it a priority.

Fighting Cancer with Nature

"I thank my dance with cancer, three months after our marriage in 2001, for opening our eyes and making us put our bodies and minds back into balance. Bypassing the nightmare of western procedures and chemicals I chose to NOT TURN MY RESPONSIBILITY OVER to a doctor to 'fix me'. I simply fired my doctors.

"Don't look for support from your previously caring physician. He or she is required by law to recommend cutting, burning or poisoning you or they can lose their license. When their advice is not followed they will usually get upset and threaten you with death. They may be well intentioned but you must be strong. Walk out and don't look back. Even when I sent the results of many cancer free tests to my GP and specialist there was no response or interest. Hard to believe. Doctors should be interested in learning new options for their patients. I avoided western medicine except for tests, and started researching alternative methods.

"There are many genuine, effective options to suit each situation and person. The only real path is to HEAL OURSELVES, body and mind, through whatever means we decide on. Alternative methods are always less damaging to the immune system. It usually takes us years to mess our bodies up, so it takes a while to heal and balance them again. Be patient. With an optimistic, knowing attitude, and once the immune system is provided with the proper tools and nutrients, our body always regenerates and heals diseased cells. Finally, my body had what it needed to heal. Fifteen months later I had my first test clear of cancer cells. Six years later we feel better than ever.

"The routine is the same for every illness or type of cancer. Just provide your body and mind with the tools they need to heal, whether it is diabetes, M.S., high blood pressure, or whatever type of cancer. Balance and health are returned. Take responsibility and make changes. This is why a serious illness is, in fact, a gift and a catalyst for change. These thoughts are shared with love, from someone who needed to learn the hard way.

Will & Motivation

"The rate at which a person makes changes depends on their will and motivation. If you are eating fast processed foods five times a week, cut it down to three. Then eliminate it all together, replacing it with a good healthy snack or meal that you enjoy and look forward to. A little bit at a time, until you have made improvements that you can notice and feel good about. Keep trying. Even a small change helps. If you add up all the time spent going to doctor appointments, filling prescriptions, having tests, missing fun events -- it wouldn't compare to a little extra effort now in PREVENTION and staying healthy to begin with. The Chinese used to only pay their doctors when they were healthy, not when they became sick.

"If someone has been diagnosed with a life threatening illness everything changes. The stakes are higher and they need to get serious - NOW. Ask yourself, - "Do I want to LIVE or die? Do I want to waste my precious time being sick and in pain?" Don't just give yourself excuses and 'try'. DO IT!

Chemicals Kill the Immune System

"At the same time I had my biopsy for cervical cancer, two friends were diagnosed with cancer. After a lengthy discussion about the options of alternative methods to consider, one friend decided to opt for full western treatment; surgery, procedures, chemotherapy, etc.

With an immune system killed by the chemicals, and discouraged by the painful procedures, he died within one year. He chose the path he believed in. We all do. Another friend decided to opt for alternative methods and did well for six months. Impatient and not really believing in the methods he had chosen, off he went to his doctor at the first problem; who filled him with fear about dying and did a surgical procedure. Fear took over. All our friend's work with cleansing, juicing, etc. went down the drain. Back to square one. After that point he only half heartedly followed the alternative methods. He was dead within nine months.

"A person has to research THEM SELF and develop a plan of alternative treatment that he or she believes in and KNOWS and TRUSTS will work. Clear your mind and connect. Get rid of the naysayers in your life. Make serious changes. Know that there will be ups and downs.

Surround yourself with supportive, positive influences: select friends, family, and a knowledgeable, encouraging naturopath, who all honour your right to choose and follow whatever path. Ask them to love, listen to and support you and to leave the fear outside the door.

"Thousands of people have been successful following alternative methods. One doesn't have to look far to realise this and be encouraged by the successful results. Hopefully your friend or family member's self worth will lead them to choose self responsibility and natural methods of healing. But remember, healing only works if you believe in it and want to heal; not everyone does. Love them and honour whatever path they choose."

Chapter 39

'Animal Foods Contribute to Diabetes, Cancer, Heart Disease & Obesity'

We cut the throat of a calf and hang it up by the heels to bleed to death so that our veal cutlet may be white; we nail geese to a board and cram them with food because we like the taste of liver disease; we tear birds to pieces to decorate our women's hats; we mutilate domestic animals for no reason at all except to follow an instinctively cruel fashion; and we connive at the most abominable tortures in the hope of discovering some magical cure for our own diseases by them.

– George Bernard Shaw, Man and Superman

SHARAN is a non-profit organisation in India with the goals of spreading holistic health awareness, and an ecologically-sustainable compassionate lifestyle. It believes that all life on the planet is interconnected. By reconnecting, man heals himself and Mother Earth.

According to Dr. Nandita Shah of SHARAN, an erudite and well-travelled homeopath of exceptional skills, "It is well known that animal foods contribute to diabetes, cancer, heart disease and obesity, as well as other health ailments and diseases. During SHARAN's Disease Reversal retreats, participants experienced a significant improvement in their health and well-being by eliminating all animals foods from their diets. The work of medical professionals like Dr. Dean Ornish, T. Colin Campbell and Dr. Neal Barnard has proven that many diseases can be reversed through a low-fat, plant-based diet."

She comes up with an easy suggestion for non-believers. "Try vegan for 30 days. It's easier than you think! There are many alternatives to eggs and dairy available, which make it easy to make the switch. Try it and feel the beneficial effects for yourself. Educate yourself. Once you know the facts, you can make an empowered decision. Test the results. It's a good idea to do a complete blood report including cholesterol, vitamin B12 and D before the 30-day trial to see the positive health changes for yourself."

She counters the need for animal protein easily. **"It is easy to meet protein needs on a plant-based diet. Almost all plant foods contain protein, with some of the best sources being beans, greens, nuts and whole grains. While meat, dairy and eggs are also high in protein, they contain unhealthy fats and cholesterol."**

Disease Reversal Programmes

Twenty-seven people, including medical professionals, participated in one of SHARAN's several Disease Reversal Programmes in Gokarna, Karnataka. The 21-day program included classes on healthy eating, disease prevention, re-conditioning and cooking, as well as yoga and meditation. There were also massages, art classes and nature walks on the beaches and in the surrounding hills, and films and entertainment in the evenings. The food served was all whole and plant-based. Detailed medical tests were done at the beginning and end to monitor the changes in their health.

By the end of the programme, 13 people were off all their medications while many others were down to only a fraction of their doses. There were also marked improvements in liver function tests, and cholesterol and triglyceride levels for almost all participants. Four participants with hypothyroid problems saw very significant improvements in their levels. Many people lost weight. A full day-by-day report of the Disease Reversal Program is available for the sceptics.

"Our focus is on healthful foods, not medications. Participants receive step-by-step guidance on how to make beneficial lifestyle and diet changes which can transform their health," says Dr. Shah.

She also believes that vegetarianism is the way to be. "Many people are vegetarian because they believe it is a compassionate and healthy choice. However, many are often unaware of the tremendous animal suffering that goes into producing these products. Also, both vegetarians and non-vegetarians get the same diseases because dairy and eggs are similar in composition to meat and fish. We must not forget that all animal products have a large environmental impact too. The modern production of milk and eggs causes intolerable suffering, an early death for cows and hens, and implies the killing of male calves and chicks.

For at least 10,000 years, from Rome to Egypt to China to today, the chicken has been a part of folklore, history, meal traditions, even religion. Ancient Egyptians were reportedly among the first to master "artificial incubation," allowing them to raise a larger number of eggs for food. In ancient Rome, chicken farmers used mixtures of wine-soaked bread or cumin seeds, barley and lizard fat to fatten up chickens. Prior to the 1920s, poultry was raised as a hobby in the United States, but not so much as a food source – the fact that you could eat them was incidental. Then farmers realised that they could simply add vitamin D and other vitamins and medications to chicken feed, and "modern" chicken farming was born.

Adds Dr. Shah, **"In an economically competitive market, egg-laying chickens and dairy cows are artificially stimulated to increase production. High productivity shortens their life spans. Cows can live up to 20 - 26 years but dairy cows are slaughtered at five years. The lifespan of a chicken is five-six years, but an egg-laying hen is spent after a year-and-a-half.**

"Like any mammal, cows produce milk only when they give birth. They are artificially inseminated so that they can keep producing milk. Male calves are by-products of the dairy industry and are killed for veal and leather. Rennet from their stomach lining goes to make cheese. Male chicks are also by-products because they cannot produce eggs. Their little bodies are ground up to make meal to feed their sisters.

"Dairy cows are confined to small spaces, fed hormones and antibiotics to increase their milk production, and hooked up to machines which cause pain to their udders and frequent infections. Hens are confined to dark, crowded cages. They are forced to live in their own filth and their beaks are cut off to prevent them from pecking at each other.

"If you truly care about animals, the environment and your own health, vegetarianism is not enough. Go vegan to make a difference to the way you feel, to the future of planet earth and to the animals."

Chapter 40

'Do-Nothing Farming' *vs* Genetically Engineered Foods

Life is either a daring adventure or nothing.

-- **Helen Keller**

As I end the book, I am reminded of Masanobu Fukuoka, the celebrated Japanese farmer, philosopher and author who launched "do-nothing" farming in 1938 and pioneered the highly acclaimed One-Straw revolution. He later became a spokesperson of the global natural food and lifestyle movement. I had the privilege of meeting him in Mumbai. He was a farmer of citrus and grain and used conventional farming strategies with reasonable results.

One night, as he lay on a hill overlooking the harbour, contemplative and exhausted, he heard the cry of a heron and the flapping of its wings as it soared away. That moment something hit him hard. Call it *Satori* or *Buddhahood* but a great realisation hit him. As he explained: "In this world there is nothing at all.

"I could see that all the concepts to which I had been clinging, the very notion of existence itself, were empty fabrications. My spirit became light and clear. I was dancing wildly for joy. I could hear the small birds chirping in the trees, and see the distant waves glistening in the rising sun. The leaves danced green and sparkling. I felt that this was truly heaven on earth. Everything that had possessed me, all the agonies, disappeared like dreams and illusions, and something one might call 'true nature' stood revealed. I think it would safely be said that from the experience of that morning my life changed completely." Empowered by this realisation, Fukuoka had bumper harvests. He adopted a strategy called "No farming farming" in which he didn't interfere with nature. His message was simple – just observe nature's principles.

GE Foods

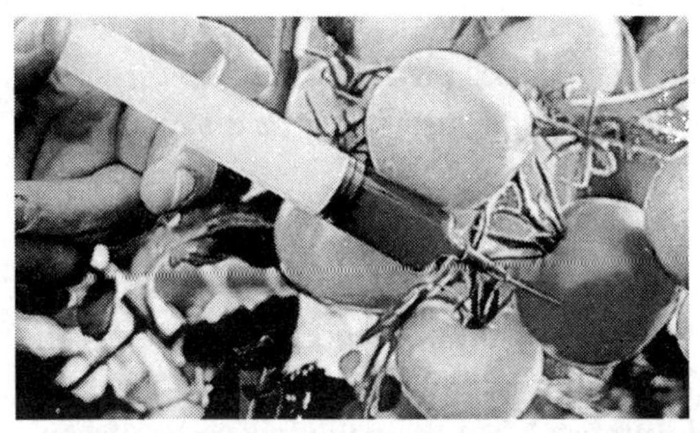

Fukuoka's words are even more relevant today with the onslaught of Genetically Engineered foods or GE foods. Besides potential health effects due to the genetic alterations to the crop, several harmful agricultural chemicals will be used on the soil resulting in its destruction. More importantly, toxic chemicals such as 2, 4-Dichlorophenoxyacetic acid -- a main ingredient of Agent Orange – will wreak havoc. (Agent Orange is the combination of the code names for Herbicide Orange and Agent LNX, one of the herbicides and defoliants used with lethal results by the U.S. military as part of its herbicidal warfare programme in Vietnam).

All this could well destroy the soil and even the genetic make-up of the crop. If the soil itself is deflowered, the crop will most certainly be compromised. As a consequence, the cell structure of the human body may change or be subject to new travails leading to new diseases. This should be interesting, if not devastating.

Not too long ago, Bt toxin originating from genetically engineered Bt crops were found in 93 per cent of pregnant women tested and 80 per cent of umbilical blood in their babies. More recent results from a German study shows that people who have no direct contact with agriculture have significant concentrations of glyphosate in their urine. Glyphosate is the active ingredient in many broad-spectrum herbicides.

Urine samples collected from city dwellers in Berlin all tested positive for glyphosate, with values ranging from 0.5 to 2 nanograms per milliliter (ng/ml), which is five to 20 times the permissible upper limit for glyphosate in German drinking water. Research published in 2010 showed that the chemical causes birth defects in frogs and chicken embryos at far lower levels than those used in agricultural and garden applications. Glyphosate has also been linked to decimation of intestinal probiotics, endocrine disruption, DNA damage, developmental and reproductive toxicity, and more.

There is also documentary evidence that there is frightening lack of life in an Iowa field growing Genetically Engineered corn. There are no birds, insects of any kind or bees. Bees have been dying off around the world for a decade now from a phenomenon called Colony Collapse Disorder, or CCD. A third of the U.S. food supply depends on the honeybee. GE crops and chemical agriculture in general are prime culprits in the disappearance of bees, other insects and butterflies.

There is global resistance against GE foods. Hopefully, good sense will finally prevail. We will have to wait and watch.

I end the book with The Mother's take on immortality. "The cells which can vibrate in contact with the divine Joy are on the way to become immortal. The body doesn't feel immortal, but the cells feel to be eternal. We have been created for immortality and we want immortality!"

Maybe, Just Live Natural!

Several decades ago, when the world wasn't as connected as it is today, and when the marvels of science were yet to make their imprint, Dr. J.M.Jussawalla, a young Parsi doctor from a family that immigrated to Bombay from Pakistan (then British India) had a simple dream. He wanted the world to return to nature and to good health. A lot has happened in the interim. The circle is almost complete. His cry seems to have finally found ears from a planet on the edge!

Chapter 41

The Birth of a New Race: Cracking the Immortality Code

Every child begins the world again.

--Henry David Thoreau

As we look into the future, let us cast an eye on what is being called -- *Children of the New Dream*. According to Drunvalo Melchizedek who is researching this phenomenon, "There are three different kinds of children emerging in the world today that I have been able to identify. The first are called the *Super Psychic Children of China*. The second are called the *Indigo Children* and the third are called the *Children of AIDS*."

Melchizedek is particularly interested in the third group -- the *Children of AIDS*. According to him, many years ago, at least 10 or 11 years ago in the US, there was a baby born with AIDS. They tested him at birth and at six months and he tested positive for AIDS. They tested him a year later and he still tested positive. Then they didn't test him again until he was six, and amazingly he was completely free of AIDS. He was taken to UCLA for further tests and to better comprehend the change that had taken place and it was discovered that he didn't have normal human DNA.

Melchizedek points out that in the human DNA we have four nucleic acids that combine in sets of three producing 64 different patterns that are called codons. Human DNA all over the world always has 20 of these codons turned on and the rest of them are turned off, except for three which are the stop and start codes. Science always assumed that the ones that were turned off were old programmes from our past. This boy had 24 codons turned on — four more than any other human being.

Disease Free

The child was tested to see how strong his immune system was. A very lethal dose of AIDS in a petri dish was mixed with some of his cells but his cells remained completely unaffected. The researchers kept raising the lethalness of the composition and finally went up to 3,000 times more than what was necessary to infect a human being. Yet, the child remained completely disease free.

Intrigued, the researchers started testing his blood with other things like cancer and discovered that this child was immune to everything! Then they found another child with these codons turned on and then another one then another one -- then 10,000, then 100,000, then a million of them and at this point. Finally UCLA made a calculation. By watching world-wide DNA testing, they estimated that one per cent of the world has this new DNA which breaks down to approximately 60 million people who are not human by the old criteria.

It is also believed that even adults have this 'capability'. Those researching the topic believe that there are many people showing up with this new alien DNA; they believe that a new human race is being born on the earth that apparently can't get sick. The explanation is that it is a very specific emotional, mental body response -- a waveform coming off the body that is causing the DNA to mutate in a certain way.

There are apparently three parts to this phenomenon, according to Melchizedek, "The first part is the mind that sees Unity." It sees the Flower of Life. It sees everything interconnected in all ways. It doesn't see anything as separate. And the "second part is being centred in the heart -- to be Loving." And the "third thing is to step out of polarity -- to no longer judge the world." As long as we are judging the world as good or bad, then we are inside polarity and remain in the fallen state, he says.

Melchizedek believes that these people (with the new DNA) have somehow stepped out of judging and are in a state where they see everything as one and feel love. Whatever they are doing within themselves is producing a waveform that when seen on computer screens looks almost identical to the DNA molecule. So the researchers think that by the very expression of their life that these people are mapping with the DNA -- resonating it – they are changing these 4 codons and thus becoming immune to the disease. They might be immortal too.

What is even more remarkable is that the entire process may have started with one child who put it into the grids and it is now in the subconscious of the earth and is accessible to anyone. With meditation and deep prayer, others have connected to this on a subconscious level.

Apparently, a new race of humans is being born!

Over 60 years ago, Edgar Cayce, one of the most documented psychics in history, predicted our current earth crises. But he said we possessed the power to change those circumstances by the nature of our being which could or, rather, should include balance, godliness and patience. For Cayce, Christ Consciousness (which you could also call Buddha, Kwan Yin, or messianic consciousness) was the pattern that we were to follow in relating to ourselves, and each other. The task was simply to bring the divine light to earth and live from a higher plane.

List of Dr. Jussawalla's Books and Booklets

Books

1. Prevention is Better than Cure – 1961
2. Healing from Within – 1966
3. Living the Vegetarian Way – 1971
4. The Natural Way of Healing – 1974
5. Natural Dietetics – 1979
6. Heal your Mind, Heal your Body – 1981
7. The Key to Nature Cure – 1983
8. Vegetarianism -- 1985
9. Medical Dietetics – 1987
10. Integrated Healing Arts – 1988
11. The Art of Healthy Living – 1993
12. Nature's Materia Medica – 1994

Booklets

1. The Message of Nature Cure – 1939
2. The Message of Nature Cure to Suffering Humanity – 1949
3. Nature Cure Movement – 1954
4. Nature Cure – Foreword by Morarji Desai – 1956
5. A Case for Nature Cure for the Govt. of India – 1958
6. A Case for the Promotion of Nature Cure in the Third Five-year Plan – undated
7. Food Guide – undated
8. Some Proved Methods of Nature Cure on Prevention of Disease for the Govt. of India – 1965
9. What is Nature Cure? – 1986
10. The Human Workshop – 1990
11. The Vegetarian and Vegetarianism – Pros & Cons – 1993

SELF-IMPROVEMENT/PERSONALITY DEVELOPMENT

STRESS MANAGEMENT

RELIGION/SPIRITUALITY/ASTROLOGY/PALMISTRY/PALMISTRY/VASTU/HYPNOTISM

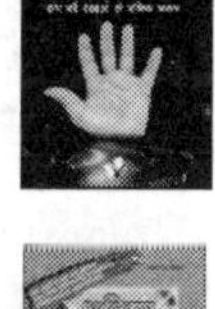

FICTION

JOKES

Contact us at sales@vspublishers.com

PARENTING

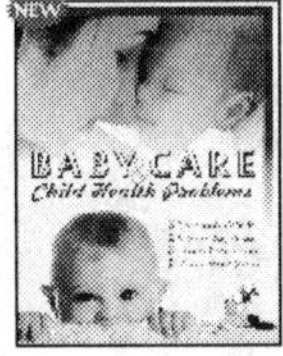

FAMILY & RELATIONS

COOKING

HOUSEKEEPING

Homely guide to 1000 + domestic tips to keep skin shining, utensils clean, jewellery sparkling, rectifying small plumbing & electrical defects, keeping clothes moth-free, banish nasty smells and dressed-up interiors neatly.

WOMEN ORIENTED

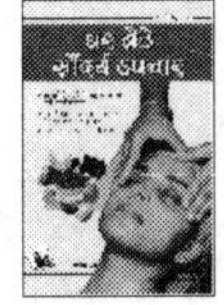

GENERAL HEALTH & BEAUTY CARE

ALTERNATIV THERAPY

FITNESS

PERFECT HEALTH & AYURVEDA

A Set of 4 Books

DISEASES & COMMON AILMENTS

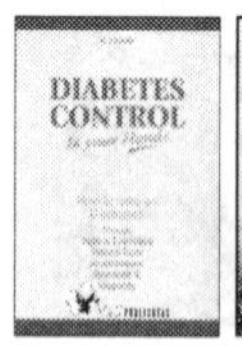

CAREER & BUSINESS MANAGEMENT

CONCISE DICTIONARIES

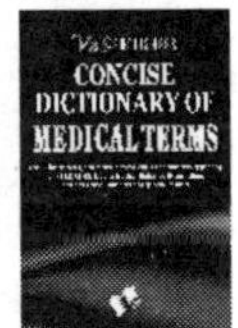

Contact us at sales@vspublishers.com